Recovering From Life

Recovering
from
LIFE

Discovering Joy Through
Courage and Enlightenment

LORIJEAN

Sage
Creek
Press

TRAVERSE CITY, MICHIGAN

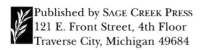Published by SAGE CREEK PRESS
121 E. Front Street, 4th Floor
Traverse City, Michigan 49684

Publisher's Cataloging-in-Publication Data
LoriJean.
    Recovering from life: discovering joy through courage and enlighten-
    ment / LoriJean. – Traverse City, MI.: Sage Creek Press, 1998.
        p.   cm.

    ISBN 1-890394-14-9
        1. LoriJean.   2. Women alcoholics—United States—Biography
        I. Title.
HV5293.H86 A3 1998   97-62352
362.292'092   dc—21   CIP

PROJECT COORDINATION BY JENKINS GROUP, INC.

02 01 00 99 ◆ 5 4 3 2 1

Printed in the United States of America

This book is dedicated to the memory of Jack Boland, minister, teacher, and recovering alcoholic. He inspired us, encouraged us, and showed us that a joyous life is possible no matter what we have experienced.

On March 4, 1992, his death, like his life, left the inspiring message to "March Forth," and set me on a path of discovery I never could have imagined. He shared his experience, strength, and hope with us. I will be forever grateful.

For information on books and tapes by Jack Boland, contact:

Church of Today

P.O. Box 280

Warren, MI, 48090-0280

Also, to "The Children of St. Jude," who show us that life is a valuable gift worth fighting for. By purchasing this book you are contributing to the research that is helping to eliminate the suffering of children. To make a donation or to become a St. Jude Partner in Hope, write or call:

St. Jude Children's Research Hospital

P.O. Box 50

Memphis, TN 38101

(800) 822-6344

"...a non-profit, tax-exempt corporation whose purpose is to care for children stricken with catastrophic diseases, to conduct medical research on those diseases and to raise funds needed to allow St. Jude Children's Hospital to accomplish this."

Do it for the children.

CONTENTS

FOREWORD

When I first began reading LoriJean's manuscript I thought to myself, "This is an interesting and introspective portrayal of a recovering alcoholic, but it's most certainly not about me." And then I read some more. "Boy, she really struggled with her alcoholism and her recovery has been a roller coaster. I feel blessed that I haven't been so consumed."

More reading, and the words began to do their work. I think it was the loyal accounting of her dreams that finally moved me beyond ego, permeating the surface of my psyche, much like my own dreams attempt to do every night.

Soon I began to recognize myself in LoriJean's self-portrait—remembering my own times of obsession, my experiences of confusion, fear and inadequacy, my own struggle with needing to control and my inevitable surrendering to God. I am not an alcoholic, although I am a child of an alcoholic. And like LoriJean, I, too, am recovering from life.

Recovering From Life is, first and foremost, a courageous and authentic telling of the inner and outer life of a recovering alcoholic. Those who know themselves as recovering alcoholics will find a valuable mirror in which they may see themselves more consciously. LoriJean's journey may very well inspire others to look a little harder at themselves and their own lives with a self-forgiving heart.

This is also a book about the healing power of the journaling process. As one reads LoriJean's journal entries and dream accounts, the reader becomes a personal witness to a profound healing. Alcoholics Anonymous, daily meetings and the twelve-step process work hand-in-hand with the writing to lead LoriJean through the darkness into more enlightened—and infinitely more peaceful—times.

I had the honor of reading LoriJean's first book, also titled *Recovering From Life*. This was before she declared herself an alcoholic. It had a lot of wonderful wisdom in it, but no sense of "having been through it." This is actually her second book, and according to LoriJean, has very little of the first one in it. I guess I would have to disagree.

Her first book of the same name was like an affirmation. It reflected a vision of where her spirit wanted to be. The second book records the often challenging experience of manifesting that vision. I believe her first book led her into recovery. The second book led her through it. And that journey has made all the difference.

As I finished her book early this morning, I decided to fall back asleep to see what my dreams would tell me about the book. I dreamt about searching through houses for something—I'm not sure what—and about cleaning up messes in other people's houses where I kept leaving my own footprints through what I had just cleaned. And then there was the dream about a biology test the next day that I hadn't studied for, and that "not showing up for it" was probably the best solution. This dream series ended with a cardinal appearing in my dream, which has always been a symbol of my father's presence, and a clear voice saying, "Now you can wake up."

As I woke up, remembering my dreams, the message was clear. I'm living in recovery, too. There is little difference between LoriJean's inner journey and mine...and I'd venture to guess...yours. Only the expression is unique. Like the trees she talks about at the end of the book, we are all reaching towards the light.

And so, dear reader, may you find your own life more illuminated by your journey through this book. I must warn you, it won't always be easy...or comfortable. But it will be worth it.

So are you.

Mary Knight

ACKNOWLEDGMENTS

First and foremost, to my best friend and soul mate, my husband, Gregory, for riding the wild roller coaster with me the past fifteen years, and for taking care of me until I could take care of myself. For supporting me, not only financially, but emotionally and spiritually. For loving me when I didn't love myself, and for believing in me when I was full of doubts. But most importantly, for recovering with me.

To my daughter, Megan, for putting up with me, for laughing with me, crying with me, and for growing up with me. You are a gift from God, and a best friend for the rest of my life. I love you with all my heart.

To the rest of my family for loving me and supporting me, even when they didn't know what to do with me. To Mom and Dad, my sister and brother, for loving me unconditionally and always believing in me, and to Kassie Jo for reminding me of myself.

To my "Nurse Practitioner" who has treated my mind, body, and soul! To Mary Knight, for the faith and encouragement, and to all the people who have touched my life and helped me grow, I love you all.

In memory of Charlotte Carter, thanks for the dreams, and Judy Dickinson, thanks for the spirit. You are a part of who I am....alive in mind and heart.

Last, but not least, to my Guardian Angel who inspires me, protects me, and reminds me why I'm here.

Grace Prayer

For Thee I thirst.
Into Thy hands I commit my spirit
(my soul, my body, my life,
this problem, all unforgiven states).
Thy will is my will.
Thy will be done through me.
Heal me at depth.
Reveal that which needs
to be revealed.
Heal that which needs
to be healed
so I can glorify You, God,
and live in the fullness of grace.
It is finished.

For more information contact:
WINGS OF SPIRIT FOUNDATION
5767 Arapacho, Suite 711
Box 345
Dallas, TX 75248

Chapter 1

IN THE BEGINNING

Promise not to laugh. In 1992 I wrote a book called *Recovering From Life*. I finished it in 1993. In 1994 I quit drinking. For over fifteen years I was virtually an every day drinker. Oh, I quit every now and then, for a week, thirty days, and I was always going to quit on New Year's Day.

One year I quit until my birthday in April. I did it, and then I drank from April to January. The next time I made it to my husband's birthday, which is January 14. After that, I quit quitting.

My name is LoriJean and I'm an alcoholic. I call myself an "addict," because I'm addicted to many things. I'm the youngest of three children, all of us born by the time my mom was nineteen. We knew our parents were younger than other parents, but that's just the way it was. We thought it was cool. My sister and brother were teen-agers themselves when Mom was still in her twenties, Mom and Dad were both in their thirties when they became grandparents.

Because my parents were so young I grew up with lots of grandparents. I had five grandmas who lived until I was a teen-ager: two grandmas and three great grandmas. Holidays and family get-togethers were always fun. I was surrounded by loved ones. It was a loving family, a safe place for a child.

We didn't have a lot of money, and I know it was hard on my folks trying to raise three kids. They were still so young themselves. But, considering the struggle, they did an incredible job. They loved each other and us, and they weren't afraid to show it. We ate dinner together as a family every night, and we always said a prayer first. When we were finished eating we had to ask to be excused from the table. Dinner time was great. It was a time we were all together.

I remember liking the family I was in, always feeling love and acceptance, and we had a sense of humor about things. Dad was a jokester and always had one-liners. Life was good. I don't remember being traumatized by the beatings my brother gave me, or how mean he was to me growing up. That's just the way brothers were; my friends said the same thing.

If anything traumatized me growing up, it was having red hair and freckles. I was a pale-faced, bright red-headed, extremely freckle-faced DIFFER-ENT FROM EVERYONE ELSE child, who was teased relentlessly, and left out of all the "groups." As a result, I was shy and insecure, spending many childhood moments crying, praying, and asking God why he had cursed me with red hair. In a world where being accepted was so important, especially to a child, why did I have to be so different? My brother and sister had red hair too, unlike our parents, but that didn't help at school.

Overall, I always summed up my childhood as being wonderful. I never could figure out how I became so screwed up. Then, once I sobered up and recognized that all three of us kids are alcoholics, I knew I needed to take a look at that. How did it happen? What went wrong? Where did it go wrong?

I remember realizing, seemingly for the first time, that my parents were teen-agers when they had us. Having teen-agers of my own makes it seem all the more incredible. Suddenly it seemed quite shocking that my mom was only fifteen when she got married. She was sixteen when she had my sister, seventeen when she had my brother, and nineteen when she had me. To think that my mom was trying to raise teen-agers in her twenties, and was a grandma when she was a year younger than I am now, amazes me.

Neither of my parents finished high school. Dad quit to work and Mom to have the baby. I know they struggled financially the entire time. I know Mom was stressed about paying bills and grocery shopping—heaven forbid you threw school shopping, birthdays, or Christmas in there. Dad worked as hard as he possibly could, yet it never seemed to be quite enough.

Every couple of years or so, Mom and Dad would fight over their finances. It seems Mom would let things get way out of hand before she let Dad know they were in trouble. I remember her telling him she was going to need anywhere from $500 to $700 to bail them out. Dad would yell at her and ask why she hadn't come to him when it was $100 or $200. Why wait until it was so much? Mom always had the same answer, "I don't know." She was trying the best she could, but there never seemed to be enough.

Still, I remember Christmases and birthdays as being fun. I know it was a hardship for them, but we always seemed to be well taken care of. I remember school shopping as particularly stressful for Mom, but we each got three new outfits, and we were excited. We didn't have as much as some kids, but we had more than others. I never remember feeling poor or lacking in anything.

I know my parents must have been scared to death. I know that many times they panicked when bills piled up and they had to borrow money. How could they add another bill when they couldn't pay the ones they had? I know as hard as they tried, we still picked up on their fear, felt the insecurity and the hardship. None of us ever asked for anything extravagant, we just knew. We always felt grateful for what we had.

My parents came from very different backgrounds. I never gave that any thought while growing up. I didn't seem to notice. For some reason, all these awarenesses have come as a surprise to me. Mom's family, although not wealthy, were well-known and respected in the community. My dad's parents were poor, still working to support themselves when grandma died. In exchange for rent they cleaned the buildings where they lived, and at one time I believe they cleaned the office building where my Mom's dad worked.

I look back at the two families I was born into, and the contrast is so obvious. It never was growing up. I'm grateful for the childhood I had, the diversity. So many things are clear to me now. Life has a way of bringing everything into focus when the time is right. I have such fond and loving memories of my childhood, and such sadness.

My mom was the oldest of three children. Her baby brother was only three when she "had to get married" at fifteen. It was the 1950s and that's just what you did. I was the baby on that side of the family for ten years before my cousin was born. My grandparents lived next door to my great grandparents, and my parents lived in the one-bedroom apartment in the back, with all three of us kids. We outgrew that place in a hurry, and after living in a couple of other small places, when I was three, we moved into the house I grew up in.

Mom's side of the family was extensive: grandparents, great grandparents, uncles, and great uncles on grandma's side; plus grandpa's side of the family. It was wonderful. Lots of loved ones all around. I know there was dysfunction all around too, but to a child it was nice. I will be forever grateful for that side of my family, for the love and the humor. All of us have struggled, but we have a strong faith. I love my grandparents so much, and although we live miles apart, we're very close. I write to them every week.

The only time I remember any drinking when I was growing up was at Christmas. Grandpa would make Tom and Jerry's, a tradition, and even the kids got to have one, only without the rum. Usually everyone had one and that was it. We never had wine with dinner at any family event, and other than Tom & Jerry's once a year, there was never any drinking at our family gatherings. That was a tradition I started at my own family get-togethers.

I didn't know that grandpa on Mom's side used to drink, and worked as a bartender for many years, in addition to his office job. I didn't know that his father was an alcoholic or that his sister died at the age of thirty-seven, having been married seven times. Alcohol was her downfall. By the time I can remember, grandpa had quit drinking and he and grandma were devoted to their church.

Drinking was not something I grew up with in my home either, although a few incidents which stand out in my mind, of course, involved alcohol. I never understood why my mom had such an unfavorable reaction to my dad drinking even one beer. I guess I always figured it was the church, which was against drinking. But she would turn into a bitch, and that in turn would piss dad off, and the fight, it seemed, would be on.

Since none of us were used to seeing our parents fight, they were always so loving, it was a terrible thing for us. I remember we would all be crying, listening to them yell at each other. In my mind I always blamed mom for these incidents. Never did I blame dad or the drinking, because after all he was only having one or two beers with a neighbor or something, but she wouldn't allow it. I always felt that if she would just let him have a damn beer once in awhile all of this could be avoided. It was never going to happen while I was growing up.

Once every three or four years, not very often, Dad wouldn't come home from work on a Friday. Mom always knew what that meant. He always came right home after work. If he didn't, he was at the bar with the guys for *a* drink.

I don't think my dad ever knew how to have one drink either. When he got home it was either a loud argument or dead silence, but mostly I remember them yelling. It seemed longer periods in between these incidents, I'm sure it just wasn't worth the wrath of mother.

What I didn't know, and Mom could not forget, were the early years. Dad was still a teen-ager and wanted to party with his buddies. Apparently that's what he did, at the most inconvenient of times, like Christmas Eve. One Christmas Eve in particular it was getting late and toys needed to be assembled. Dad's buddies carried him in, passed out. Mom made them dump him in the shower. He got sick, drank some coffee, and then played Santa. What a video that would have made!

I think my mom never could get over those early years, and if he even had one drink she was afraid he was going to repeat past behavior, which he was always prone to do. Her predictable reaction to the drinking, even if it had been years since the last one, really pissed him off. The combination of the three, Mom, Dad, and drinking, never mixed well.

I never saw drinking on my dad's side of the family either. There had been some problems early in their marriage, I'm told, with grandpa's gambling (I have a hunch there was drinking there, too). My dad's only brother was the "alcoholic" in the family, the one who died from the disease at age forty-seven. There are those in the family who would say he died of liver failure, or any number of other "natural" causes, but anyone who knew him, knows that alcohol killed my uncle. Not, however, before it robbed him of everything he ever worked for, everything he wanted in life.

I'm not so different from my uncle, no alcoholic is.

My dad was the youngest of four children, and to me, his story is the saddest. My Grandma Sue (Dad's mom), was the glue that held the family together. When she died the family fell apart. It was fractured long before that, and probably none of them know why.

Three of the four children are still living (it's been over twenty years since they lost their brother), but they haven't seen each other now in over a decade. I think my dad's youngest sister had to break free of her past, where she came from, early on. I know it was a painful decision for her, but it's what she felt she had to do. She lived far away and her visits were few. Once grandma died, and grandpa after that, she never came back.

My dad's other sister married an alcoholic who left her with four small children and no money. The hardship fell to my grandparents, who already struggled, working hard physical jobs for meager earnings.

Then my aunt met another man, and he seemed to be an answer to a prayer. They married and he adopted her children. He took care of them, provided them with a house and food on the table. I never liked him. When I stayed with my cousins I always had to sleep in a bedroom all by myself. The girls and I would beg to stay together, but he always separated us. He watched every move we made and was always lurking around somewhere.

He would sit in that damn chair of his and want us to sit on his lap. He would laugh and tickle us, and we squirmed about, although I inevitably squirmed right off his lap and backed off about ten feet, watching and laughing, but keeping my distance. Pretty soon I stayed back. I didn't know why I didn't like the tickle game, and I didn't give much thought to why I didn't like my uncle.

I thought he was strict and controlling, and I felt sorry for my cousins, but it's just the way things were. We, they, made the best of it. My cousin who was born a month before I was, and the one I was closest to, rode to school with him early each morning. He worked for the school system as a janitor or something. We lived a block from the school so she would walk over to my house and then we'd walk to school together when it was time. He found out about this and from then on locked her in the library until it was time for school. I was devastated, and couldn't understand it. I felt helpless and sorry for my cousin for being locked up.

But I didn't have anything to compare this behavior to. I thought a lot of things were strange but couldn't confirm anything. He was strict and he had weird ideas about things. It's just the way he was. We would soon find out he was a child molester.

That whole time in my life brings back powerful and painful memories. I was never molested by him. I don't know if it's because I backed away so quickly, or that he was afraid of getting caught. Whatever the reason, I'm grateful. But it scared me, and I couldn't believe something like this could happen. I felt incredible sadness for my cousins. I was haunted by the realization it could have easily happened to me, and I felt somehow guilty around them because it hadn't. The whole thing was so confusing. I was fourteen years old.

A lot of things were changing at that time in my life. My dad's brother had just died a couple of months before, my great grandma on my mother's side died, and about six months after that, the tragic loss of Grandma Sue. My dad believes, and so do I, that the whole mess with "what's his face" is what killed her.

Grandma was an incredible woman, and her death when I was fifteen, on top of everything else, was a blow I wasn't prepared for. I didn't handle it well, now that I look back. Grandma Sue was a tiny woman, only 5' 2", but she had a power much bigger than her stature.

I never remember her speaking of any particular religion, although she was Baptist. I just remember that she believed in God and trusted Him, and taught us the same. When I think back to how poor they really were, and then remember Grandma's attitude of gratitude and blessings, it's all the more powerful. She felt blessed and rich, she really did. She also had an incredibly tough and sad life.

Grandma was psychically gifted as well, yet modest about it. She called it intuition, and said we all have it. She encouraged "tuning it in." She and my father had a special gift and bond. I'm the same age now as my father was when she died. It seems so young. I can't imagine the pain he felt, and still feels.

Grandma was never the same after everything with "uncle." I think she knew something wasn't right, as we all did, but she couldn't imagine such a horrible thing, so she denied the feeling altogether. When it turned out to be as terrible as it was, I know she couldn't live with the guilt.

She always told us to never go against our feelings. No matter what, she'd say, listen to your feelings. This is one time she didn't, and I think she lived to regret it. She died while grandpa and her were on vacation. They'd both had physical checkups before they left, and were quite healthy actually. She was sixty-six and grandpa was seventy.

But she got sick, caught a cold while walking a friend's dog. She ended up in the hospital with bronchitis and laryngitis. I'll never forget the phone call. Grandpa called with news that not only was she in the hospital, but that she wasn't going to make it.

I remember Mom handing Dad the phone, the look of desperation on her face, and an incredible look of fear on my dad's face. None of us could believe this was happening. Dad was getting on the first plane out. He would fix this whole mess. No way was his mother going to die. I know my dad believed he could save her. We believed he could too. If anyone could, he could.

My grandma was born without tear ducts, so she couldn't cry. I remember as children she told us never to be afraid to cry, especially the boys. She said you don't know what it's like to want to cry and not be able to. It seems the rest of us did enough crying for her. My dad's a sensitive guy, cries about happy things and sad things. My mom's side of the family is the same way. I didn't have a chance. I cry at the drop of a hat.

She also taught us to never say "hate." She said it was a negative emotion that only hurts the one doing the hating. She said when you hate, you love yourself less. She taught us not to complain, or try not to, by reciting the poem, "I cried because I had no shoes and then I met a man who had no feet." She was big on being grateful for what you have.

My dad got to the hospital and found her unable to speak. She was hooked to machines. When she saw my dad, she started crying, real tears, it was a miracle, and a sign. She knew what my dad was trying to do. She knew his will could hold her there, and she didn't want that. She pushed her hands out, and with her eyes she told him to let go.

It wasn't until she lapsed into a coma, a machine breathing for her, that my dad knew he had to let go. He went down the hall and prayed, saying, "if it is Your will to take her, who am I to hold her here?" With that he felt the hand of the nurse on his shoulder saying she was gone.

After that, it would seem, I headed down a path of self-destruction, disguised as having a good time. I lived hard and feared nothing. I turned my back on the church, and sought my own way. I didn't need anybody. I knew what was best for me.

Chapter 2

THE CHURCH

So many thoughts and emotions are stirred in me when I think about the church. First and foremost, I'm grateful. I'm glad to have learned about God and the stories from the Bible. It was a loving place, a family. I had many friends within the church, and we all grew up together. The church was only a block from our house, and we enjoyed the activities and events, camp, plays, and the group for teens that met each week. I have many fond memories of the church, and many questions and much confusion.

For the most part, I accepted everything I was taught, but I see now that I had doubts about some things. I didn't understand why black people weren't allowed in the church. Although they were eventually, I was bothered by the fact they weren't always. I didn't like how controlling the church was. If you missed a Sunday, they wanted to know why. When I got my first job, I was called into the office and asked why I wasn't tithing ten percent.

I questioned the kingdoms in heaven, and the requirements for reaching the highest one. I found it difficult to believe that the only way I would be with my loved ones after I died, was if we all worked to achieve the highest kingdom. Since my father's side of the family didn't belong to this church, I found it disturbing to think I would somehow be separated from them in the afterlife.

I think that's probably the main reason I left the church when I did. It wasn't until I was working through anger in early recovery, that I discovered both grandma's death and leaving the church happened when I was fifteen. It wasn't a conscious decision, one because of the other. I never put the two together. But now it's clear. I see exactly what happened. Grandma died and no way was I going to have anything to do with the people who were telling me she wouldn't be waiting for me when my time came.

When the whole mess happened with what's-his-name, I was extremely bothered when the church questioned the girls, asking them why they let him do it to them. I was enraged and confused.

I had studied the church seriously. Up to that point I was very religious. I wanted to be a good girl. I wanted to follow the church. But the more I heard, the more questions I had, and pretty soon it didn't seem to be the place for me. I still loved God, and I was not walking away from Him, but I had to find a different way. I was sad. People I loved were being hurt, dying even. I was disappointed with life. There wasn't much I felt I could be sure of. I see now how vulnerable I was to addiction. The downhill spiral, I believe, began here.

Chapter 3

EATING

I see now that the whole eating disorder thing started at that vulnerable age of fifteen, when everything else in my life was changing. I didn't realize the magnitude of it then, but I do now. First of all, I never thought it would be an issue for me, food, eating, not eating, dieting, being overweight or underweight. It wasn't something I was conscious of while growing up.

I was a toothpick until I hit puberty. Pictures of me as a kid are funny. I had bird legs and twigs for arms. I was tall and straight as a pin. My mom was heavy for as long as I can remember. My sister fought her weight as well, fat jokes were her burden to carry as a child. But I don't remember thinking too much about that, the fact my mom and sister were heavy and my dad, brother, and I were not.

I remember liking vegetables a lot, and candy and desserts sometimes. It wasn't something I gave any thought to. I ate when I was hungry, stopped when I was full, and if I wanted something sweet, I ate it. Food was just a natural part of life. We eat to survive, and so I did. It was that very attitude that I was able to draw on and return to, later, following years of unhealthy eating and attitudes about food and weight, anorexia, and bulimia.

Things really began to change once I hit puberty. The real downfall came when I started smoking pot, and consequently got "the munchies." That's when I remember "pigging out," eating way too much of all the wrong kinds of food. Never in my life had food tasted so good, and never before had I eaten so much that I was sick and bloated, but still wanting to eat more.

I can see now that I was stuffing my feelings, and running from my life. The pot smoking and overindulging in food were just stepping stones to my alcoholism and addiction.

Consequently, because of the overindulgence in really bad foods, I had a weight issue to deal with for the first time in my life, something I never thought would happen to me. I can see now that's when I panicked, and obsessed, which I know today only made things worse. I began exercising like a mad woman, but didn't change anything else. I continued to "pig out" and in a very short time, added alcohol to my list of abuses.

I was caught up in a vicious cycle of self-destruction, and wasn't aware of what was happening to me. I thought I was partying, enjoying life, something I now had a zest for. But it was all about outside stimuli, in other words, it was all about indulging in whatever I could, so I wouldn't have to look at myself, especially wouldn't have to be alone with myself.

I was hyperactive as a child, nervous is more like it, scared to death if you want to be truthful. The more I tried to get away from myself, the more destructive my behavior became. Dieting wasn't working, and eating properly wasn't an option, because I was in denial. That's when the bulimia started. I have a lot of shame about this part of my life, but it is important for me to see where my addictions began.

The feeling that bingeing and purging gives you is indescribable. It's crazy, now that I look back on it. I didn't know *why* I was doing it, so how was I going to be able to stop? It was a feeling of power, a control thing. It was a high in itself, an escape from the world, eating anything and everything I wanted. But the high was short-lived. It ended as soon as I was painfully full. But I kept eating until I couldn't eat anymore. And then the relief. The purging was a whole different kind of high.

The feeling of control was all too short-lived, because once I got rid of everything I'd eaten, I wanted to eat again. And so the cycle went, moments of relief and control, followed by frustration and desperation. It's such a terrible feeling, to be so full you can barely move and yet still want to eat more, have to eat more. It's insanity, kind of like being so drunk and all you can say is, "Gimme anodder dwink."

Bulimia didn't fix anything for me. It didn't help me lose weight. I didn't get skinny bingeing and purging. But my weight didn't balloon out of control, as I'm sure it would have had I continued the way I was. Most of this was going on during high school, but by my senior year something changed. I have no idea what, I just know that I didn't want to binge and purge anymore. I decided I was going to start "eating healthy."

I had the right idea, kind of. I would eat one healthy meal each day and exercise moderately, (my days of obsessive exercising behind me). But the problem with this plan was I chose to eat *one* healthy meal a day, instead of *three*. As the weight began to come off, I felt so much better because I wasn't miserable from eating mass quantities of food and then throwing it all up. I felt relieved. I felt free.

What happened after this is something I think happens to a lot of people who have been overweight and begin to slim down. I had a new resolve. I wanted to lose more and more weight. I had to keep losing weight, it felt so good. And a whole different kind of control kicked in, one that said, "No one can control what I eat or how I look, except me."

That one meal a day got smaller and smaller, until eventually I was barely eating enough to stay alive. I wasn't drinking during the anorexic phase of my disease, I was just wasting away to nothing.

The comments of how good I looked turned to concern. I heard comments like, "You're getting too skinny," and "You better not lose any more weight." Then worse yet, "Your eyes look sunken in," and finally, "You look sick."

I didn't know what anorexia was. It was 1978 and Karen Carpenter's death, which brought the disease and knowledge of it out in the open, wouldn't occur for a couple more years. I didn't think I was starving myself. All I wanted to do was return to the naturally thin person I'd always been.

All the negative attention I was getting made me start thinking; and eating. But still I hadn't dealt with what was really going on with me. I hadn't dealt with me at all. So I kept eating and eating and eating. Again I gained weight. I ate too much of the wrong kinds of food, and again, I began throwing up. But I hated throwing up, and now it was "bulimia." Now it was an "eating disorder." It had a name, and I had it, so I stopped. The throwing up part was disgusting and I hated it. That's when I found alcohol as an alternative source of relief.

For the next few years I went to aerobics three times a week, stopping at the bar afterwards for a couple of White Russians to reward myself for a good workout. I went on a series of every diet known to man, while maintaining a weight of 160 pounds (my ideal weight is 130). I had replaced over-eating with over-drinking—and somehow that felt better. I didn't have to throw up and I was numbed out for longer.

The weight stayed on because of how much I was drinking, much more than I was eating at that time. I couldn't throw up the calories consumed from drinking, or at least I never thought about it, because I wasn't stuffing myself, I didn't feel "full." I wasn't eating healthy either. Many nights I drank my dinner, and then I'd be so hungry later on that in a drunken stupor I'd eat anything, often pigging out just before passing out.

On the inside this was an incredibly unhappy time for me. On the outside I was the party girl! Everyone thought I was so happy, so together, having so much fun! Sure I was a little chunky, but I was buying my own place, I had a good job, and I had my own car. I had it all, or so it seemed. I was drowning in self-destruction, putting on a smile for the world, while slowly falling apart inside.

At this point, the drinking was getting way out of hand, but I didn't know what else to do. I didn't know how else to live. I was looking for relief in a way I was never going to find it. I was overeating and drinking way too much, yet I was too tired to do anything about it. I was going to do better tomorrow, and tomorrow never came. Days turned into weeks and weeks turned into years.

I met Gregory in 1981. By 1983, when we started living together I really changed the way I thought about food. He was thin and healthy and ate anything he wanted, including snacks, cookies, whatever, in moderation—just like I did growing up. That's when I focused on getting back to the naturally thin person I'd been. I knew I was never meant to be overweight. I knew I wasn't one of those people who had to watch everything they ate. So I made a conscious decision to change my thinking, trusting that the results would follow.

I began eating three meals a day (instead of all day I joked), and I quit dieting once and for all. I also quit getting on the scales and looking in the mirror. I stopped doing everything that told me something other than the affirmations I was saying, which were, "I eat healthy. I'm at my ideal weight. I'm fit and trim." If I got on the scales or looked in the mirror I heard, "You're fat," so I steered clear. I affirmed I was happy with my body, and I quit obsessing about it.

In one year I went from 160 pounds to 130 pounds. I was eating three meals a day. I didn't binge and purge once during that year, and wouldn't for the next ten years. I maintained a healthy weight as well, give or take ten pounds. I felt like I did growing up: food was just a part of normal everyday living. So was drinking.

Chapter 4

EARLY DRINKING

Drinking was a lot of fun for a lot of years—until it wasn't anymore. In her book, *Drinking, A Love Story*, Caroline Knapp says, "Drinking made everything better until it made everything worse." It was true. But that didn't stop me. I kept looking for the next great buzz, the wonderful relief it was in the beginning. Never mind that it hadn't been that way for a long, long time. I kept searching. Once in a great while I would have a fun drunk, the harmless kind it was at first, but all the other times it was anything but.

At first it took away my insecurity. Being who I was, was never okay with me. But with alcohol, I somehow settled comfortably into my own skin. Drinking made me feel beautiful, instead of the plain person with bright-red hair, pale skin, and freckles I'd always been. It didn't matter that I had big feet and small breasts, after a couple of drinks it all seemed to fit.

My feelings of inadequacy and fear of people would disappear. Suddenly I was the life of the party! The early days were a blast, especially once I could get into bars. The lights, the music, the men! It was tons of fun and I became addicted to that lifestyle from the very start.

Something else happened, and I didn't quite know how to handle it. After being a plain Jane all my life, I never had a boyfriend in school, never ran with the popular crowd, I wasn't a cheerleader, I didn't get asked to dances, and suddenly, you might say, I blossomed. I quickly learned that there was a big difference between the way little boys think about redheads and the way big boys do. Suddenly the curse of being different became the blessing of being unique. I had too much attention too soon. I loved it, thrived on it, and made a fool of myself because of it.

I see now that I was nothing more than a bar slut, looking for love and telling myself I was loved and appreciated because the best looking guy in the bar wanted to take me home. To me, they were all potential boyfriends. I would have started a relationship with any one of those guys, but that wasn't what they were looking for, was it?

The drinking helped me forget the one before, and the fact he never called. It helped me set my sights on the next potential boyfriend. It never happened. It was never going to happen. But I kept trying, drinking more to forget how many there were.

I lost myself early on, and didn't even know it. I drank to loosen up, to relax and have fun, and to forget. When it wasn't fun anymore, I drank more to try to find the fun. When that didn't work, I drank even more so I wouldn't care.

As I look back, I see that the fun turned to despair early on, but I knew what had worked before, so I just kept trying the same thing over and over again, hoping to find the magic once again. It was never going to happen. Kind of like the definition of insanity, "doing the same thing over and over, expecting different results."

I became engaged, briefly, during this time, but he was controlling, wanted to change me, and keep me to himself. When I left work early one day, hungover of course, and went by his place, I found him with another woman, an old girlfriend that wasn't really an old girlfriend after all. I ended the relationship and he married her.

When I finally found "the one" and fell in love hard, I wasn't the one for him. I was crushed, my heart was broken. I became pregnant and honestly didn't know between two men who the father was. The one I was in love with or the one who helped me forget.

I was twenty-one years old and didn't know what to do. I had an abortion and drank even more not to feel anything. Nothing seemed the same after that, but I kept on as I always had, drinking and partying. My "encounters," although not as frequent, began to take a turn for the worse. A couple of humiliating experiences in a row and I began to like myself less and less.

One night I was following a guy on a motorcycle, headed to my house.

We'd known each other when we were kids, and now, years later, had run into each other at the bar. We were both drunk. He got stopped by the police going about 100 miles per hour.

I continued home. When I got there, another guy I had been seeing, not dating mind you, just having sex with, was waiting in the driveway, passed out. He had come to my house like always, after he'd had his party. I freaked out, realizing what might have happened had I showed up with the other guy (both had the same name by the way). I felt like my guardian angel helped me out on that one.

It turns out the guy who was waiting in the driveway was sleeping with two other girls I worked with, and he was engaged to someone else! A close call with a venereal disease and I'd had enough. I vowed to stop sleeping around, but I kept on drinking, and overeating, and gaining weight.

I was the captain of a women's pool team, and I got stopped coming home from pool night. I was so blasted I didn't even know I was behind the wheel. It's a miracle I didn't kill someone, or myself. The police officer had to practically hit my bumper, as well as shine his spotlight right into my car before I knew what was happening. I barely remember seeing a glow (I had the glow!). I managed to pull over and when he opened the car door, I fell out.

He helped me up and had me humor him by trying to stand on one foot. I did, and he caught me. He had me try the other foot just for fun, same thing. He didn't even try to make me walk in a straight line. Hell, I couldn't stand in a straight line! I remember crying and begging him not to put handcuffs on me, but he had to. My blood alcohol was .23, nearly three times the legal limit. Who needs to drink that much? Maybe I didn't care anymore. Getting blasted out of my mind, every time I went out, every day, was all I was doing anymore. I was twenty-two years old.

I guess the drunk driving got my attention, at least I thought at the time it did, but not enough to *quit* drinking. Nothing was going to make me do that. I was just going to have to find a better way to do it. Getting *that drunk* was going to have to stop, and for awhile I was better.

I started eating before drinking mass quantities (what a concept!), and I wouldn't drive if I was drinking all night. I was more aware, but I didn't slow down that much. My life hit rock bottom shortly after, when I was at a friend's house after the bars closed. There were only a couple of us in the house. My friend and another person were listening to music on headsets when I went downstairs to the bathroom. One of the guys I'd met earlier was waiting for me in the doorway of one of the bedrooms.

It all happened so fast, I was in shock. He forced himself on me before I could stop him. It was over that fast. It wasn't violent. I wasn't hurt. I was just confused. I ran from the house and drove home, never remembering the drive. I blamed myself because I didn't stop him. A month later, when I found out I was pregnant, I had a secret abortion, with serious complications that nearly caused me to have a hysterectomy. I kept this all to myself.

I was very, very sick, but I didn't tell anyone for about eight years. The first person I confided in was my friend whose house it happened at, and later my husband. I blocked the whole thing out of my mind, like it had never happened, until years later when a dream about giving birth to parts of a baby prompted me to deal with it, and heal from it.

My life hit an all-time low after that. I was probably the most unhealthy I'd ever been. I was overweight, and drank excessively on a daily basis. How I kept a job I'll never know. I was numb. I didn't care. I couldn't feel. That time in my life is still not real clear, even today.

They say in recovery our minds and bodies heal, and things that we didn't remember suddenly come back. That's exactly what has happened with so many parts of my life, except that period. It's all foggy. I remember very little, until I met my husband.

I already knew him from work, but when we started seeing each other outside of work, my whole life began to improve. I started to feel again, to care again. I felt comfortable with him, and safe. He was just a friend, but a friend I really needed at the time. He already had a wife and two children. Somehow that made him safe for me. For the first time it wasn't about sex. I had to learn that. I'd been doing everything backwards. He was good for me, but I don't know how good I was for him. Little did he know, he was in for the ride of his life!

Chapter 5

THE UGLY YEARS

The next two years were the worst of my drinking, and the most destructive. I call them "the ugly years." Greg's marriage ended. He moved in with me, and within six months his two children were living with us permanently. They were three and eight. The ugly years were a contradiction of raising a family and partying like crazy.

I worked as a secretary, Monday through Friday, 8:00–4:30, while Gregory worked rotating shifts at the same facility. Each month we had two days off together. I went from being single, to being a single mom. I was with the kids more than anyone. I'm not sure how I felt about everything at that time. I was twenty-three years old and not at all happy about the kids coming to live with us. In fact, I wanted to end the relationship.

I didn't know what else to do. I didn't want any children, I never had. The kid's mom came to Greg in early November and said she couldn't handle it anymore. By the first of December both the kids and the house would be his responsibility. I wanted to run. And I did run, for about an hour. I'd finally found the love of my life, and I wasn't about to give him up, no matter what the cost.

So, by Thanksgiving our love nest became a family home, and my life changed forever. I did good the first year, only stopping for a couple of drinks after work before picking the kids up from day care by 6:00 p.m. I made dinner every night, kept a clean house, and did lots of little laundry. I managed to work a full-time job while drinking every day, more on the weekends.

Six months after the kids came to live with us we moved back into their old house, their old neighborhood. Everything was the same for this family, as it had been just over a year before, only the woman had changed. I often thought how that must have seemed to the neighbors, to the children! The eight year old seemed the most affected, and the one we had to work with the most. That's another book, but the next eight years were filled with calls and meetings with the school, visits from the police, numerous trips in and out of court, counselors, doctors, and so called "specialists." Looking back, I didn't handle it well.

Jeremy was a good excuse for me to drink. Depending on how many calls I got, and how bad he was that day, was how drunk I got that night. Suffice it to say, I wasn't coping. The first three years continued to get worse. If Greg was on dayshift and was home with the kids, my "happy hour" turned into three, and progressively I got more irresponsible.

I held it together when I really had to. If he was working swings or sleeping because of midnights, I manipulated my responsibilities around my drinking, or vice versa. The kids got picked up when they needed to be, they were taken to soccer practice (I never missed a game), teacher conferences were held, dinner was on the table, breakfast ready in the morning, and clean clothes were in the closets. What they didn't have was a sober mom. They didn't have a mom who would sit with them and hold them, or talk with them.

Mornings were pretty fun. I never wanted the kids to be rushed in the morning. I wanted their day to start off on the right foot. There was time to eat, get dressed, take our time. Mornings were good. Jeremy caught the bus from the day care center at first, so I took them both there on my way to work. Later, he caught it near the house and just Megan went to day care. I would get off work at 4:30 p.m., race to the bar for as many White Russians as I could drink in an hour-and-a-half, and pick them up, usually late, by 6:00 p.m., when the day care closed. I'd drive with them in the car! Thank God we only lived a few blocks away, but still, I cringe at the thought.

Even more devastating are the times I had "to go" White Russians in the car (they used to do that). One at least, sometimes two, to get me through the evening. I couldn't go to the bar with the kids, but I remember putting them in the car and driving a couple of blocks to get a "to go" drink or two then return home. I thought that was perfectly acceptable. After all, I was home with them. I fixed their dinner and put them to bed. What more was expected of me? Yikes.

At this point, their birth mother was taking them once a week for a couple of hours, usually to a movie and fast food for dinner. That gave me a couple of hours to drink at the bar, if Greg was working, and if he wasn't, we spent rare time alone. I remember resenting her for not taking them overnight, so I could keep on partying of course, but her weak attempt at spending time with her children (two hours a week was ridiculous), began to wear on me. I resented being the major caregiver for these two children, even though I'd grown to love them and call them my own.

The relationship between their mother and me grew increasingly strained, and she had me to answer to every time she showed up late to get them, which was nearly every time. I continued to push her into spending more time with them, to no avail, and my resentment grew deeper. The problems we were having with Jeremy didn't help. His desire to live with his mother was the source of his rebellion.

He would wait at the window on the days she was coming to get them, and when the scheduled time came and went, he would get increasingly angry, raging as each car passed that wasn't hers. On the days he really raged, you could guarantee the visit wouldn't go well. He was so hard on his mother, reprimanding her and being angry the whole visit. It got so that every time she brought them back she had a bad report on him, and I was getting tired of getting him back meaner and more ornery than when he left.

We tried not letting him go the next time if he behaved badly, and that worked for awhile, but it wasn't worth what I had to go through with him when she drove off with Megan. And I was even angrier, because I didn't get a break at all.

One time she showed back up shortly after taking both kids. She was bringing Jeremy back because he was so bad. I'd been drinking, of course, and was just about fed up with her not dealing with her children, especially Jeremy. I told her she wasn't going to see them if she didn't learn to deal with them. I asked her who I could call when he misbehaved, who could I dump him on? No one!

It got uglier. The fight was on. I slapped her and pushed her out of what used to be her own house! The fight continued at the neighbor's, when Jeremy came back crying that she was going to take them to Texas. The neighbor broke us up and she left, horrified I'm sure. I returned home to hysterical children who'd seen it all.

At the time, I admitted to being sorry that I had let her make me lose control, but I wasn't sorry I had hit her. Today, I'm very sorry, and I've made amends the best I could. Things would continue to get worse for the next year or so: Jeremy's behavior, my drinking, the relationship. I began spending more and more time at the bar when Greg was home with the kids. Always I would promise to be home in time to fix dinner, and more often than not I wouldn't make it home until 9:00 p.m.

The fight would be on, not because Greg was mad at me for disappointing him once again, but because I was ugly and wanted him to be mad at me. I wanted him to yell at me, to hit me even; but he never would. So I would. I see now that I was so angry at myself for my behavior and lack of responsibility, yet I didn't know what else to do. I loved him so much, the kids too, but I just didn't like my life. I didn't like my choices.

It was one thing to have the family I never expected to have, but it wasn't the perfect family, and I didn't want to deal with that. I certainly didn't want to see my part in the dysfunction. There were instances when Greg and I would go out together, without the kids, and drink and party. I would usually get ugly once I got too drunk. It was never because of him, always because of me. I think it had to be my own self-hate, my own disgust about the drinking and the fact that I couldn't stop, no matter how hard I tried.

It was during one of these fights that I began throwing and breaking things. I may have even hit him this time. I did that a couple of times, so out of control, the alcoholic in me raging. Although this wasn't frequent, it happened. A few nights of not coming home at all, and I'd pushed too far. I was asked not to come back at all. It was a wake up call I never expected.

This was March of 1986. Since I'd sold my mobile home when we moved into the house, I had no where to go, except my folk's, something I never thought I would have to do. It was the worst time of my life. I cried myself to sleep every night. I missed Greg so much. I must admit I was enjoying the freedom from parenthood and the problems with Jeremy, but I missed the kids terribly, especially Megan, because she'd been with me since she was three, and had never been an ounce of trouble.

One day when I went to visit, she came running from the neighbors, calling, "Mommy! Mommy!" My heart was broken. What was I doing? I had to make some decisions. I knew that Gregory was valid on everything he could no longer live with. If we were ever going to make this relationship work, I was going to have to quit drinking . . . so much. I was going to have to quit going to the bars, unless we were together, and I was going to have to keep my word. It wasn't a hard decision. I had to have him back, them back. I was miserable by myself, and problems or not, I loved the kids.

Gregory wasn't going to let me back that easy, though. At first I was still up to my old ways, even though I wasn't living there. We were still seeing each other, but I continued to disappoint him at times by not showing up when I said I would, if at all.

I remember one night I was supposed to come for dinner and he ended up finding me at the bar playing pool with an old boyfriend. I acted like I wasn't doing anything wrong. I felt like I wasn't. He came back to the pool tables, gave me a look I'd never seen before, and turned and walked out. That would be the night I'm told, that I showed up at the house late, drunk, driving of course, and demanded he let me in, which he didn't. I went out to the car and honked the horn, waking up the whole neighborhood I'm sure, until he came out and made me stop. I'm told I drove away, pissed off. (It's such a glamorous life, isn't it?) I don't remember where I went after that, probably back to the bar. Scary stuff.

I guess it had to get worse before it got better, and shortly after that I knew I needed to make some changes. I weaseled my way back into the house while his parents were visiting from California in June. I never left. Four months later we were married, with Jeremy as best man and Megan as bridesmaid and flower girl. It would end up being the best decision I'd ever made. And if there's such a thing as getting one's drinking under control, that's what I did, although I never stopped.

Chapter 6

CONTROLLED DRINKING

Once we were married I started drinking at home. The bar life caused too many problems. I continued on as captain of a women's pool team, we played on Thursday nights. That was my night out, and I milked it for everything it was worth. Greg couldn't understand why I had to close the bar every Thursday night. I couldn't understand how he could think I wouldn't, after all it was my only night out anymore. We had a few disagreements about that, but it wasn't going to change. I wasn't going to change. Didn't he think it was better than it used to be? What did he want from me?

Ten months after we were married, we packed up everything we owned and moved from Idaho to Michigan. The night before we left, Jeremy made one last attempt to get his mother to let him stay. Like all the times he'd tried to get her to let him live with her, she said no.

Once we got to Michigan, we had plans to stay in my cousin's cottage. It was small, but we made it a comfortable home our first year. That's the year I drank White Russians by the pitcher. Every day I drank, and that seemed to be acceptable to my husband. After all, I wasn't going to the bars anymore, and I was keeping up with my duties. My house was spotless. I handled the bills and the shopping and cooked the meals. Everything was in order.

I even started running a couple of miles a day. We lived in the country, with a river running through the yard and all kinds of wildlife everywhere. Deer wandered into the yard. It was the most peaceful year I'd ever had. Life was very good for me that year, drinking and all. The problems with Jeremy were still there, but it didn't seem as bad as it had been. I think being away from his mom made it a little easier for him to bond with me, because he didn't feel like he was betraying her. It was one of the best years that Jeremy and I ever had.

A year later we moved to a house in town. I began working at a real estate company, and things seemed to be going pretty good. But the problems with Jeremy continued to get bigger, as he did. Before we knew it, we were involved with the Michigan court system. I was still drinking at home, but the bar was always a big draw for me. I found a bar downtown that I was able to persuade Gregory to walk to on Friday nights for happy hour. It was always so busy that we didn't really like it that much. Still he would go if I wanted to (I always wanted to).

If I had to go downtown for something, like to the bank or the dime store, I would always stop at the bar and have a White Russian or two. No one ever knew about that, it was my little secret. Some days I went specifically for the bar, but kidded myself that I had other things to do as well. By this point in my drinking career I was very content to drink alone, in a bar, in the early afternoon when I was often the only one there. It was my "reward." For what, I don't know, but that's what it felt like; a reward.

Before long the game center right behind our house was sold and turned into a sports bar. Yippee! I was in seventh heaven, much happier about it than I let on to Gregory. We were both glad to have somewhere a little closer for Friday happy hour, which was, of course, not nearly as important to him as it was to me. He indulged me, he always indulged me.

I can remember going downtown on my days off for whatever reason, and stopping at the bar for a couple of drinks, and then upon returning home, depending on the time and how soon the kids would be home from school, go to the sports bar for another one.

Some days I remember getting home to meet the kids from school only to leave shortly after that to "have a drink with a friend." By this time, I had met several people at my job who drank, so if it wasn't my idea to go after work, it would be theirs. We could always count on someone. I justified this because it was just behind the house and the kids knew where I was, and I left the number for them.

Some days I remember them calling me at the bar when they got home and found me gone. I was always surprised they knew where to find me. Ha!

This was my phase of deep denial. I was kind of hiding it from Gregory, but not caring that the kids knew. After all, I was an adult. It was only an hour or so. I was always back in time to fix dinner and before Gregory got home from work.

Some days, if someone asked *me* to go for a drink, I would leave Greg a note, or tell the kids to have him come over. I guess I thought it was okay as long as it wasn't my idea. There were a lot of drinkers at work, so Friday nights were usually a party, and most of the time Gregory knew where to find me. I would have dinner already in the crockpot or something easy to fix in mind, so I could handle it being wasted. If I did get too wasted, we ordered pizza. Usually I tried to have dinner prepared ahead of time if I knew I was going to the bar. That way I didn't have any guilt.

There were only a couple of incidents during those years, when I got too drunk or stayed too long, didn't fix dinner, whatever, and the fight was on. Because of me, mind you, never Gregory. It was my own guilt I think, but whatever it was, it was horrible. It was like the ugly years had come back to haunt me, and it gave me one more thing to be remorseful about in the morning.

Luckily, these incidents were few and far between, since I was trying so damn hard to keep my drinking under control. My wonderful husband reminded me of one of these alcohol-induced fights in which I slapped him across the face. He, in turn, slapped me (because last time I hit him he vowed the next time he would hit me back). I slapped him again, he slapped me, and it could have gone on and on as far as he was concerned. He said I was pissed and stomped off. I vaguely remember the incident. We laughed good and hard when he refreshed my memory. One more reminder of the insanity of this disease.

The last couple of years of my drinking, it was the big fight every day, between myself. Should I go to the bar? No, you don't need to. But I want to. No, you shouldn't. What the hell? I'm going. My time for this was usually around 2:00 p.m. The kids got home after 3:00 p.m., but some days I was there at 1:00 p.m., and occasionally I was there for lunch.

Sometimes my arguments with myself would hold out almost long enough, and then at 2:30 p.m. or 2:45 p.m. I was racing over there to suck down a quick White Russian and return home, like nothing was going on. It was a battle between my evil twin and me.

The last couple of years of my drinking I switched to wine, because I could get more for my money. Still I had the bar addiction and the White Russian addiction. I'd usually have one, if I had enough money. If not, I had a glass of wine, then back home to the bottle in the fridge, which I sipped (yea, right) while fixing dinner. I quit my job at the real estate company the summer of 1992 in order to write a book.

Chapter 7

THE BOOK

I guess my hope and dream to become a serious writer was always there, yet I didn't consciously make it a goal until 1991. The idea of writing a book, I thought, began at that time, but I've found in going over my journals that the dream was there much earlier.

It seems as though my soul was speaking to me, even as I drowned it with alcohol and fear. Alcohol quieted the fear, until ultimately it nearly destroyed me. As I look back at the dream unfolding, it amazes me that I had it as together as I did. I actually wrote every day, full-time, that first year after quitting my "real" job in June of 1992. I actually wrote a book.

Oh yeah, the book. How funny. I wrote a book called *Recovering From Life* *before* I quit drinking, *before* I got into recovery. What was I thinking?!! Oh, humility. Well, it's where I was. My intentions were good. I was right on a few things. I knew the book was a gift. What I didn't know was that the book was a p-r-o-c-e-s-s.

I didn't know God wanted me to quit drinking first, to admit I had a problem. I didn't know I wasn't really in recovery. I thought I was. I believed, and still do, that we're all in recovery. We are all recovering from life. That's not sleep we do each night, it's recovery! And God knew we would need it at the end of each day. (We recover, children recharge.)

What I didn't have a clue about was what recovery "from addiction" was all about, and that I qualified. I spent that first year, mid-1992 to mid-1993, writing my book. I spent every day writing, except weekends which I spent with my family. I got up early with my husband and saw him off to work and

31

my daughter off to school. I straightened up the house, which was already in impeccable order, showered, and went to work.

It was a time I remember fondly, a special time for me, finally realizing a dream. I was a writer. That was my job. I was free to write all day long, instead of trying to fit it into my busy life, never having the time I really wanted or needed. It was a dream come true, yet I felt unworthy. Finally I could get this book out of my head!

For months prior to quitting my job, I had been preparing to write the book, without knowing it. For the first time in my life I was learning to relax, if only for a little while each day. My ritual became a nice soak in a hot bath, candles burning, and meditation music playing softly. Oh, I almost forgot, a glass of wine on the stand.

I did this every night for a long time. It fed my soul so much. That's when my head began filling with information contained in the first book. It would just flow into my head, as if someone were reading it to me. It sounded good. It made sense. I was overwhelmed with how much was being given to me, and I didn't know what I was supposed to do with it.

After awhile, all I knew was that I had to write it down. I had to get it out of my head or I would go crazy. The seed had been planted and it wasn't long before I had quit my day job and was writing full-time, fighting feelings of unworthiness and guilt.

After all, other people had to get up and leave the comfort of their homes, work at jobs they hated, travel on winter roads that were treacherous, follow what other people told them to do, when they were told to do it, while I, well, I had the good life. I could start my day whenever I wanted. Granted, I was up and at 'em earlier than most people start their jobs, but I could break whenever I wanted. I could work in sweat pants and slippers, with my kitty curled on my lap or stretched across my desk.

If I was tired after a long stretch of writing, I could take a nap, which I often did, all the while feeling guilty as hell because my life was so charmed. I never felt worthy. I fought that the whole first year. I was afraid to feel excited about my life and what I was getting to do with it. I see now that those feelings of unworthiness are what prompted my second year, the one where all I did was drink.

But first I want to talk about the nine months I was actually writing the book. It was an experience and an adventure I hold dear to my heart. It was the way things were supposed to be. Whether or not the first *Recovering From Life* has anything to do with the finished product, is doubtful. It seems that most of the book was written *after* the original was completed.

I didn't know what I was going to write about each day. I started this new adventure in June. It was warm and I would write out on the front porch first thing in the morning. I'd have my coffee, and life was good! My heart was filled with elation at the wonderful life I was living. I wrote about whatever came to mind. The writing flowed and I filled notebook after notebook.

To this day I still find myself drawn to the front porch on warm summer mornings, where I have a chance to write the old fashioned way. It reminds me of those early days, before I got my word processor, which was a going-away present from my friends at work. They collected over $200 and gave me a gift certificate. I put it on layaway, the check covering over half the cost of the machine. A month or so later, I had a new word processor.

This was the life! Now I was getting serious about this writing thing. I could write a lot faster on the word processor, and it was then that I really immersed myself in "stream of consciousness" writing, which was almost trance-like. I wasn't consciously thinking up anything, I was just writing what came to me, as fast as I could get it down. The whole thing just "kind of happened."

It was a magical time for me. Writing a book. Wow. No experience. Didn't even know how I was going to put it together, how to break it into chapters, what to call them. I didn't have a clue what I was doing, and yet it just "happened." When I was done writing, apparently I was done writing.

I remember I stopped one day, finished what I was working on, saved the file, turned around and saw all the typed pages and handwritten notebooks laid out on the bed, and it was like, okay, the writing part is almost done. I knew I had more work to do on one of the chapters. It was a Friday afternoon. I'd been writing since early morning and I was tired. My little Saushy was stretched out across my desk, sleeping.

I was struggling with this chapter. I couldn't seem to bring the right emotion to it. It was an important chapter, and I wanted it to be meaningful. I jotted myself a note and decided to let it rest for the weekend. I felt so sleepy I could barely keep my eyes open. I laid down and Sausha got on the bed and licked my cheek. As she did this I went immediately into a deep sleep. When I woke up she was asleep beside me.

Monday morning I found her dead under the front porch.

I couldn't believe this was happening. She'd been my buddy while I wrote the book. She wasn't used to me being home during the day, and once I quit my job, she followed me everywhere. Now, I was just about to finish the book, and this happens?

I couldn't bring myself to go into my office for three days. My last memory in there was of her sprawled across my desk. Finally, I had to. I sat down at my desk and immediately saw the note I had left myself the Friday before. It said, "Loss of a Loved One." The chapter I was having trouble bringing enough emotion to was about grief.

I've lost a lot of people in my life, suffered some devastating losses, but it had been awhile. Time does have a way of healing the heart, and it was hard for me to totally recall the initial grief and devastation that you feel when you lose someone close to you.

So, here I was, feeling so much grief over a little animal. But she was more than that to me. She was my buddy, and this was a very personal loss. I was so angry at God. I felt responsible, thinking that if I'd been able to write that damn chapter, Sausha wouldn't have had to die. Why was this happening to me?

Somehow, through it all, I trusted that all things happen for a reason. I cried and prayed to God, saying that I didn't like what had happened, but I trusted Him somehow, damn it! I trusted Him. It seemed like forever, but just over a month later we got Cali, so much like Sausha it was amazing. It took awhile, but we all adjusted, and before long it was perfectly clear that everything does indeed, happen for a reason. We were so grateful for Cali, possible only because of Sausha's death.

A year later I wrote a story about Sausha; it was very healing for me. But right after her death, before we got Cali, I was in turmoil. I felt a deep sense of loss. The book had been such a positive experience, I was so excited about my writing and about life itself, but now I didn't want to play the game anymore. I was no longer having fun. After those first few days, I made myself pick up the pages of the book that were finished. I began reading them, editing them.

Time seemed to fly and I was grateful for the distraction. It was positive reading, and I felt nurtured. The words no longer seemed to be for others to read, instead they were written for me. That's how I got over the grief of losing my little writing buddy.

The work on the book kept me involved, plus the chapter about loss was easy to relate to, and write about. After that, the order of the pages just sort of happened. The chapters found their places and titles. There was more editing and re-writing, and before I knew it I was printing out a finished product. It had been nine months from start to finish.

A typical day for me was writing until about 2:00 p.m., sometimes 1:00 p.m., depending on how early I started. Sometimes I would nap for about a half hour before going to the bar, sometimes I went straight to the bar. As I look back now, I see that I felt it was my "reward," no excuses about it. I deserved it. After all, I'd put in a good day of writing, and after Saushy died, I *needed* that drink in the afternoon.

Once I actually finished the book, well, it was time to celebrate. I was proud of myself. I knew I wanted to write a book, had to write a book, but it was also something I had doubted in myself. Could I really do it? Would I really do it? And I had. I spent the next few months trying to get it published. I thought it was good. I really did. Parts of it are good, it's just not the book it was intended to be. Not my intentions, mind you, but the one who gave the gift.

People had warned me about rejection slips, how harsh they could be, downright mean sometimes. But I wasn't afraid of them. I'd prepared myself for that. I never felt my book would be accepted right away. I sent out several manuscripts at a time, switching envelopes and cover letters when they were returned, and sending them out again. It never got me down. I never doubted it would get published. My rejection slips are some of the kindest and gentlest let downs I've ever read. They were encouraging. I don't remember it ever becoming discouraging. I don't remember making a conscious decision to stop sending out manuscripts either, but sometime in that next year I did. I also stopped writing.

Chapter 8

LAST YEAR OF DRINKING

Now, years later, I've been afraid to look at what I wrote during that time, afraid of seeing how sick I really was when I wrote the book. Yet, I know that so much of my writing does not come from me, but rather "through" me. I do not take credit for much of what was given to me that year.

After the book was completed, or so I thought, I'm pretty sure most of what I did was drink. My disease progressed to the point that I knew I had to do something. It became frightfully clear I was not going to be able to get my drinking "under control" as I had tried so hard to do for so many years. I wasn't yet ready to admit I was an alcoholic, but I could no longer deny that this thing was getting worse instead of better. It scared me to see where it was heading.

I've often said that the last year my life got in the way of my drinking. I remember my 2:00 p.m. drinking time moving to noon. I remember having a drink with lunch a lot of the time, and a lot of the time no lunch. Nothing else was important it seemed, and I had never felt that way before. I always believed that alcohol and drugs "enhanced" my love of life, my deep-seated joy for living. But now it seemed the joy was fading, and an ugly fog was moving in.

No longer was alcohol working. No longer did it bring the relief it always had. Hell, I couldn't even get drunk at the end. There was never going to be enough alcohol to do the trick. Thank God I hadn't discovered that a few slugs of vodka would do the trick quicker than mass quantities of wine, or I very well could have, would have, sought out that relief.

For me, it just wasn't working anymore. I didn't have it in me to search for that next something that might. After all, I'd been a heavy vodka drinker for years. I only switched to wine the last two years because it was cheaper and I wasn't working. I could drink a lot more for the money. I could buy a whole box of wine for a little more than what two White Russians cost me at the bar.

I guess my phase of buying kahlua and vodka, mixing up White Russians by the pitcher, was too telling on me. I could go through a couple of fifths in no time, and that was even too costly compared to wine by the box. Besides, it was a little too tempting to start drinking early when those "chocolate milk" drinks went down so smoothly. I could never drink wine before noon, but I could mix up a frozen White Russian and think I was having a milk shake!

For me, the scary part of my drinking was the feeling there wouldn't be enough. As far back as I can remember my drinking was always a "need." That's what bothered me the most. That's the thing that had the potential of making me an alcoholic. The panic, the relief.

The ability to go for a drink after work was a fix, something I had to have. Holidays and family get-togethers required the proper supplies: wine, or kahlua and vodka, whichever the case may be. It was a feeling of peace and calm inside when I got it, a feeling of anxiety and fear until then. As soon as my booze was secured, I was fine. I was calm. Life was good. The anxiety would leave me once I had my goods, but that was about to change as well.

The last Thanksgiving before I quit drinking was the one that my mom says warned her of a serious problem. We had made our usual stop at the store for my "supply." When we got to Mom's I put the wine in the freezer, because it was warm. A few minutes later she opened the freezer for something and the wine fell out and broke all over the floor. Well, as my mom says, there was a look of panic on my face. And I remember that panic. It was a panic! And I was pissed at her. How could she have broken my bottle of wine? What was I supposed to do now?

I remember the feeling. What I didn't realize, was that it wasn't normal. I remember my sister ran downstairs to see if she could find a bottle of something, anything. When she came up with it, I breathed a sigh of relief, and the day went on. Mom said that was the first time she realized this thing might really be a problem. That was her warning sign, not mine.

That Christmas was the next warning sign, and one that did get my attention. I telephoned my grandparents when I was drunk. Why is it that we drinkers don't want people to know how much we drink, yet we always want to call people when we're drunk? Anyway, that's what I did. I don't remember anything I said to them, I only remember hanging up and being embarrassed because I knew I was slurring my words and I had no idea what I had said. I then called my mom and told her I'd talked to them. She said, "You did?" and she sounded distressed. I was almost too drunk to notice, or to feel bad, but not quite. The memory haunts me still.

After drinking virtually every day for over fifteen years, I quit drinking the following March. Like most alcoholics, I hid my drinking; but I'm afraid it was getting to the point where I wouldn't have been able to hide it. I drank around everybody. I wasn't a closet drinker, I just hid how *much* I was drinking.

I did my best drinking in the kitchen. I was spending more and more time in there, baking more and more. I'd drink a glass of wine while fixing dinner, and for all anybody knew, it was my first glass. Little did they know I'd already been to the bar earlier in the afternoon and had two or three White Russians and at least that much wine. I'm only now beginning to realize how good I was at the game, and how much my alcoholism was progressing.

I worried that I drank too much for years, but like every other alcoholic I've ever met, I was just sure I could get it "under control." The last year my drinking really increased. I couldn't get enough. I was going through a bottle of wine in no time flat, and since I'm a conscientious recycler (absolutely refuse to throw a bottle in the trash), I was faced with a sobering realization about how much I was drinking.

I remember being at the recycling center and emptying a bag full of glass into the bin. Mounds of wine bottles spilled into the pile. It was shocking to see it like that: all that wine, me, drinking alone. I felt a panic, the thought that maybe this thing was getting out of hand, that perhaps I wasn't going to be able to get it under control after all. I had to think fast! Denial! That always works. I have to get smarter about my drinking. I have to move on to the BOX OF WINE.

There were eight bottles to a box. I was in heaven. Little spout. Free flowing wine! Security! Well, it worked for a minute. That first box seemed to last forever. I thought I'd found my answer. The second box seemed to go a little faster. But I could replace the empty one with a full one during the day when no one was home, and the cardboard could be broken down and flattened out to fit inconspicuously amongst the recycling. I was so clever. I had it all figured out.

Then the next box seemed to go way too fast. I couldn't believe it. I realized then, for the first time really, that this thing wasn't going to get any better. In fact, it was going to continue to get worse. I didn't know about alcoholism as a progressive disease at that time, but I knew something was happening—and it was out of my control.

That, I believe was the beginning of the end. I'm not sure how much longer I drank, how many more boxes of wine I went through, but if I remember right, it happened pretty quick once I'd moved on to the boxes. I think I bought four, maybe five in all.

I remember thinking that when I made the decision to quit drinking that March night, that I had dumped out what little was left in the box. I think I even said that at a meeting early on, but I'm afraid that's not what happened. I, like most of the alcoholics I know, never poured out a drop of alcohol. I'm sure I drank every last drop of that box and *then* surrendered to the thought that maybe I needed to learn to do life without a drink in my hand.

It may not have been as low of a bottom as some of us suffer before getting sober, but it was my bottom. I will never forget the feeling I had inside of desperation and hopelessness. I had finally hit the bottom I needed to hit. Me, Miss Positive, Miss Know It All, everything you ever need to know about how to live a joyous life, while slowly killing yourself with alcohol.

For me it was the end of everything I ever thought I had control of. It was an emotional bottom that took me lower than I'd ever been, as far from the life I was after as I could get. But I'm grateful that's what it took for me. I'm glad I didn't lose my marriage or my children or my home, like my cousin did. I didn't lose my life like my uncle did. I think of alcoholism as a sleazy snake, weaving its way in and out of people's lives, disguising what it really is.

Leading up to the day I quit drinking was horrible. My husband had been working downstate, only home on the weekends, so I was drinking a lot more than I would have had he been home. It was easier for me to isolate from my daughter and drink in private upstairs. I kept it together enough in the evening to do dinner and then would retreat upstairs to......what? I don't know, all I know is I hid and drank.

I was working at the bar behind the house on the weekends, and I remember that night in March. I could hear some commotion coming from outside. There was a negative feeling surrounding that night, the bar, my life. I'd been drinking all the wine I could from the box in the fridge, and still I couldn't numb myself, still I was feeling hopeless.

I was sick to death from the sweetness of the wine and yet I couldn't stop refilling my glass. I wanted to kill that box, no matter how much was left in it. I just kept drinking and drinking. I looked out at the bar and there was a fight or something, several people from inside gathered around, and I just felt such negative energy.

I was frightened, paranoid almost, like something terrible lurked all around me. It was the most horrible feeling I've ever had. Somehow I realized this was what my life had become: a life of dependency, where nothing else mattered but drinking. Numbing the pain was no longer effective. For the first time in my life I prayed the right prayer.

I always knew there was something wrong with my drinking, how I drank, why I drank, the need. I had no trouble with the first step of Alcoholics Anonymous, even before I knew what it was. I had always been "powerless over alcohol." What I didn't know was that I would always be powerless over alcohol.

Finally, my lifelong prayer of, "God please help me quit drinking *so much*," became a prayer of, "God, please help me quit drinking." It was that simple. I felt instant relief, a calm that I very much needed that night. The fear lessened, and I felt a slight sense of hope.

The next day felt different, I knew it, but I was still cautious. I wasn't quite sure how to proceed with my day or my life, without every thought and focus being on when I could drink, should I drink, or I won't drink, oh what the hell, let's drink! I seemed lost the first few days, an eerie calm came over my life, and yet the compulsion to drink had left me. I felt relief.

I continued to feel relief for the next six months. The "pink clouds" I would learn, though they were not going to be pink for very much longer.

Chapter 9

FIRST YEAR SOBER

We were remodeling our house, ripping out old lath and plaster so we could re-wire, insulate, and replace windows. We began this last winter when Greg was laid-off. I wasn't much help. I was still drinking. In fact, he did it all. I'm not sure what I was doing. Somehow I stayed busy, *looked* busy, until he went back to work in early March. Then my dad started coming over and the two of us continued ripping out old walls, until he went back to work in May.

That's when I started stripping the oak staircase. It was one hundred years old, and had twenty-seven spindles, two large posts, and four layers of paint. I stayed really busy for the next few months. I see now, this was how I dealt with not drinking, or in other words, how I avoided dealing with why I drank in the first place. I stayed extremely busy. So busy I didn't have time to think about my life, and what it was going to feel like without my buddy, alcohol.

In June I quit the bar I'd been working at part-time for the past year, which was a really smart move. It got me away from that atmosphere and one step closer to learning how to live my life without alcohol, especially since it had pretty much been my life until this point. Things continued to be pretty good for a couple more months. The only problem during that time was that I wasn't feeling good physically. I'd quit drinking and felt like I had a hangover when I woke up most mornings.

By late summer I was getting about two migraine headaches a week, and I was tired all the time. I thought, this is the thanks I get for quitting drinking? I told my husband many times that I felt just like I was hungover. I had a lung infection from working one day without a proper respirator and breathing plaster dust; but I continued to smoke cigarettes!

I finally got an antibiotic for the infection, which helped, but the other symptoms remained. Finally in September, at my husband's urging, we had the furnace checked. They shut it down, saying we were being poisoned with carbon monoxide. Since I was home all the time, I was the most affected. Had we turned the heat on, we all could have died in our sleep.

It was this same time that I went to my first AA meeting, and my recovery and my healing began. The physical healing that usually takes place the first year after quitting drinking was hindered by the carbon monoxide, so about the time I started feeling better physically, the pink clouds burst, and emotionally and spiritually I was a wreck. I know that God's timing is perfect, and that's why I found my way to AA when I did. If it weren't for that, I'm certain I would have started drinking again.

My first meeting was a step meeting at my church, held once a week on Tuesday nights. A friend of mine got into some trouble and was court ordered to go to the meetings. When she told me, I said I'd go with her. *For her*, you see, because after all, I wasn't an alcoholic, and even if I were, I wasn't anymore. I hadn't had a drink in six months.

Another friend of ours who had been in the program a couple of years before, but was back drinking and happened to have a really bad hangover the day we were there, agreed to go with us. I remember saying on the way there that I wasn't going to say I was an alcoholic. I said I would admit to having a drinking problem, but I was not going to say I was an alcoholic (that word again, the one I'd avoided all my drinking life).

They went around the table and everyone shared their stories, told how they came to sit at these tables. I was told to look for the similarities, not the differences. I heard my story in every one of theirs. I was surprised to hear "God" in the readings, in the steps. I heard this was a spiritual program. I was shocked. The meeting opened with a moment of silence and the Serenity Prayer. It was a comfort. I couldn't believe what I was hearing.

Some people have a problem with the God thing at first, but that was the most comforting discovery I made at my first meeting. I'd been on a spiritual journey for many years, I'd just taken a few murky detours along the way. I realized early in recovery that winding up here was part of my spiritual path, but I was surprised. I felt like I had finally found my place, I belonged, and I had no trouble saying, "My name is LoriJean and I'm an alcoholic." They were the most freeing words I'd ever spoken.

After my first meeting, I never stopped going. It seemed to help so much. But then the holidays hit, my first Thanksgiving, Christmas, and New Years without drinking. We went to the company Christmas party and I was tortured by the free bar. It was right behind our table. I noticed every glass of wine that went by, and every person drinking one.

I gave in. I "slipped," as they say in AA. I had my husband get me a glass of wine. One won't hurt, we both reasoned (he hated to see me suffer). But it wasn't okay. My body told me with the first few sips. I had poisoned my body with alcohol for too many years and now I'd given it a break for nine months. My body said, "No." I felt nauseated right away, that old drank too much feeling.

We left and went dancing, just a couple of songs before going home, but I felt queasy the rest of the night. It was something I needed to have happen. It seems after finally starting to feel so good, getting physically sick was all it took for me not to want it anymore. The compulsion was never as strong after that, and from then on I started feeling like I had a choice about drinking. Instead of thinking I can never drink again, I knew I didn't want to.

The holidays were still difficult. Although I wasn't aware of it at the time, I ate my way through them. After it was said and done I'd gained over ten pounds. On January 1 I decided to quit smoking cigarettes. Maybe not so smart. I started smoking when I was fifteen years old, and aside from one time when I quit for three years, it was a daily addiction as strong as my alcoholism.

Giving up the cigarettes would be the thing that almost did me in. It thrust me into a decision about recovery that I wasn't sure I wanted to make. I was suddenly, painfully, aware that I didn't have a clue how to live life sober, and yet the old way was clearly not an option, having failed me in the end. I was pissed. I didn't want to drink again, but I couldn't imagine not drinking.

I began the rough roller coaster ride that is familiar to all those in early recovery. I was not having fun! It's like it says in the Twelve Steps and Twelve Traditions, "The pains of drinking had to come before sobriety, and emotional turmoil before serenity." Well, I was in turmoil all right. Week after week I showed up at the meetings, barely hanging on, talking about how useless I felt, how non-functional I'd become, how this just didn't seem to be working.

Again and again it was suggested that I attend more meetings, but I didn't think it would help. I'd never imagined myself in recovery in the first place. I avoided it like the plague. The fact that I was going to a meeting every week was more than anyone should expect of me. But still I suffered. Finally I'd heard it enough, "go to more meetings." I was told about a women's meeting that met the next day at noon. Maybe I would try it. Here's what I wrote that day:

Today is Tuesday, February 14th, my hardest day yet. I have NEVER felt as out of sorts as I have today. If this is part of recovery, fine, then I really do need to go to more meetings, if it's not, I'm doomed. (Just kidding). But never have I felt so restless, useless, apathetic, lethargic, and I wondered all day what I'm supposed to be doing and why I can't do it.

I didn't want to do anything I managed to do. I did Yoga (hoping it would help), ate a good breakfast and took my vitamins, took a hot shower and then didn't know what to do next. Oh, it's been a weird day. Sad like, but not really. I don't know what I'm trying to say. I can't believe I'm writing. It's 5:30 and I have to put dinner in the oven (don't want to do that either), but I have to do something! I'm having a really hard time with how I'm feeling right now. God this is hard.

(Later) Well, I'm back. Dinner is over and the dishes are done, all reluctantly. This is depression! I realized it while I was making dinner. Everything I had to do was a struggle, life is a struggle at a time like this. I couldn't do anything right either. I kept dropping things in the kitchen, I used the wrong pan, nearly forgot to put the fish in the oven, and did forget to do the rice so I had to do a quicker kind.

It was all a struggle. And yet my mind wanted to rationalize and remind me of everything that's good in my life (and it is), but that matters not! I told my husband I've felt empty all day. I don't think he liked hearing that. I don't ever want to feel like this another day. I can't imagine people who suffer for years, their whole lives even with depression.

I know this is brought on by my alcoholism, its got to be. I remember someone asking me at the meeting if I was suffering from depres-

sion. Of course I said no right away, but now I really have to ask myself
if it was just denial. Does the fact that I've never had depression before
mean that I just don't recognize it? I mean, this is really something different for me, and I don't like it one bit!

I wish I would have remembered to look for some books on recovery while I was at the library yesterday. It's the most helpless feeling
I've ever felt. I have laundry to do, things I've never minded before. I
always liked keeping the house clean, everything in order. I like running
a household, writing, but I don't like anything when I'm like this. I just
want to curl up and go to sleep.

While fixing dinner I just wanted to cry. I wanted to break down
and sob, feeling sorry for myself for feeling so sorry. I'm just going to
pray. I have already today, maybe not sincerely enough. I think I was
too depressed to ask for help. Anyway, I'll be all right. I'm going to the
women's meeting tomorrow at noon and see if it helps. If it does, I may
be going every day. I laugh to myself at the prospect, but it wouldn't surprise me.

I've been back ever since.

Not only do I go to the women's meeting, but I'm also at noon meetings
at least three other times a week, sometimes four. To this day my recovery
consists of a meeting every day, and that works for me. Somehow I had
missed a common saying to newcomers, "Ninety meetings in ninety days." I
didn't understand when I heard, "Keep coming back." I didn't know it was
because I would need to.

I remember early on, when they asked if anyone had an anniversary, and
someone said they had fourteen years. I was astonished. I remember thinking, you mean I'm going to have to come here for the rest of my life? It
wouldn't be long before I found myself saying, "Thank God I have somewhere to go for the rest of my life!" The next year was touch and go, *with* a
meeting every day, much of it in the "white knuckle" stage, but one day at a
time I didn't pick up a drink.

Aside from eating to get me through those first sober holidays, I also
shoveled snow. Obsessively. In fact, my father-in-law told my husband, "She's
a human snow shovel!" I shoveled our walks, the lady's across the street, the
other lady across the street. Some days I went around the corner and shov-

eled Greg's folk's. I shoveled a path out to the garage, double-wide, out to the alley. I cleared a path for the postman! I didn't see a thing wrong with what I was doing.

I loved it out there. It was so peaceful. I see now that I would have done anything not to have to go back inside and be alone with myself. I didn't know how to live, so I shoveled snow. At least I was being productive, and helpful! I didn't recognize I was running while I was in the midst of it. But when winter rolled around again, it became very clear. I didn't know how I'd been able to do it. That year I could barely shovel our walks, single-wide. The mailman had to go around, and the widows across the street, well, someone else would have to take care of them. But who? Wasn't this *my* responsibility? I felt guilty. (Work on my codependence was yet to come).

I couldn't help if I wanted to. I wanted to, but I just didn't have the strength. For the first time in my life I felt physically exhausted. And guess what happened that very day? I looked across the street, as I did every day in winter, to see how bad Mrs. T.'s walks were, and I saw the kid next door to her shoveling them. Turns out she was letting him park his car in her car port and he agreed to shovel her walks.

I looked down to Mrs. L.'s and hers were already done. Turns out her next door neighbor was re-building his garage and she was letting him use hers, in turn he was keeping her walks clear along with his, using a snow blower. I couldn't help but smile. I finally realized I didn't have to take care of the world. I was being told to take care of myself, and the rest would be taken care of. I felt that a power greater than myself was slowing me down, forcing me to stop running. I had to. I was too tired.

Chapter 10

RECOVERY BEGINS

I've been going over more of my journals. Of course, I found much more than I remembered. I had been going to meetings for not quite two months, sober over seven months, and was just beginning to ride the roller coaster of early recovery.

November 9, 1994

I'm so afraid. I'm learning so much. I want to know more. I didn't think I was an alcoholic. I knew I had a drinking "problem," but I thought it was something I could get under control. I tried for all those years without success. It's because I couldn't admit I was an alcoholic, but now I can. And now that I have, I can begin to recover.

My drinking was so important to me that I would do anything to get it under control, anything so I wouldn't have to quit. I just had to learn HOW to drink and everything would be okay. But it wasn't, and now I know it never would be.

What was I so afraid of? What did drinking "fix?" What was it I expected to get from drinking? What was I running away from? Why was I so afraid?

I may never know the answers to these questions, but I know this, I was looking for drinking to answer all my questions, and I see now that it only created more questions. It created more frustration and drained me of my self worth.

I guess what I need to know now, or what I want to know is not so much WHY I drank, but how do I go on from here. How do I learn to handle life in a different way than I've done in the past. I have an opportunity to learn how to really live, and to enjoy life like I never could before. I've made a lot of mistakes. I've hurt people I dearly love, and I've hurt myself. I've done things I'm not proud of. Now it's time to heal. I'm afraid, but not nearly as much as when I was drinking.

Oh, how much time I've wasted. But, how much of life I've yet to enjoy. I don't have to be afraid anymore. I don't have to be controlled, or controlling anymore. I feel free. I am free. I am an alcoholic. I am a recovering alcoholic. I have a chance to make it.

Three days later I wrote my first official 4th Step. It was the best "house cleaning" I could do at the time, but it barely touched the surface of what I needed to deal with, and heal from. I owned up to "the ugly years," and made amends to the people closest to me, the ones I'd hurt the most. I was throwing monkeys off my back right and left, it seemed, and although I was a bit overwhelmed, and had a hell of a lot of work ahead of me, I still felt I was somehow on the road to freedom.

This was in November. By the end of the year I was struggling. The holidays were hard. I was out of sorts anyway, and Greg and I were trying to figure out how to relate to each other now that all the rules had changed. The house was torn up, and so was I. A lot of changes had occurred in our lives, things were all messed up. I was impatient with everything.

I didn't know it at the time, but I was just trying to get through my days without doing what I'd done most of my life, medicate. Going through that process of withdrawal is a full-time job, but none of us knew that at the time. Everybody (including me) wondered why I wasn't working. I was barely hanging on. I wasn't drinking, but that's all. This is what I wrote:

I'm sitting here in my office, if you can call it that, I can see through to our bedroom because there are no walls. This is the second winter I've had pink and yellow insulation covered in plastic for walls in my bedroom. This is the second year I haven't had a closet in my bedroom, or even on the same floor! This year we have no bathroom upstairs. There are no walls either. There ARE however, 3 new windows, and they are wonderful.

My office area is particularly a mess right now, has been for awhile. For a person who likes things to be in order, it was all falling apart. It started with Gregory's back injury in August. He was off the whole month, bedridden and unable to work on the house.

He returned to work the first of September, only to get laid off three weeks later. Financially it was stressful, then you throw Christmas in there and it was a little scary. I tried hard not to worry, and everything worked out all right in the end, but it just didn't seem like Christmas, not to me anyway.

I hardly enjoyed my tree at all, and I didn't put out any of my decorations because of the remodeling. And it didn't snow! First time since we've lived here. No white Christmas. 1994 just wasn't going to be my year. But, I told myself, next year will be different.

Gregory & I have had some trials, but nothing we haven't been able to resolve. We're both trying to work through some issues, his with me and the fact that I wouldn't get a job when we needed the money so bad. I rationalized that I couldn't get a job because I didn't want anything to interfere with my writing, yet I wasn't writing. That issue finally came to a head about a month ago.

We yelled and screamed at each other, and when all was said and done, we came to some kind of an understanding that I was doing what I needed to be doing, and the only thing I could do. Then I had to take a look at myself and the fact that I hadn't been writing. I've been dreaming some pretty powerful dreams lately, and the messages have been clear. So much is going on, and it seems I'm always on the verge of being overwhelmed.

In going over my dream journals, I realize I began writing my dreams down in recovery. I was surprised to find that my dream world mirrored what was going on in my life, and they both felt out of control. The following dreams began at the same time I started going to meetings, the same time everything started falling apart.

I couldn't seem to write. I couldn't seem to do anything I felt I needed to be doing. I didn't know what the hell was happening to me. I have always dreamed a lot, but my dreams were getting so crazy. I was remembering them so well, I knew I had to start writing them down.

I dreamed I was running from at least two gunmen and they were spraying me with bullets. I seemed to be running from house to house, seeking protection. All of them were vacant, empty except for maybe one piece of furniture. The house where they caught up with us (now my sister was with me), had just a table in it and we both dove under it. We were sprayed with bullets anyway, and I thought my sister was dead.

My body was riddled with bullets too, but I was still alive. Suddenly a friend of mine was there. He was bending down, telling me to lie still until help arrived. He was holding a cloth over a bullet hole in my chest. I remember laying very still, slowing my breathing to barely nothing, so I could reserve my strength to live.

I felt much sorrow knowing my sister was dead at my feet, and then she got up. I did too, but the gunmen were after me again. My friend and my sister were gone now, and I was running to another house to try to get away from the gunmen, but it was no use.

I knew I was never going to be able to get away from them, no matter how many houses I ran into. They were all vacant and no one was around to help me. I resigned myself to the fact that I was going to die. I was shocked and surprised that I would die so young, when I was so sure I would live to be one hundred. I resigned myself and was okay with it. I knew I was not going to run anymore.

That about says it doesn't it? A house represents the body, the physical self. My house is pretty empty. A table represents a place of activity. What am I ready to do? Shooting in a dream represents killing off aspects of self, and often bullets represent words. Running or being chased in dreams means running away from self's creations, running away from me, and my work (running from words). Finally at the end, deciding not to run anymore. Hallelujah!

A few days later I dreamed I was in a big, old theatre, the kind where live plays are performed, a theatre like I remember from childhood, only much bigger than ours was. I was reading a script where I only had a few lines and I knew them all well. I was ready to "go on." Suddenly, I was in hysterics, trying to find my script only moments before I was to perform. I couldn't for the life of me remember my lines! And they were so simple! No one else could find their scripts either. My mind was a total blank and I was incredibly panicked.

I ran around helplessly, begging people to find a script, but none could be found. I felt doomed. Then, suddenly, I found a script, reviewed my lines and we had already performed the show. But now it seemed we were to repeat the show a second time, right away, yet two of the actors were missing. A male and a female, and everyone seemed to know where they were, but weren't about to admit it. It was a "secret," where they had sneaked off to and what they were doing. Everyone knew but me.

I was becoming increasingly agitated, not only because the play was about to go on, but also because the people around me were clearly "playing dumb." Finally I said, "Fine, I'll find them myself." After all I had went through—forgetting my lines, searching for a script, doing a show—I wasn't about to have the second show ruined by two irresponsible adults indulging in "physical pleasures" while there was serious work to be done. It was very clear in the dream what the two were doing.

I found myself on the third floor, the hall was big and wide and had many rooms, all with the doors closed. I opened a bedroom door, only to find the two were, in fact, in bed having sex. They were shocked to see me and both sat up, covering themselves with the sheet. I proceeded to chew them out, saying that while we had important work to do, and they knew it, here they were......excuse the french but the dream was very frank...I said here you are FUCKING, and I yelled the word, shocking both them and myself, because I never refer to sex with that word and I can't stand it when anyone else does.

The next thing I know I'm heading down one of the aisles in the balcony and walk smack dab in the middle of a shooting gunman. In fact, I find myself sitting down in the aisle, in the middle of two heavy-set girls in jeans. I was also wearing jeans. As soon as I sat down I realized I had picked not only a very bad time to come into this area, but also a bad place to sit down. We were on the front line of fire for the gunman. I knew there was no way he was going to miss hitting me. But I felt as if there was a possibility that I wouldn't die, even though I was definitely going to get hit.

The gunman then began spraying us with bullets. I remember thinking as I felt the bullets fill my legs, if he'll just (and this part sounds terri-

*ble to me now), but I thought if he would just keep shooting in other direc-
tions, if he would start shooting other people I won't die. I'm shot, but I
could survive. Now my human, awake self would never want him to shoot
other people instead of me, but it was a real fight for survival.*

*Then, much to my dismay, I heard the gunman re-loading while he
remained in the same place. I was also aware that he had a lot more
ammunition, and I knew at that point that this man had no intention of
just wounding anyone. He was out to kill. At that point I knew I was
going to die and I thought of how pissed off (that's what I thought) my
family was going to be because I was supposed to live to be a hundred. I
remember being really shocked myself that I was going to die. The "oh
well, I'm going to die" feeling was the last I remember before waking up.*

This dream told me many things. It made me laugh. The feeling at the
end of the dream was surrender. It was the old me, the sick me, being the
one to die. The theatre, being a place where creativity is expressed, represents my writing, specifically the book. That's the part of the dream that
makes me laugh. The couple in the dream that was fooling around instead
of getting ready to perform, and my explicit language describing them, said
to me, "Quit fucking around and get the show on the road."

The part where I know my lines, then suddenly don't, and can't find a
script anywhere, shows I'm afraid I'm not going to be able to perform well.
I won't know what I'm doing with my writing, as well as with this new, sober
life. Again, the shooting represents killing off aspects of myself. I guess there
was a lot to kill off!

A hall represents access, privacy, transition (going from one room to
another). How well do the parts of myself connect? Rooms in a dream represent places in our minds, parts of ourselves. The dream told me there are
many closed doors on my upper level. The bedroom represents my private
self, my intimate self, the real me, and that, it appears is where all the fooling around is going on.

Everyone in the dream "playing dumb," represents the part of me that
is trying to pretend I don't notice I'm not working, and it tells me I'm not
fooling anyone.

I dreamed I was walking by a house that looked strange. There were boards nailed to it where they shouldn't have been, and it seemed an upstairs window was boarded up. Suddenly I realized that our friends in Idaho (whom we miss very much), lived there. I went in and was so happy to see them; I hugged them both. I noticed as I went in, the house was a big mess.

I certainly know that I need to clean house, both physically and spiritually, and the upstairs window being boarded up could represent my reluctance to check out those "upstairs rooms." As much as I want to explore my spirituality, I guess it's a fear of the unknown. Possibly fear of my own power. But my life is definitely in disarray right now. Maybe I not only need to clean my house, but unboard some of those upstairs rooms!

The next dream I had was of a house, a very lovely, intricately detailed house. I only saw the outside. This, I believe to be my higher consciousness, my dreams, hopes, and desires. It felt good seeing this great house.

Later that night I dreamed that I was being instructed, along with other people I didn't know, about the activities and arrangements that would be made for this trip or outing we were all going on. We were told there was going to be a newlywed couple joining us for this "special" weekend, and that made everyone really happy. I thought, "What a great place to enjoy a honeymoon."

The place we stayed in was a huge, fancy hotel with big open staircases and huge, open hallways. I had been wandering around, checking the place out, and just genuinely excited about being there, about being able to get away and forget all my worries.

I kept passing a cute, blond guy who would smile shyly, keep his eyes on me, but wouldn't speak. Then I was going up a staircase as this man and his wife were coming down. Either he or she said something about how I hadn't been very friendly or something, or how I hadn't talked to him. I said, "Well you haven't talked to me," and with that his wife took him by the hand and led him up to where I was, as if she were fixing us up, bringing us together.

Then I was standing out in front of my room, the door was open and I could see my sister in front of the mirror, putting on make-up and get-

ting ready, I assumed for dinner or whatever fun thing we were going to do. I looked down the hall and saw a young man carrying his bride into their room. I told my sister, "The newlyweds are here!" She said she had already heard that they had arrived, and she was excited too.

I seemed to be just hanging out in the hallway, checking out who was coming and going. There was an elevator with wide doors to the left. They opened and out came a beautifully-dressed couple, their outfits matched and were Napoleon-style, brilliantly colored aqua, the most beautiful color I had ever seen. They were familiar to me, from junior high school. I was surprised to see them together, although they made a very handsome couple. I said I should get a picture of them, because their outfits were so spectacular. They were newlyweds too, and these were their wedding garments.

Immediately after that I found myself driving a big old semi flat-bed truck. I had to maneuver it through two lanes of a bunch of other big trucks, and the road was being worked on. There were huge holes in the road, big enough for the semi to fall into. There was a hole on one side of the road and then the other. I zig-zagged back and forth with only enough room to swerve in and out with the semi.

I was having enough trouble driving this thing as it was, but it was made harder and more stressful because I could barely reach the pedals, and the truck kept dying and I was having a heck of a time stretching far enough to put the clutch in to start it again (and again and again). A couple of times I got out and was walking because the road was too rough to drive on.

There was a cute, long-haired, dark guy, maybe an Indian, who was directing traffic. There was also a black man without a shirt on in one of the holes. He was working. I kept trying to maneuver the semi in and out of traffic, dodging holes, and trying to keep my foot on the pedals, especially the brake. I hit the semi in front of me several times. In fact, my driving was so bad I felt like I was driving a bumper car! I got so frustrated trying to drive this thing, and I could see the road was even rougher ahead, so I got out and started walking again.

The Indian guy said, "Are you just going to leave your truck there?"
I said, "Well I didn't think I could get through."
"You can," he said.

"Oh, okay," I said, and I ran back to the truck and got in. Again, I was stressed out and started driving recklessly, because the darn truck was so big! I was running it into the semi in front of me and worrying about avoiding the huge hole with the black man in it. I felt extremely frustrated, scared, stressed, and inadequate!

A hotel in dreams represents a place of transition or change, a stopping over place. What part of me is in transit? This makes sense to me, especially since in my dream I was "hanging out" in the hall. Steps are ascending consciousness, or descending, but since I was going upstairs I think that's a good sign. I feel like I am continually climbing, even if I stop on a floor for awhile.

I also read more about guns. They represent emotional explosions, so I'll have to do some thinking about that, since I've had a few dreams about guns and shooting.

The color of the wedding garments represents spirituality, healing, and the "perfect couple" represents a need to work on relationships. The excitement about having newlyweds around also shows that work on relationships, especially marriage is indicated.

In reading further about clothing I find that "quality materials and clear beautiful colors" are usually positive symbols. The married couple's Napoleon-style outfits were definitely quality material, very rich and extremely well-made; beautiful, blue-green, heavy material, almost like what would be used to make drapes. I also read that "wedding garments" could mean spiritual integration.

And how much clearer can the "trying to drive a semi" be? That dream was a metaphor for my recovery. That's exactly how I've felt trying to live this new life, think this new way, get to know me. It's all unfamiliar. I've never done it before. Learning to do life sober feels exactly like that dream. It's all I can do to keep the damn thing on the road!

The next night I dreamed about a series of bright, white lights, blinding, and filling the whole area. There was a door, free standing, like the frame and the door standing there. Someone opened the door, which let in the blinding white light. It was a man. He had long hair and a beard. He wore a white robe with a rope around the waist. It was Jesus. His hair and beard were darker than I've seen in pictures, but it was definitely Jesus.

Having Jesus open a door to a bright light for me is a wonderful message. It was encouragement that I needed very much at this phase of my recovery. Today was exhausting yet exhilarating. I wept and wept this morning as I faced the things I want to change. It was as if I were saying good-bye to some old ways, and it was painful and draining. It was a process of surrendering. I knew I was growing.

The next night I dreamed that a famous actress was killed in a car accident. I remember feeling really sad because I liked her. I felt sorry for her family, and her boyfriend who was also an actor.

Again, I related this to a "death" of a part of me. A celebrity representing recognition, fame. Do I want to be recognized? Do I fear recognition? Ooh. I hope it's the fear that was killed in the car accident.

Then I had two dreams close together about an old girlfriend of mine. If I were to describe her I would say she's somewhat of a rebel, a "bad girl" if you will. She's mellowed out a little, but she's still drinking and drugging. In both dreams we were in the valley, surrounded by mountains. It was very difficult to make our way out, even with proper vehicles.

The first valley had a ton of snow, the second one was green grass and beautiful mountains. We were down in the valley (way down). The first one with the snow we were trying to get out on some big snow tractor or something, but it kept tipping over. My friend appeared to live in a cottage in the valley. In the first dream it was urgent that I get her out of there before we got buried in snow. The second dream it didn't seem we were trying to get out.

This dream shows me that I still felt a need to save the alcoholics in my life. I was beginning to realize how much anguish my codependence was causing. I was trying to stay in my own program and detach with love. It felt really good if I could do it, but my need to save everyone was still there. Maybe the second dream showed my progress from the struggle down in the depths, trying to save my friend, to the beauty of the green grass and gorgeous mountains, and not trying to get her out.

The next night I dreamed I was in a very big house with many rooms. I remember checking out the lower floor, but don't remember what I saw. I remember seeing in one room, once we got to the upper floor, a couple of people, seemed like young teen-agers, laying on the floor watching television. I could see them laying, facing the doorway. I could see the light from the TV, but couldn't see the set itself.

Then to my left I saw my cousin in one of the rooms. She's the one I lovingly refer to as "air head." She was dancing around like a person in a mental institution who had lost it. She was in "never-never land." Then it seemed I was in the kitchen, but it wasn't finished or anything, kind of like in the middle of the hallway or something.

The floor was quite a mess, unfinished and unsafe, with boards here and there, the floor beneath showing through in spots. I was at the sink or cupboard and then I spilled a pitcher of water onto the mess of a floor. It was a big mess and I knew I needed to get it cleaned up as quickly as possible or it would not only ruin the floor, but ruin the downstairs.

Trying to get down in the floor, to where the water spilled, was not easy. My dad and someone else stood behind me. My dad offered to go down and clean up the water, but I insisted on doing it (it was clearly dangerous). I got down, was sitting on a floor beam, legs hanging down, and was wiping up the water when the boards beneath me cracked and fell an inch or so.

It was clear to me it wouldn't hold my weight much longer, and to stand or kneel in order to climb back out would certainly cave it in. I thought I needed someone to grab me by the arms and pull me up, but I knew no one could do that.

In interpreting this dream I relate to the "airhead" in one of the rooms. I certainly have been mindless in a few areas of my life. When I think of teenagers I think of the "do nothing" way they can be, lazy even, so I know there's a part of me like that. The floor tells me that my spiritual foundation needs some work. I'm not on very solid ground. The kitchen represents nourishment and productivity. It's still in the hallway, but it's under construction. I'm learning that I have to clean up my own messes, quickly, before they get worse. But I still believe no one can help me.

So many changes were taking place inside me, and I was healing, and dealing with emotional pain. Again, my dreams said it all.

I was in a hallway and there was a bathroom about in the middle, that no one ever used. It was dark and appeared newly-constructed. I used it and water flooded all over and down the hall. I was telling someone what had happened, but I didn't see anyone else around. Then it seemed I was in the house across the street, and something seemed really scary, spooky, and dark, but I don't know what it was.

Again I find myself in a hallway, a place of transition. A bathroom represents a place of cleansing and release. Water representing emotions, and the flood, an overflowing of emotions. The scary feeling at the house across the street tells me I'm really afraid. I'm not too sure I can do this recovery thing. I'm afraid to deal with overflowing emotions.

The dream continued. Now I was going to see the minister of our church. I really had to talk to her because I had married someone else, someone who is like a brother to me. I showed her the ring. It was all weird, sticking way up, made of pewter.

Then I couldn't believe what I had done and I quickly took off the ring and began searching for my wedding ring. I couldn't find it amongst a bunch of cheap costume jewelry in a side pocket of my purse. Suddenly I had the ugly pewter ring on again. I asked the minister how it got on my finger. She smiled and said, "I put it there." Then I couldn't get it off and I panicked. I cried and cried because I love my husband so much. How could I do this?

At this time I was beginning to see my marriage for the valuable thing it was. The panic at marrying someone else and trying to find my own ring amongst a bunch of fakes, tells me it's time to pay attention to something I've always taken for granted.

My husband put up with an incredible amount from me for twelve years of my active alcoholism. Finally, I was able to see how lucky I was to have him during those years, and how much he protected and took care of me. I was a reckless alcoholic. I shudder to think what might have happened if it weren't for him. I was getting an incredible amount of awareness at this time, and I was a bit overwhelmed. My dreams were busy too.

The dream I had last night was very strange. It seemed to last all night. It began with me walking in our town, although no where particularly familiar. I was walking up hill. Everything seemed to be hilly and set on weird slants. I was walking up the road with Suzanne, a bartender where I was a waitress ten years ago.

We realized the roads were cracking and water was seeping through, covering the streets. All the water was running downhill. We suddenly knew this was a terrible thing. The best way I can describe it is if you imagined a globe or a ball that was filled with light. There were cracks in it and you could see the light shining through. That's what the streets were like, the whole town even. In every crack you could see water, and it began flowing out more and more, as the cracks grew wider and wider.

It was clear the whole place was going to burst wide open. I panicked and exclaimed, "What have they done? They've built the town on a lake!" We knew we had to get out of there. We headed down and could see a path off to the left, leading where we needed to go, but it looked dangerous to me, even though Suzanne headed that way. A man was there who was familiar to me. I think I had seen him on television or something. He was cute and seemed like a really nice guy, but I knew he wasn't to be trusted.

Suzanne wanted to trust him. She wanted to go with him when he offered to help us down the path to safety. He was driving a big tractor or some kind of farm equipment, something with a fork-lift or maybe a scoop on the front of it. I said, "No, we couldn't go that way because water was already running down there too. It looked treacherous.

"Let's take this way down," I said. Right next to the treacherous path was a door that I opened, and found stairs leading down. This was clearly our saving grace. I was in a hurry, fleeing for my safety. I looked and saw that I didn't have any shoes on. I reluctantly raced back up to get them.

I hurriedly put them on. They were wet and I was standing in the flooded water. I looked down. I had put on two different shoes, because it was night and I couldn't see very well. I had no time to change, so I quick-

ly looked and found the matching shoes, as well as a sweatshirt that was my husband's. I knew I couldn't leave it. I rolled the shoes up in the sweatshirt and took off.

The other two followed, but I was ahead of them. Against my better judgment I kept stopping to make sure they were still with me. I was impatient. A couple of times I began walking back up the stairs until I could hear them. I would holler for them to hurry. "Let's get out of here." I would again begin running down what I can best describe as a spiral staircase leading into the earth, with "doors and floors" at each turn or level.

The weirdest part was that each level was like a little round living area, small, for one person. It was as if we came in the back door at the end of a spiral, walked around the circular "home" and out another door on the other side to another set of spirals. It seemed we went down part of the way, and then began a climb up, but in the same fashion as before.

Then Suzanne turned into Barb, a bartender at the only other place I'd ever been a waitress, about six months ago. The same ritual went on as I hurried through the spiral maze. Then I either stopped or waited or headed back to make sure they were still behind me.

Each floor I came to and went through, other people's "houses" (it was almost like trespassing), was different. Some were really neat, tidy, and cozy. One in particular I loved, and I commented on it to Barb. I said, "How cozy and comfortable it would be for just one person living alone." It was like a little doll house.

Other floors were cold and damp, and in need of paint and repair. Some were outdated, and one in particular had a room off to the right. It was a living room with a Christmas tree in the corner. In fact, that was all that would fit, because all these little houses were extremely small, like they were built and stacked in the middle of a giant tree.

Barb wanted to show me how the Christmas tree looked lit up, but I was nervous we would get caught. She plugged in one cord and the light at the top of the tree went on, but nothing else. Then she picked up another cord and plugged it in. Only one light on the tree went on. She did this a couple of more times, but only one light would come on at a time. The third time a light came on, but the light at the top of the tree went out.

I was getting more and more nervous. I looked to my right and saw the lady who lived there walk by, but she apparently didn't see us. I told

Barb, "Someone's home. Let's get out of here." We (Barb and I; I don't know what happened to the guy) went around a few more floors.

When we were first coming down Barb was locking each door behind us. That made me nervous. I said, "I don't think you should do that. What if we have to get back out that way?" Then I realized she was locking the doors from the inside, so we'd be able to unlock them and get out. Then I worried, "What if other people from the surface need to escape this way?" So Barb quit locking the doors.

At the next place she kept trying to take a pair of bronzed baby shoes, only they were ladies', too small for me. She kept saying, "Here's your shoes." She would start taking them off their holders, and I kept saying, "Those aren't my shoes."

We came to a place where it seemed there was a trick to getting out. As Barb opened a closet, I psychically knew exactly where the switch was, way up high on the right behind some towels or something. I reached in and flipped the switch, proud of myself for knowing something I had no way of knowing. The door was released and on we went.

Finally we came to the top. We had traveled down, then up, around and finally ended up again, like in a safe part of town. I looked ahead, feeling tremendous relief at being able to see the outside world through windows in this bigger, brighter house that was the last stop, the end of the maze, so to speak.

As I headed for the sliding doors I realized I didn't have the shoes or sweatshirt. I panicked and headed back to retrieve them, but quickly decided they weren't worth it. If I went back in I may never make it out again. I felt lucky to have actually made it out in the first place.

I feared it was too good to be true, that when I got to the sliding doors they'd be locked or something. But when I got to the glass, it slid right open. There was a screen. I thought, "Oh great, the screen is probably locked." But when I tried it, it opened right up.

When I got outside there were three horse-drawn carriages parked and waiting. They were large, capable of holding about twenty or more people. The first one looked pretty full, but my friend, Sally, was on that one, saving a place for us. Now Barb was Susie, and she wanted to ride the one in the middle, right in front of us, because the driver was really cute. We had a dilemma because Sally was waiting on the other carriage.

We hesitated too long and it left. We saw another carriage coming down the street. We looked, and the one Sally was on also pulled away. Then another carriage passed, going in the opposite direction. As it passed I noticed Sally's boyfriend in the back. He was wearing a tuxedo. He was all dolled up. A sweet young thing in a sexy, short party dress cuddled up next to him. They held hands and entwined their legs. Everyone noticed but Sally.

This part doesn't surprise me, because in real life Sally is about the only person who doesn't seem to know her boyfriend cheats on her, although we all think it's more that she doesn't want to know. Thus the dream shows her looking the other way as he rides by with another woman. I remember feeling great relief that I was out of the maze. The whole ordeal, from start to finish, was very stressful.

Boy, this dream tells me a lot of things. I'm realizing why it's so important to write dreams down, because while they may not make sense at the time, often they become clear later. I was just over eight months sober when I had this dream. Looking back, I see that it painted quite an accurate picture of my recovery.

The hills represent a comfortable progress, an easy climb. The water represents the emotions. The lake represents contained emotions (seeping out). The flood depicts an overflow of emotions. I felt like I was going "down, down, down," yet I came up on the other side. The shoes have to do with grounding, so the dream was telling me I was going to be wearing two different shoes for awhile, while carrying the spares. As far as my husband's sweatshirt, maybe that was a symbol of my codependence; still wanting to carry some of his stuff, which, of course, in the end was not worth going back for.

The books on dream interpretations that I read talked about spiral meaning evolution, cycles. Exactly. My worrying about whether the other two were behind me, tells of my need to take care of other people, but the desire to take care of myself was strong. It was stress in the transition taking place, both in the dream and in my life.

The cozy, comfortable house represents the cozy, familiar house of self, the desired self. The cold and damp, old and rustic houses represent emotional chill, a lack of circulation, discomfort, needs work. The fact I was nervous being there, like I was trespassing, tells how uncomfortable this new life felt at first, like it wasn't really mine. Intuitively knowing where the switch was to continue on, reminds me that I will always know what to do next.

Christmas represents celebration and reunion. What do I wish to reunite with? The tree represents a structure of life. Where in my life am I ready to grow? Lights represent illumination and vision. What am I ready to see? Apparently only one thing at a time, lest I overload.

The relief of having escaped the maze is exactly how I've felt about my alcoholism. I've often said it exactly like that, "If I went back I may never make it out again. I felt lucky to have actually made it out in the first place." Fearing that the door would be locked showed that I didn't trust things would get better. I might need to come back this way. It was also a reminder that things would work out.

The horses, I believe, represent power, and choices for me. It would seem that early recovery for me would mean a lot of work, feeling that I was going down, when actually I was heading up. I went through rooms that felt cold and uncomfortable, and wanted to hang out in the cozy ones. Spiraling at times, I felt like the maze would never end. Yes, that dream foretold of my early recovery, including emerging safely on the other side.

That was the last entry in my dream journal for four months, but I was back to my regular journaling. I was also experiencing more and more peace and serenity, yet not always able to recognize it.

Chapter 11

WAKING UP

January 7, 1995. I've been feeling kind of neutral, no emotion like. I know there is so much I'm going through right now, so I'm trying to nurture myself and do the best I can. I quit smoking, and like drinking, I'm taking a day at a time until it no longer consumes my thoughts at all.

The drinking was a big problem for a long time. I didn't realize how big of a problem. In fact, there's a lot of things I didn't realize, but now I can begin to explore and discover who I really am, and make some positive changes so that I can do the work I need to do.

January 9, 1995

I've been thinking about life, about my problems, and how I've let them consume me. I was reminded how insignificant they are yesterday at church. I'm worried about being a little short on money while Terry, our fill-in minister for the past several months, is losing his wife to cancer. Judy, the most wonderful woman any of us are fortunate enough to know. I love her so much, and for the first time yesterday, we all realized that she is in fact, dying.

The cancer which began in her breasts is now in her bones, and the latest report shows it's in her liver. Terry resigned so that he can care for her. They made such a perfect couple. They were so young and vibrant. They came to the church and before long were in charge of the children's program. I'm so thankful that they spent the time they did with the kids because I know that my daughter and my niece are blessed to have known Judy.

I can't believe she's dying. She was so vibrant, so colorful, from her outfits to her two different colored eyes. She was full of life and laughter. She was loved by everyone who knew her, and it seemed she had so much living yet to do. It seemed that "Terry & Judy" were just getting started.

Going to church yesterday put my life in perspective. I have no problems. Money is not a problem. I have a wonderful, loving and healthy husband and children. My parents are still alive and healthy. All the most precious things in life are in order for me. I feel so silly for feeling sorry for myself the past few months.

(Later) Life scares me. I guess it's okay to admit that. In fact, it feels good to say it. It's like coming out of denial, surrendering.

Still struggling with letting go of the old life, I write...

Today is Friday the 13th of January - Good thing I'm not superstitious. I'm feeling torn about something. I'm having the urge to go to the bar. Not to drink, but to see the old gang. I've been going back and forth with myself all afternoon, the familiar war, the one I've always had with myself about going to the bar, only this time I'M NOT DRINKING!! Why on earth would I feel exactly the same feelings (and guilts!) about something that there's nothing wrong with?

I've had absolutely no desire to go to the bar since I quit drinking, until now. Greg is downstate, and Megan's gone so I didn't have to fix dinner (something that usually interfered with my drinking!). Maybe that's what the feelings were all about. Maybe there never was a time when I should have been going to the bar, maybe I was always putting my drinking before something else, and just maybe because of that, there was always guilt associated with going to the bar.

Whatever the case may be, I was really weirded out by the feelings I was having, and I didn't quite know what to do. I felt trapped again, afraid to make a decision for fear of making the wrong one. And just like always, I ended up going to the bar just to shut off the arguing. At one point I took my shoes off and was going to make a cup of cappaccino and I was staying home!

But I never made the coffee, I ended up putting my shoes back on and off I went. I stayed for about an hour and a half and then decided I'd talked to everyone I wanted to, drank all the soda water I could hold, and breathed all the second hand smoke I could take, so I went home, feeling good, feeling happy to have seen a few old friends, and even happier that I didn't drink, didn't want to drink, and was glad I quit smoking!

It's strange though, there seems to be so much more to this recovery thing than I ever imagined, and I keep discovering, or noticing for the first time, behaviors that I had no idea were there. This is good, I have to be able to see a behavior to change it. The best thing is I'm ready to feel. I'm ready to wade through the unacceptable behaviors and make the changes necessary to get what I really want out of life.

January 17, 1995.
I don't have to drink anymore and I don't have to smoke either. Every day I'm taking more of my life back from dependency and addiction, fear and frustration. Today at least, I'm not afraid to look at all the ugly stuff I want to get rid of. The feelings I'm dealing with now are guilt, unworthiness, and fear. The longer I go without drinking, without old controlling behaviors, the stronger I feel. For the first time since I was a teen-ager, I feel like I'm growing up.

I'm coming to terms with all the games that alcohol plays, and played for 15 years in my life. It takes on a life of it's own, and it has more control than any drinking person can imagine. I know that until I got away from it, nothing was going to change (in terms of spiritual understanding and growth).

Everything in life revolved around it, and it literally consumed the thoughts of this alcoholic, so that everything was dependent on that first drink of the day. When will I be able to have a drink, what time is it? What time is "proper" drinking time not to be considered an alcoholic? Every function and activity had to include alcohol. My security blanket. A necessary tool for living life. It's cunning like the AA program says. It takes control of your life and you don't even know it.

(Later) You know, as I was making my lunch and doing some laundry, I noticed how calm and peaceful I'm feeling today. How different I seem to be moving through my day. And I couldn't help but notice how much of my house is out of order right now. Finished or not, I have much work to do.

That's what I was thinking about when I was making lunch. It doesn't matter anymore. I don't have to worry about it. I'll get everything back in order. I don't have to beat myself up about things, I don't have to do it all right now. I always had to do everything right now. For the first time in a long time my mind feels in order. I can feel the confusion diminishing, and I can feel the power and the guidance and the wisdom within me. I'm finally getting out of my own way and the answers are coming.

January 18, 1995

Went to the meeting by myself. The girls aren't going anymore. Ironic. I thought I was going for them in the first place, now it has nothing to do with them. I love the meetings, we all gain strength from each other. I'm learning how to do life without drinking, I'm discovering everything that alcohol covered up. I'm ready to feel it all. I can't believe the difference in my thinking from last week to this. How fast things change. How wonderful it is when it does.

January 20, 1995

I've been so afraid. I've shut myself off because of fear. Many times in my life I've wandered off the path, tried to find my own way, forgot how to listen, got lost and stopped moving. But anytime I quiet myself and listen, the answers come. It's by daily, conscience contact with God that I'm able to get out of my own way, and it's then I can begin to live. I know for me, I have to take it an hour at a time, a minute sometimes. But with each letting go, with each surrender of a negative thought or feeling, faith and trust are strengthened. I've been too afraid for too long, to do anything but trust now.

January 23, 1995

The most beautiful time of the day is dawn. This morning I was out shoveling snow at 7:30 and there's something so peaceful about that time of day. Especially in winter because everything is so pure and white. The street lamps have a soft glow to them, and aside from a few cars going by, it seems the world is still asleep.

I was feeling a little nervous and uptight this morning and I have no idea why. Of course it's really my usual, the unsettled feeling I've fought all my life, but with all the prayer and meditation I've been compelled to do lately, I've found a way to quiet it. My goal is not to have control at all. I want to learn to breathe freely and feel calm and peaceful virtually every moment of my life.

I've discovered that shoveling snow at 7:30 in the morning will do it! Especially when you shovel someone else's walks for them, that really does something to bring about peace. I'm going to strive to keep this feeling with me. I'm often torn when I'm settling in to write, and today seems especially difficult. I'm aware that I let fear keep me from it, and that causes anxiety. I know how much calmer and peaceful I feel when I'm writing. But today I'm feeling like the demon fear is trying to once again sabotage my efforts.

I talked to God first thing this morning and asked Him to take charge of my life today, and tell me what He would have me do. I know I need to calm myself and listen. I just need to listen more. Sometimes I get myself all worked up over life. Over the everyday, ordinary events that most people deal with. I have too high of expectations for myself and I've got to learn to LISTEN, and follow my inner guidance. I'm tired of trying by myself anyway. I keep screwing up. I blow it every time I try to handle anything by myself. I'm too easily affected by other people's words and actions, and I stick my nose (concern) where it doesn't belong.

I've got to discipline myself to keep my focus where it needs to be. The answers will come when they are needed, and I'll be prepared when I get there. I'm ready to start fulfilling my dreams, accomplishing my goals, improving my life!

January 25, 1995

I'm feeling all sorts of emotions right now and I'm not sure where my thoughts are. Yesterday morning I got out to shovel a little later than I wanted to. It was pretty light out, the street lamps were off so I missed their soft glow, but it was still peaceful and quiet. It was so calming, with everything snow covered and pure white.

I shoveled our walks, Mrs. T's, Mrs. L's, which seems to be my ritual lately and I love it. It feels good to be out at that time of morning, dawn, God's time. There's just something about it. It especially feels good to help out two sweet ladies that have lost their husbands and live alone. My whole life I've found myself with friends like these.

From the time I came into this world with very young parents, and was raised with so many grandparents, I find I have older friends, always have, and I relate especially well to "grandmas." I was walking back home and I looked down the snow covered street and houses and just felt the peace of the morning. I was in front of my walk way when I turned and noticed that one solitary lamp was still shining.

I watched it with a peace and calm, as if it stayed lit just for me. I started to go in, but turned and stopped to watch it again. I felt certain this time that the lamp was meant for me, and it was as if I could hear the words, "you see, you never have to worry, I will always keep a lamp on for you." As soon as I heard those words I felt so good inside, and I smiled. Then the lamp went out and I went inside.

Those are the special kind of moments where God speaks to me, but many times I'm just not quiet enough to hear. When I am "listening," it's amazing how quick He is to reassure me that's He's there.

This morning I got out while the lamps were still on. The glow of the sunrise could be seen along the skyline. That wonderful color that is dawn, scattered with clouds and glimpses of light brushing their edges. The half moon stared at me through a snow covered tree, and I was in awe of the beauty of this sight.

But I felt nervous, I felt scared. I've been feeling it more and more, and stronger it seems. I'm hoping for the possibility that it's one of those things I'm about to get rid of, so it seems bigger than it is. I'm hoping this is part of recovery, and that my fear, my uneasiness, are about to be replaced with a longed for calm and peace of mind.

I'm filled with emotion much of the time, either that or breathtaking fear, nervousness, scattered thoughts and difficulty shutting it all down. I'm going to pray unendingly, I'm going to LISTEN for my answers, and I'm going to trust God like I've never trusted Him before. I need to learn to take care of myself, nurture myself, before I can take care of anything else.

January 26, 1995

I'm letting circumstances get to me. I can't seem to put a clear focus on my life. I've felt so out of sorts this past 10 months since I quit drinking. I've let a lot of things stand in the way of my goals. I have a lot of work to do and I know it. There are many things I've been unable to keep up with that I could before. I'm just finding out what it means to really feel, without any painkillers.

I want to start living my life triumphantly instead of fearfully. I'm not healthy enough yet. I'm working on it, and I'm getting better, but it's a minute by minute thing right now. It's been a challenge just accomplishing the things I need to do. I'm not secure with who I am yet. I still feel a need to stay within my comfort zone. I've widened it from where it was a month ago, but I'm still keeping things quiet. Nothing wrong with quiet.

January 28, 1995

Right now, in this phase of my recovery I feel like a person trying to fly five or six kites at the same time, and keep them all in the air. I can't take on any more kites right now. I have to take baby steps for awhile. I never expected recovery to be like this. I'm kind of embarrassed that I wrote a book called "Recovering From Life," being clueless and all. That was my first lesson in humility.

All the things happening in my life right now, continue to amaze me. But I really do need to take things slow. I can't go getting my mind all busy in a bunch of directions. I can't fly five or six kites at the same time anymore. I have to learn to focus better. I have to relax and meditate more often. Yoga is another gift. I just started doing it and it feels really great. The breathing is really helping me to calm down.

I just get way ahead of myself in my mind. I worry or think about too much, unless I pay attention and quiet myself. I know I won't always have to be so attentive to my emotions, but right now I'm feeling nervous and scared. I'm not going to numb these feelings with anything anymore. I'm just going to feel. And that feels uncertain, so I'll take it slow, but I'm going to keep moving.

(Later) I have everything any sane person could want out of life, and still I've felt uneasy. Still I had to drink, smoke, and indulge in just about anything I could get my hands on, for what? The longer I go without drinking, the healthier my mind and body become, the clearer I can see all the things I've been blind to for so long. Every day I'm feeling stronger and healthier, but I know I have a ways to go.

I still have some obsessive tendencies, I still have some behaviors I'm barely noticing, yet they are beginning to come into focus. I'm dealing with a lot of old feelings I didn't know were there, and I've got a whole bunch of new ones coming at me. But everything is okay. This is life. I'm living it now. I'm feeling it now, and I feel strengthened somehow. I'm feeling less scared and nervous all the time. I'm going to conquer this thing!

February 2, 1995

I've let fear keep me away from this desk all week. Look what I was just talking about last time I wrote, and then fear does it again. I've struggled this week. I'm getting healthy for the first time in a long time, I can feel it. I'm growing up emotionally. I just keep asking God to free me from all my addictions and help me not to be afraid to live, and I'll take life a minute at a time and keep reminding myself that God is with me, and I'm right where I'm supposed to be.

February 3, 1995

I wrote my first story today. It was about Sausha. It felt so good to write again. I was amazed how much it healed my heart.

February 7, 1995

Two years to the day that Sausha was killed. Could that be why my first story was about her and her death? Well, anyway, I'm still afraid to write. I find myself doing everything BUT writing, and I'm very aware of it. It's become painfully apparent that I'm still keeping my good from me. I'm stopping myself from doing all the things I want to be doing.

February 10, 1995

I accomplished next to nothing yesterday. Didn't write a word, didn't make myself even go near the office. I didn't do Yoga and I was dragging, restless, lost, and literally unable to do anything. I didn't want to read, write, anything! I laid down at 11:30 and slept until 2:00. Then I barely got it together by the time Meg got home from school.

My emotions have been on the old roller coaster and it only got worse when Gregory got home and said he was getting laid off. I didn't say much to him, but went right upstairs and cried and cried. So much for faith, huh? Anyway, I didn't realize that he was hurting worse. I was so busy feeling sorry for myself I forgot that he was the one who's disappointed. He thought his job was secure. Actually, I'm glad he's laid off. It's supposed to get really cold next week and I didn't want him to have to work in it.

I have to believe that everything I'm going through is part of the process, and that everything will start falling into place for me soon. If anyone would have told me that recovery entailed so much, I would never have believed it. I would never have believed I would go through so many emotions, feel so scared; yet feel such strength.

Next month will be one year since I quit drinking (amazing!). Maybe then I'll start making a little more progress in my recovery than I have. I want to get back to being motivated, busy. I don't want my thoughts always consumed with killing the pain, and battling back and forth trying to stay sober. One day at a time they say, and maybe that's what I'm forgetting. I either get too far ahead of myself or I spend too much time in the past, regretting.

That's what kept happening to me yesterday. I kept remembering all these terrible things I did, and some of it was over 10 years ago. I've got to let it go. I've got to forgive myself, because I know God has forgiven me. I've got to forgive myself so I can move on.

I'd like to say that's what I did, but it isn't. This is when I didn't do any writing. There are three months between the above entry and the next one. What I remember feeling during this period is debilitating fear and desperation.

I felt like I was unraveling, "white knuckling" it, and barely hanging on one day at a time. I remember struggling through each day, going to meetings and being told a day I didn't drink was a successful day. I didn't buy it. Somehow I kept coming back, day after day, feeling like I wanted to die.

Greg and I were having more trouble relating to each other than we'd ever had, yet somehow we knew we could work it out. We knew we could learn this new way of doing life. I was becoming more and more aware of how important he was to me and how much I needed him in my life. As hard of a time as we were having learning to communicate, he was my strength. I had tremendous hope for us.

I dreamed that Gregory and I were on a cruise ship. The section we were in was filled with tables and chairs and the room was filled with AA friends. Gregory and I danced through the crowd, as graceful as Fred and Ginger. He held me in a loving embrace as we danced around the room.

I remember feeling so proud that he was my husband. I was pleased to show off our love and our good fortune to have each other. Then we separated. He went to one end of the room and I sat down at a table with three people playing cards. As one of them talked about a ship capsizing, I realized they were talking about us. Before I could say anything, we began turning over.

At this point I knew I needed to be with Gregory. We needed to be together, but as I turned to go to him, the ship flipped over completely. Everyone and everything toppled. We were now crawling around on the ceiling. I felt panic and a desperate need to find Gregory, scared that he may not be okay. I hollered for him, praying just to hear his voice. Nothing. I hollered again. This time he answered from somewhere in the middle of the room.

The lights had flickered on and off, but were out now. I began crawling toward Gregory. Then it became painfully obvious that we were running out of oxygen. If you've ever been in a situation where you couldn't catch your breath, you know how frightening it is.

The air became thicker and thicker as I made my way toward him. Halfway there I realized I was going to die and prayed for it to be over quickly. I thought, "Maybe, just maybe, I'll wake up in the hospital. But please God, let me pass out now, before I begin gasping for air that can't be found."

I just needed to find Gregory, to die with him if we must. As I reached him, he said, "Don't worry." With that he reached above his head, where there was a small square window, and he cranked the handle and let in fresh air.

This dream had a very simple, straightforward message for me. As long as Gregory and I stay together, I'll be okay. Should we separate, however, my whole world would turn upside down. He is the very air I breathe.

Then I had a very reassuring dream. At first I didn't recognize the man that was with me, yet I did know him. He was extremely tall and very thin, as he embraced me while we walked. My head was level with his waist. As we traveled along, we came to different disasters or rough spots in the road. With each one the man would pull me to him in a reassuring and loving embrace, hugging me, and literally taking all the fear from me, drawing it out with each hug. Then we would go a little further.

The dream consisted of smooth roads and rough areas, running into construction and destruction. The man walked with me in the smooth areas and hugged me tightly to himself with reassurance over the rough spots.

I realized the man was Jesus. He had long hair and a mustache and wore a white robe. He was unnaturally tall and thin, and he hugged me all through my dream. Alas, all through my life.

Now my dreams were getting really busy. There was so much going on and I was remembering them all. I could get the meaning from some parts, but others didn't make sense. I'm so glad I wrote this next one down. The dream's messages are clear to me today.

I was parked at my daughter's friend's house. It was the turquoise Maverick I had in the early eighties, my first car. I was parked on a steep, short driveway. My daughter was waiting in the car as I talked to a man outside. I was attracted to him in a surreal sort of way. There was something mysterious about him.

I kept Megan waiting and she was becoming impatient. She didn't like me giving this stranger so much attention. Then she was gone. I knew she had gotten mad and walked home. I told the guy I could give him a ride to where he needed to go.

Then we were in a building, like a huge department store. He wanted me to meet him in a half hour. I was already running late to get home and fix dinner. I was worried about how I would get out of the house again. But, after dinner was too late for this guy, so I decided to stay with him now and just be late for dinner.

It kept getting later and later, as I tried to find my way out of this building to my car parked out front. The guy was gone. I could see my car through windows and from balconies, but I couldn't get to it. The build-

ing resembled a hospital that had been turned into offices. I went into office after office trying to find a way out, but no luck. I worried about how late it was getting and my frustration grew. I was caught up in something I wanted to get out of, but I couldn't find a way.

I knew if I could just make it out of the building I could get home. I only lived around the corner. I came out of one room onto a balcony with a moat below and a cement wall and a chain link fence on top of that. I could darn near reach out and touch my car, but could not get to it.

This went on and on. I could see a great deal of construction going on outside, roads and buildings being built. My frustration was mounting. It was getting later all the time. I saw a clock on the wall which read 7:15 p.m. I knew I was expected home at 6:00 p.m.. It was later than I thought and I knew I was in trouble.

I was able to find my way out of the building a couple of times, but once outside I was disoriented. Nothing looked familiar. I was turned around, confused. Nothing was where it was supposed to be. Street names were unfamiliar. I traveled a bit, got lost and scared, and turned back. My frustration mounted as I realized it was getting later and later. I wasn't going to be able to find my way home.

A big city was being built where my little town used to be. I could see J.C. Penneys, two stores, one like the old one from my childhood, and a new, bigger one. I looked at one last street sign and didn't recognize it. I was getting weak and sick with fear and confusion. I knew I had to go back into the building, find out where I was and call Gregory to come and get me.

I went in. It was a hospital. There was a nurse behind a counter and a doctor behind her. I asked him where I was. What street was this? I needed to call my husband to come and get me. The doctor repeated the name twice, as I tried to comprehend and write it down; but I couldn't think straight. The third time I asked him to repeat it, I began to feel really bad.

My mind was a blur and my legs began to collapse beneath me. The doctor said to the nurse, "She's not well. Get her to a bed." At that point I collapsed into two people's arms. They put me on a couch. I was out of it. My eyes were closed and my body was limp; although I was aware of everything around me. I just couldn't move or open my eyes.

Then I came to and tried to call Gregory, but I couldn't figure out how to get an outside phone line. I picked up the receiver and heard people talking, so I hung up. I tried again, pushing a button on the phone. I heard a dial tone, thank God. But immediately the line clicked dead. I was frustrated and too ill to keep trying. I hurried to the couch, so I wouldn't pass out again. It seemed like I was in a waiting room.

A nurse came and sat at my feet with a chart. I asked her to please call my husband, but she said they wanted to find out what was wrong with me first. They were perplexed, until I told her that every time I got the least bit hungry I felt absolutely famished and that I shook and felt sick, barely able to "hurry up and eat." (This had been true).

She said, "Ah, ha," and began writing. I somehow knew that this wasn't a serious condition, but could be if it was left untreated. She left to go do something and I looked into the room across from me. It was dark, but I could see about five or six black children, girls I believe, with the whites of their eyes showing through the darkness. They were looking at me with sad, blinking eyes.

They were all in one bed, facing different directions, though all of their heads were turned toward me, watching. I could see no bodies, only heads, and they were all identical. It was kind of frightening. I woke up.

Crazy dreams, huh? This one tells me a lot. Since turquoise in dreams represents healing, I feel that's what my old car represents. The healing, from the old to the new. The same with the old Penneys and the new. They indicate change, improvement.

The stranger I was flirting with represents something lacking in my relationship with myself. The store represents choice, offices represent a place of work. It seems I was "stuck" in the place of work, just out of reach of my healing, my spirituality. Many obstacles between me and the car. And the offices were outdated, so was the hospital, but outside was all new construction.

The big city being built where my little town used to be is a metaphor for my recovery, of moving out of an old, comfortable place to a bigger, brighter place. But there's a lot of work to be done, and a lot of confusion, frustration, and fear. The man in the beginning could have represented a distraction from what I'm supposed to be doing.

I'm most disturbed by the dream's indication that it's later than I think, although that too, motivated me to get busy. It is later than I think. It's later than any of us think. Ask anyone who's nearing the end of their life. We're here such a short time, and I know I wasted enough time in my disease. It's time to get on with my life.

Hospitals represent healing and confinement. Illness in a dream is a sign of emotional ill health (not serious, but could be if not treated). The dream indicates how tired I am, how important it is to take care of myself, and that I have to ask for help. The fact I'm always trying to call Gregory shows me how much I've depended on him, and not being able to reach him tells me I've got to learn to take care of myself.

Not being able to find my way home indicates how lost I feel on my journey, and the fear I have of not being able to get there. The dark room with the many heads tells me there is something very dark and frightening in one of my rooms, yet the fact they are children may indicate the problem is basically harmless, or easily repaired. I now believe it represented the 4th Step work I hadn't done yet.

Last night I remember being reassured, calmed, and centered, but I don't know by whom. I do know I felt everything was going to be all right. Then I remember dreaming about a friend's baby, he wasn't breathing. I began working on the lifeless child, while the parents stood, helpless. I began breathing into the baby's mouth, filling his lungs with air. We watched, hoping for signs of life. Nothing. He was pale with dark circles around his eyes. The child clearly looked dead.

I breathed into his lungs again, this time harder, and then felt air come from his tiny nose. His eyes fluttered beneath closed eye lids. We were relieved, grateful, humbled, and emotionally drained. His breathing was shallow and we knew he wasn't out of the woods yet, but he was alive again!

A baby in a dream represents something new, a new life or way of life. I breathed back life into something that was dead. That baby represented me.

May 2, 1995. Last night I dreamed I was at a retreat, so there was a feeling of love and acceptance. We were in a circle and I could see an angel

*of some sort flying around. The Inn illumined the color of yellow, even
though it's actually painted a blue-green color. I was reminded of sun
shine, love, and acceptance.*

*There was an older couple there. Then I was at a house and the phone
rang. It was a friend from group. He asked if I had time to talk. I was waiting for a friend from childhood who I hadn't seen for a long time, to come
over, but told him yes.*

*Just then she pulled up in a big yellow car. The next thing I knew I
had just left him on the phone when he really needed someone to talk to.
I felt bad, but I was looking so forward to seeing my friend after fifteen
years.*

This dream came at a time in my recovery when I was beginning to see
that it was indeed love and acceptance that were the keys to peace and serenity. The color yellow represents clarity, so the dream confirmed this awareness. Perhaps I still have work to do, though, blending the old with the new
and getting my priorities in order.

At this phase of my recovery one thing was clear: I was after peace and
serenity—and I was willing to go to any lengths to get it.

Chapter 12

WEEDING THROUGH

May 5, 1995. This is the weirdest thing in the world to me, recovery. I thought that if you were an alcoholic and you quit drinking, you weren't an alcoholic anymore. And I certainly knew to stay away from AA, because although I knew nothing about it, I knew "those people" could never, ever drink again. I wanted no part of it.

I didn't know anything about alcoholism. I knew my Uncle Jack was an alcoholic and he was dead at 47. That's what happens to alcoholics. I knew that alcoholism was a disease. I knew Uncle Jack had it. Poor Uncle Jack. I'm sure glad I don't have it! And my sister doesn't know how to drink right, and neither does my brother, and I need to quit drinking "so much," but thank God none of us are alcoholics.

I had just returned from a spiritual retreat with the church. Judy died on April 21st, the day after my birthday and two days after the Oklahoma City bombing. She hadn't been doing very well for awhile, but many of us felt the reason she "left" when she did, was to take care of the babies lost that day. It somehow made it easier for us to let her go.

May 7, 1995
(Sixteen days after Judy's death - Thirteen months sober) – I'm overcome with emotion. I feel loss and despair, yet strength and hope. Judy was with us at the retreat, I felt her in the meditation room. That's the rea-

son I spent as much time in there as I did. While I was in there I was flooded with memories of Judy that I had forgotten. Times I spent with her, and conversations we'd had that I'd forgotten about. I was overcome with gratitude at having been able to retrieve those lost moments, now preserved in my memory forever.

The service at church today was done by the retreat people. Very special people sharing a very special experience. It was truth and honesty. It was from the heart. It was sharing life's experiences with each other and encouraging healing. That's what I'm feeling going on with me lately.

So much healing. So many hurts I didn't know were there. So much learning to do. I'm just amazed at the process. I'm just amazed at life, and so thankful that I'm finally getting some directions, a simple map that tells me where to go, how to go, and how to BE, today.

Much of what seems to be coming up for me lately is FEAR. And surprise of all surprises, worthiness. Where I once felt incredibly comfortable and at home at meetings, I'm feeling separate, like getting somewhere and finding out you don't belong there, or worse, don't deserve to be there.

So I wonder, is this a bad sign for me? Am I getting stinking thinking that could eventually lead me to think I could drink again? I think not. I see myself continuing to recover . . . . forever. I recognize my feelings of not fitting in, or not belonging there, are trying to tell me something. I have to look closer at my issues, what I think about, what bothers me and why.

I know what bothers me right now is how unorganized I've become where once I was Miss Perfection. I can't stand looking around at piles of books and stuff everywhere, furniture that needs to be dusted, floors that need to be swept or vacuumed, and not feeling like I have the energy to do anything about it. This makes me feel worse. I want an orderly house. That's a part of the old me I really liked. I want her back! Just her organizational skills!

The promises say that feelings of uselessness will disappear. Well, Hallelujah! Because I've been having feelings of uselessness for several months now. I used to drink a lot in the kitchen, making dinner or baking. Always had my glass of wine (or three or four) while in the kitchen. And boy, did I have fun! I loved cooking, I loved baking, I loved cleaning the kitchen while I was at it! I loved doing all these things at once!

Now I've found it's very hard for me to function in the kitchen. Now I have a hard time doing more than one thing at a time. My timing, which used to be perfect, is all off. I get confused, I have anxiety, I feel overwhelmed! Sometimes I feel really stupid when I'm in the kitchen trying to cook dinner. Recipes I've been making for years suddenly seem complicated. And I'm just not having as much fun in there as I used to.

But thank God since I've been home from the retreat I've been trying to keep that peace and serenity with me. One of the ways I've been able to do that is by listening to my meditation tape. I turned it on in the kitchen while I was making lasagna, which at best makes the biggest mess. But with my tape going, next thing I know I'm putting it in the oven and the cupboards are clean and dishes are done. There's hope for me in the kitchen after all!

I dreamed I was in a huge building. It was brand new. It was mostly bare, but nice. The halls were really wide, almost a room's width across. They were long and open, and brand new, made with light reddish-brown bricks. There was new carpet, tan or light brown, that was pleasing to the eye.

The top floor wasn't finished yet. It was a mess, with boards, supplies, and buckets of paint. Everything was strewn about, so I had to climb over stuff to get through. I knew I needed to get downstairs, because the upstairs wasn't finished yet.

I was in the new, beautiful part. Then I found myself up in the wrong stairwell, only they weren't stairs, it was a ramp, and again the area between the walls was unusually wide and open. There were building materials scattered all over the ramp. There was a big window at the top, where I could see the sky. The stairwell was bright with the light from the window.

I was afraid of getting caught up there, because I wasn't supposed to be there. I heard a door from a lower level open. I knew I had to get down—FAST. I made my way down the ramp as fast as I could, trying to step over and around the debris that was strewn about. I was going so fast I almost fell. I slid and kicked some supplies down a bit.

I almost made it down, when the person I had heard open the door was there; but he was just passing through. It was the builder. He was in white painter's coveralls and a white painter's hat. He was carrying a tool box or something for his work. He looked up at me, and I felt embarrassed at being caught doing something I shouldn't.

I told him I somehow got turned around and ended up in the wrong part of the building. I was apologetic, but he could have cared less, barely slowing down to hear me at all. He went another way and disappeared. I came out into a huge hallway and began making my way down the hall. I came across a ramp, where a stairway should have been. Although it looked nice and finished, I paused briefly, and told myself this would also lead up to an unfinished part. I kept going.

I reached the end. There was a lady standing at the foot of an escalator. A lot of people were going up, because a new store had just opened up there. (The ground floor I had just walked through reminded me of a cross between a hospital and a mall.) The colors were nice, light brown, and it was comfortable and safe in there.

The lady standing by the escalator worked there and was handing out tickets to get into the store upstairs. It was like she worked and lived there. I said, "How lucky for you. You can get absolutely everything you would ever need, all in one place. You'll never have to leave for anything."

And she said, "Except for one thing they probably won't have, and I just have to have it."

I said, "What's that?"

She replied, "Eye drops."

It seemed a big deal to her. I said, "Oh, think positive. I'm sure they'll have even those." There was a big window, ceiling to floor, between the escalators and the lady and me. I could see people through the window, heading upstairs. There were several sets of escalators next to each other.

I liked that dream. It told me that parts of me are brand new and beautiful. Soft brown represents hard work and propriety. The feel and look of the color was pleasing to the senses. It felt like serenity to me. Although I don't have as much of it as I want, I'm well on my way to having more of it.

The big and open hallways, and the resemblance to a mall symbolized choices. The stairs symbolized ascending; the ramps, grounding; the escalators, aspiring; the windows, vision; and the eye drops, clearer vision. The dream was a message of hope. The fact that I felt embarrassed at being caught in the unfinished area, knowing I shouldn't be up there, told me that I accepted the construction as a process. I know that I can't jump ahead to parts that aren't finished yet. I also see that there are building materials laying all around. I'm learning acceptance.

The only thing I remember about my next dream is that people were putting a safety harness on me. It resembled my husband's climbing belt. I knew I was going to be perfectly safe.

I was hoping for a reassuring dream, and that's certainly what I got. By this point I'd been sober for over fourteen months. I was learning so much. I felt so busy, trying to absorb it all without getting overwhelmed. Awarenesses and changes were coming right and left. I was learning so much. I had so much more to learn.

I was beginning to work on my codependence. I was becoming increasingly uncomfortable thinking and worrying about other people. I knew I was going to continue struggling, unless I learned to take care of myself, and let others alone. I bought books on codependence, and learned everything I could, so I could get better. I felt that I suffered from the disease of codependency before I ever picked up a drink.

June 2, 1995. Last night I dreamed I was in school. I was new there, but my first class made me very comfortable. The teacher was attractive. Switching classes was somewhat stressful, trying to find my next class. The halls were filled with students. I sat in one classroom with my notebook, angel book, and purse. I had to keep hold of my "stuff."

Then I was switching classes again and suddenly realized I didn't have my notebook, book, or purse. I went back to the last classroom and someone had taken them. I was so worried about someone finding my private notebook. I looked around the room, and on a table I found my purse. I was relieved about that, but still very upset about my book and notebook being stolen.

Then I was worried and uptight about the possibility of being late for my next class. I made my way through the hall, went up or down some stairs in a stairway with a door, and was relieved to notice on my schedule of classes that my first period and last period were with the same teacher. I knew he liked me so he wouldn't be mad if I was late.

I took advantage and went into the ladies' room to brush my hair, and put on some blush and lipstick. There was a girl in there and she said something about how good I looked. I told her I was thirty-five and she couldn't believe it. It was like I was going back to high school and I was really too old to be there. I was excited to be going to that last class with that teacher.

Well, that dream told me a lot. A school, of course, represents a place of learning, so it's only fitting that I find myself in a school. They say we stop growing emotionally when we start drinking or using drugs, and when we get sober, we go back to where we left off. It's fitting that I find myself back in high school even though I'm *thirty-five.* That made me laugh. But it's true. I don't feel thirty-five, I feel about sixteen.

The teacher in the dream, again indicates learning, and perhaps my attraction to him reveals my hope that with the learning might come some enjoyment! Being unable to find my class, afraid I'm going to be late, all indicate the fear I have that I'm not going to know where to go, or I might be late. Still so unsure, so untrusting.

I still need to carry my "stuff," my valuables, represented by the purse. The notebook is a source of anxiety once it's out of my possession, because of my fear of exposure. This shows how vulnerable I'm feeling, and how important it is for me to hang on to some of my stuff. The need to fix my hair and put on make-up tells me that I'm still worried about appearances, especially since I don't wear make-up normally. My hair being in my eyes tells me that worrying about appearances is messing with my vision. And both have to do with, what am I covering?

June 3, 1995

I need to, and want to, get rid of my need to control. I don't want to worry about whether Susie's working Debbie's program, or Cindy's working everybody else's program, or the fact she isn't committed to her marriage. It's those crazy, wild controlling feelings and I don't want them! I want peace and serenity. I've had a glimpse of it for the first time in my life, and I want to make it a major part of my life.

June 5, 1995

I spoke at church yesterday and it went great. For the first time since my recovery began I felt like I was headed in the right direction. Today, however, I'm feeling lost again. I didn't really want to do Yoga, but I did it anyway and was glad. I got showered, dressed, ate and went to my meeting. I got home and just couldn't seem to motivate.

It's a gorgeous day out, but I feel in a slump. I really don't like feeling this way. Unmotivated, that's the only way to describe it, and it sucks! I just don't know what I want to do. All the things that can be done, or need to be done, I don't feel like doing. In fact, I can't think of anything I feel like doing right now.

I was motivated by alcohol for so many years, I guess I don't know how to motivate without it, or some other drug. I just hope that waiting out the old behavior pattern will make way for the new. I just wonder how long is the appropriate amount of time to allow myself before thinking it's depression or something. I've always been such a busy, orderly, and motivated person, it's really hard for me to take this lazy, disorderly person I've become. But I guess I just don't know what to do about it.

I realize I've been in denial about it for months. I didn't want to talk about it at meetings and I didn't want to write about it either. That would mean I would have to admit it's what's really going on. I can't ignore it anymore, and maybe looking at it will help. In fact, it has helped. I can't understand why I've resisted. I guess it's fear. I guess I'm more afraid than I realized. Afraid of what, I'm not sure, but the fact is I've been immobilized for some time now. I need to set goals, make lists, even if it's only one thing at a time, one day at a time.

Last night I dreamed there were a bunch of people, including all of my family, traveling across the frontier in wagons (not covered). Each wagon seated a lot of people. It seemed that one whole wagon held my entire family (more than there actually are), even a couple of children that were mine. Somehow I got separated from them.

The next thing I knew I'd been left behind. I knew that my family did-n't know I was missing, and now they were long gone. Clearly there was no way to catch up to them. I was very distraught. I remember feeling very frustrated that I wasn't where I was supposed to be, and couldn't seem to get there. Then it was as if I remembered it was a dream and I could change things. I wasn't frustrated anymore. I knew I could get out of this mess.

This dream is much clearer to me today, then it was at the time. Abandonment relates to leaving behind an old self, release from control of the old self. Since it was my family I was separated from, I see that the dream showed me I would need to detach from them, and like the end of the dream, I have the power to change it and everything will work out.

That describes perfectly what has happened. I got healthy enough to be able to relate to my family in a way I never did before, thus the separation (of the old way). The part of it working out okay describes the way we're learning to relate to each other, without judgments or expectations, just acceptance and love. It didn't happen overnight.

Later that same night I dreamed I was in a huge cafeteria or ballroom or something, and we were the caterers. My sister was busy putting things out on the dessert tables. I seemed to be helping someone clean up, but mostly I was just following her around. I knew I better act busy, so I began taking the serving spoons out of all the huge salad bowls. There were fruit and jello salads, and they were all full, even though we were cleaning up.

At first I thought I should leave the spoons in them, but realized someone would be covering the bowls with foil. The lady in charge seemed to be busy, and we knew we had to keep busy too. Then I found myself with both hands full of dirty silverware. I didn't know where to put them. I found myself back in the kitchen and the boss showed me a big stainless steel sink where I could stack the silverware upright for washing. It was clear that my heart wasn't in my work. I was just doing what I could to get by.

Sounds familiar. I feel like I don't know what I'm supposed to be doing, yet I feel like I need to look busy. I feel like I'm doing just what I need to get by. Maybe the fact I was a caterer in the dream (serves people) and was gathering serving spoons, says something about how uncomfortable I am serving others. In other words, how self-centered I can be. And the fact I found myself in that position indicates I will learn how to do it. (The promise that says I will lose interest in selfish things and gain interest in my fellows.)

Again, my dreams mirrored what was going on in my life. I thought I would feel useless and uncomfortable in my own skin for the rest of my life. I was tired of being tired. I wanted some sort of guarantee that things would get better. I got it at meetings. They said if I kept coming back it would get better. They promised.

June 6, 1995

I got back from my meeting where I shared AGAIN about this stuck place I seem to be in. One day I feel like I'm in that "contented sobriety" they talk about, and the next I feel very uncomfortable in my sobriety. I don't know how I'm supposed to feel. I don't know what I'm supposed to be doing. Everything seems like a chore.

Chapter 13

CODEPENDENT & MORE

This was the period when my codependence was beginning to cause me trouble. It was becoming more and more apparent that as long as I was more concerned about how other people were living their lives, I wasn't progressing in my own. I knew I had to back away from some friendships that were no longer good for me.

I was extremely frustrated and disappointed at this time. Life didn't seem fair. I didn't feel supported by people who felt I needed to get a job, do something! I DIDN'T LIKE HOW NON-FUNCTIONAL I WAS EITHER, but as soon as I could get it together I wanted to write! Until then, I was doing the best I could. I was still too concerned about what other people thought, but I was learning. Later that day I wrote:

So, I have a couple of people close to me who don't understand me. Maybe the fact I want to write for a living just isn't good enough for them. If you don't go to work for someone else and get a paycheck every week, it's not a job, and anything else just doesn't cut it. So, I guess the old "feel sorry for me" self resents the fact that everyone doesn't take me seriously. Oh well. I got that off my chest, I feel better. And you know, I'm going to quit beating up on myself about the house and everything else. I've got to quit caring what other people think.

I want to get out of this slump I'm in. At least I could defend my writing better if I was writing. Part of the problem has been my own guilt over not doing what I fought so hard to be able to do, what I've been trying for three years now to defend. I quit my job in June of 1992 to write my book. Well, here it is June of 1995, and aside from the first year, I've accomplished darn little. I've been ignoring the problem hoping it will go away, and "stuffing" it only makes it bigger! Oh, I feel so much better already!

June 8, 1995. Last night I dreamed I was shoveling snow. I was at the next-door neighbor's and my husband was helping me. We cleared a section and it left a big, gaping hole that we knew someone could fall into and get hurt. I said I better try to fill it in, but when I tried to shovel, the ground was so frozen I couldn't even chip away anything.

Gregory also tried, but we couldn't budge an inch. Finally, he put a tarp down and roped off the dangerous area. I was up on the ground and he was down on the sidewalk (it resembled a big hole about six-feet deep). I was afraid I would fall in, and sure enough, even though I stayed away from the edge, I was pulled toward the edge and began to fall. I tried to stop myself and Gregory was there with his arms open. He said, "I've got you." I let myself fall into his arms and he lowered me down safely.

Once again, guess who was there to catch me when I fell? It was a bit of reassurance I could never get enough of.

A few days later I was sad again. I was trying to let go of my need for other people's approval, trying to back away and let go of friendships that meant a lot to me but were no longer working. I was sadder still that my husband and me were not connecting.

I didn't know how difficult it is on the spouse of an alcoholic when the alcoholic stops drinking. I wasn't aware that the codependent fears abandonment, once they no longer have to take care of the alcoholic, and that they often push their spouse away FIRST, to avoid what they feel is an inevitable break-up. I was so caught up in my own recovery and change, that I was shocked and overwhelmed to find my husband was as sick as I was. And, like me, he didn't have a clue how to get better.

June 12, 1995
Wow. Challenges. I should be upstairs with my husband right now, but

I'm not, because he doesn't want me up there. He said he doesn't know if he wants me anymore, I'm getting too spiritual, too weird. I love him so much, and yet I'm so frustrated. We've basically been together since the first time we began stealing moments whenever and wherever we could, to talk and get to know each other. He's the first man I ever got to know real well before I slept with him.

That was over 12 years ago, and although the years have been difficult at times (my drinking played a huge roll in all but this past year), and eight of those we struggled with Jeremy, our beloved "problem" child, until he went to Idaho in 1991, but all in all they've been really good years. We have a strong love and are devoted to each other. We get along well, we like the same things, and aside from the ugly years, we never fight, until now.

I can't believe that after 9 years of marriage, it would be spirituality that separates us. I just can't fathom such a scenario. If we got through the years of my really abusing alcohol and drugs, then about 7 or 8 years of relatively calm years considering I was practicing "controlled drinking," we certainly should be able to get through this, right?

I was controlling, and manipulative, I was also loving and caring (sometimes), how crazy! If he functioned that well through all of that, no wonder he doesn't know how to deal with me now. Maybe he's right and this new and improved me isn't his type. What then? What if he's not the new me's type? What if we don't even like each other?

He's resisting right now, that's for sure. He doesn't want to do feelings. He doesn't want to get in touch with anything more than he's already in touch with. He doesn't need to grow any more spiritually, he's spiritual enough. In fact, he was just fine before I went and dragged him into recovery.

June 14, 1995

Well, two days have passed and nothing has changed, well, I've changed. A bunch. Greg & I haven't been talking really, and that's strange, but I'm dealing with a lot of other feelings too. I'm coming to terms with a whole bunch of feelings of unworthiness and inadequacy, regarding my writing. I'm sad that I don't feel supported, but I let go, because my writing does not depend on anyone's support of me. It would be nice, but I can get along without it. I know there are some things I'm going to have to do alone. Well, me & God. And you know what? That's just fine with me.

June 15, 1995

Boy, things sure are changing for me this week. It's a learning week, and each day has been an experience. I feel my Higher Power right in the midst of things, in spite of appearances. Here I've been putting this whole thing my husband's going through this week, on his shoulders alone, never realizing that his reaction and behavior recently is because of my alcoholism. More and more I'm seeing how my life, and the lives of others have been affected by the fact that I drank, and now I'm in recovery. It's incredible.

This disease of alcoholism is so powerful, and the dynamics of every one of my relationships is changing forever as I change. My husband doesn't know how to deal with me anymore, not that I'm so difficult to deal with, mind you, I'm calmer and more easy going than I've ever been in my life, but it's taken him 12 years to get used to the way I was, and now that I'm different, he doesn't know what to do. Then a friend hands me an article which spoke to the spouse, saying, just because the alcoholic sobers up doesn't mean they're going to leave you. It talked about his fear, saying, it's hard to lose an alcoholic.

I was shown exactly where Gregory is right now, and what a surprise it was to realize this whole thing was really about me and not so much about him. I never dreamed it was typical behavior for the spouse of a recovering alcoholic. I was relieved to know that what he's feeling is normal and that it doesn't really mean he doesn't want me anymore, or that he doesn't love me. There's a lot I can do to heal this situation. God is so cool. I've been shown a lot of things these past four days that have convinced me there is a Higher Power working to change and improve my life, especially my marriage.

I've learned that I can't expect anyone to follow my lead. I can't make Gregory deal with his issues and I shouldn't want to. My job is to be the best person I can be, and love my husband unconditionally, providing a safe place for him to heal. He can't help feeling what he's feeling right now, he's afraid! All the rules have changed. Nothing is as it used to be for us. This requires change of him, and maybe he doesn't want to change. Maybe he's finally adapted to the way things were and he was comfortable, forget that we were both sick, he knew what to expect. My job is to be patient with everyone in my life, and pray!

June 18, 1995

Boy, what I'm feeling, and what I'm reflecting on right now is so powerful, I don't know if anyone, besides another alcoholic, can understand what it's like to be an alcoholic, to feel like I've felt the past 14 months.

I was upstairs having a panic attack which was brought on by a phone call from my daughter's birth mother. There's nothing new to me about these attacks. I've had them all my life. It's fear. I've come to recognize that fear has played a huge role in the why behind my drinking. But fear of what, I'm not altogether sure. What I do know is that since I've sobered up, I'm working through all that fear, and hopefully these panic attacks will be a thing of the past.

As I was sitting in a chair in my bedroom, doing my Yoga breathing and calming myself down, I found myself caught in an incredible reflective moment, one that found me in disbelief, not only because I'm an alcoholic, but because of what this disease is, and does, and can be. And how hard it is. But not as hard as being bound by alcohol, bound by addiction. I'm truly an addict, powerless over all drugs, anything, everything, I tried 'em all, but alcohol was my lifeline, my buddy.

Alcohol was my drug of choice, and before long I had no choices, other than should I drink, shouldn't I drink, ending with always drinking. What a battle I was fighting, and life was hard. Staying in control was hard, monitoring my drinking was hard, planning my drink schedule, hiding how much I drank, and the constant worry, and self-criticism, followed by over indulgence and then cover-up, was hard.

I don't think anyone but an alcoholic/addict, can know what torment that is. And it spirals. Downward. There's a big possibility you won't make it. I know I wouldn't have, not if I kept on drinking. Alcoholism is a fatal disease, and one that holds tight to its victims till the very end. Unless we break away first. I escaped. That's exactly how it feels to me. I was caught in the trap of alcoholism, and I was completely blind to what was happening to me.

It's a scary thing to be bound by alcohol, especially looking back. I'll never be "cured," and I guess that's what I was reflecting on, the intensity of this program of recovery, and the simple fact that this is a one day at a time, for the rest of my life, program. It's the hardest I've ever worked for a goal, and the most rewarded I've ever felt in my life.

I've calmed down now, by the way, and that in itself is proof I'm on the right track. I got too far ahead of myself, that's what alcoholics do, and a resentment builds, and we have to slow down, put first things first, keep it simple, and talk about it, write about it, go to a meeting, or take a minute to say a quick prayer. That's what my life is like, as a recovering alcoholic. They say keep it simple, because it's the simple things that throw us off.

I thought I had everything so together when I was drinking. For 15 years my life improved, or so it seemed. And my life *was* good. I had a loving, supportive, and more than tolerant husband who never knew me not to drink in over 12 years. I was working at home, pursuing my dream of writing, and raising a teen-ager. But now I feel like I'm starting over, from the bottom.

That's okay. I missed a lot, and now I'm learning to experience my life, one moment at a time. I never knew it would feel like this to be an alcoholic, to be in recovery. I didn't know I was so weak. I never thought I was that strong. I didn't think I could feel so sad, or ever get that mad. I never dreamed I could feel such peace and serenity. I didn't expect to feel grown up, to be calm, show love, and feel free.

I don't know why I became an alcoholic, maybe no one ever knows for sure, but I know that today I feel extremely blessed by this disease, and it wasn't always that way. To look back and see what I've been through since the end of March, 1994...it's been quite a journey.

The following dream began a series I would have about my cousin. She's the one who was born a month before me. I miss her terribly and I worry about her. I was especially disturbed by the dreams I had because our grandma was psychic, and the gift runs in the family. I wasn't sure they weren't psychic dreams. I feared I was picking up on what was really happening with her.

I dreamed we were standing at the foot of the steps to the hospital, when suddenly a bee or a flying bug or something bit her or stung her and in a matter of seconds she collapsed in my arms. I carried her up the steep flight of stairs and into the hospital, where I frantically searched for a doctor—someone—who could help her.

I knew we were running out of time and that if she didn't get help soon she was going to die. There was no way I was going to let her die. I was screaming and crying, running with her in my arms, but no one was around. I woke up crying.

I know my cousin is an alcoholic, and there's a part of me that feels she will die from this disease, the same as our uncle did. I love her so much, and I would carry her and help her if I could, but she's so far away. She doesn't think she needs help. This dream was very upsetting to me, and it drove the seriousness of this disease home. Why did I escape, when my uncle and others did not? The whole thing became suddenly REAL.

The reality of this disease got me thinking. I was finally ready to look back on my self-destructive years of drinking with an open mind. In fact, I was reflecting a lot on the past, somehow trying to come to terms with it.

June 19, 1995

I was a party girl. Boy was I. I loved to party! My sister & I used to say, "Party! Party! Party!" The words have come back to haunt me. But I laugh when I look back to where it all began, and what fun times those were. Fun, with consequences. And it was for those times, those unforgettable fun times, that I continued to search, on a quest for a fun-filled and fulfilling life. Yep, it was down those murky roads of alcoholism that I trekked, searching to enhance my life. I liked the way alcohol made me feel.

I've had a chance now to look back over those years, in particular while raising the kids. I've had to think about how my drinking affected our lives, especially Jeremy's, since he was already an angry little boy when he came to live with me. I was strict, there's no doubt about it. Too strict if you asked me today, but back then it was my way or no way.

Through all the years and all the counseling, even parenting classes (court ordered of course), and although I begrudged everything at the time, we got a lot of help along the way. Jeremy seemed to slip through the cracks somehow, but we learned a lot about being better parents. That seemed to have lessened the anger and resentment I had toward him, so in that respect I improved (screaming attacks and slapping frenzies were no longer acceptable). But I kept right on drinking, and I could always count on Jeremy for a good excuse to get drunk.

When I was still drinking White Russians regularly, I would frequently overindulge. I used to say, my limit is three, and I always have four. I wasn't trying to be funny, I was just stating facts, and didn't have a clue what that was saying about me. Many times over the years I felt I was addicted to White Russians themselves. It wasn't that I drank too much, it was that White Russians were too good. So I struggled day in and day out. Always going to slow up, never going to quit. I needed it too much.

I was like a junkie with my booze, especially the last few years. I knew it wasn't normal to depend on a drink so much, think about it, look forward to it, and then feel guilty about giving in to it. But alcoholic? No way. I'll get this thing under control, shape up and learn how to drink right, and the need will go away.

But it didn't go away, it got worse, just as it always must. Until I finally prayed the right prayer, and asked God to remove this crazy compulsion from my life. Take away the relentless voice that tells me to drink, help me stop the madness that keeps running through my head. Help me stop drinking.

Ha! Turns out that was the easy part!

I dreamed I was trying to escape, or sneak into, or blend into the crowd with another person, in order to get into a building. The two of us were hiding behind cars and dodging guards, trying to get across the street and into the school. Suddenly I broke away from the other person and slipped into the crowd of people coming and going. I knew right away that I was free. I fit in. No one was going to pick me out. I belonged there and was going to be able to walk right into the school.

This dream was very significant to me because it showed that I'm breaking away from codependence. I'm ready to worry about myself and let everyone else worry about themselves. The "fitting in" makes me think about AA, about recovery, this new life. Finally, I feel at home with the other students.

Wow! What a dream I had. We were at this house and Jeremy was here visiting (yikes!). I don't remember too much about it, but he was being fine, no serious frustrations, just a slight uneasiness. Megan and I were in the backyard when we noticed two men sitting by the tree. They were different, almost transparent, like someone was showing a slide of them against the tree.

One was telling the other something. It had to do with us. Then I realized they were angels. I said that to Megan. We knew it was true, and turned to our left to view a big movie screen superimposed over our house, up on the second floor and roof. As we watched, we saw a small angel with wings fly around the person on the screen, and then pick them up and carry them away. Megan and I were holding onto each other tightly, fascinated by what we were seeing and feeling.

Suddenly we felt it, weightlessness. All at once we were being lifted by the angels. We were in awe as we flew effortlessly around the backyard. What an experience for us to share. Meg's eyes were wide with wonder, her mouth open in awe by what we were experiencing. Then we were inside, going over what had just happened. It was an incredible experience for us.

I was making arrangements for Megan to visit her birth mother. I questioned when Jeremy was returning, so perhaps we could schedule it for the same time. I remember worrying about this "return" trip for Jeremy, fearing they were going to tell me that he had no intention of returning to Idaho. I couldn't wait until Greg got home to share the experience Meg and I had of flying with the angels.

This dream was a gift. I believe it spoke of the relationship that I would have in recovery with both my children. Megan would "fly" with me, enjoying an extraordinary spiritual experience, one of weightlessness, of letting go. Jeremy, on the other hand, still causes uneasiness, and I'm fearful I may have to deal with him again. This told of the work I would have to do on the relationship. It wouldn't be the same as the relationship Meg and I share, but it wouldn't be so bad (no serious frustrations).

June 20, 1995

I'm sitting out on the front porch. It seemed strange when I wrote the date. It took me back to June of 1992, I was sitting right where I am now, doing exactly what I'm doing. Although it wouldn't have surprised me three years ago to know I would be sitting out on my front porch writing, I do think it would have surprised me to know I'd be working on the book. I found myself remembering back to those first days writing full time.

I remember most of my life, having a yearning, a need in fact, to write, and I kept journals as far back as I can remember. But I never seemed to have enough time for my writing, and when I did write it was always in volumes. But just as many times I can remember not taking the time because I had too much to say. I'd catch up when I got some free time. It just never seemed that writing was a priority in my life. In fact, I can remember many times feeling guilty because I was spending too much time writing, filling too many pages. Those little diaries you get when you're a teenager were never enough for me. I always felt I was squelching my writing, until that summer of 1992 that is.

Even then it took me months to allow myself to write without feeling guilty, without feeling I should be doing something else. I have a good idea where that comes from. I think it's past life stuff. My grandmother was a writer, so writing was always encouraged in this life, but there has always been fear, uneasiness and guilt associated with my writing.

One day about 6 or 7 months ago, maybe longer, I was at my word processor writing when I had a vision, memory, whatever you want to call it, but in it I saw myself as a young boy. He was dressed in knickers and wore a cap. The room and furniture seemed to be from the 19th century. I (he) was sitting on the floor, crouched by the bed, writing on a note pad of some sort. I want to say it was England because of the clothes, but I don't know why I say that.

I can picture him clear as day, but have trouble describing it. He wore knee socks, and the word "lad" comes to mind with this boy. Then in my vision I hear the sound of the father coming down the hall. He's been drinking like always and is yelling before he reaches the room. He wants to know what the boy is doing and says he better not be wasting time with that writing again. Hard work, not writing, gets you through in this world!

I see the boy hurriedly shoving the writing tablet under the mattress. I never see the father come into the room. I can feel that the boy writes out of a deep need to do so, and can't seem to stop even though the father thinks it's a waste of time. For whatever reason I saw what I did that day, it made perfect sense to me, and finally helped me understand where those feelings with my writing may have come from. Suddenly I felt a block had been removed.

After finishing the book, and trying to get it published, I put it on the back burner and focused on some serious isolating and drinking. I began working weekends and special occasions at the bar. That ended up being a turning point in my drinking. I was burning out on the place, and didn't have the desire to go over there afternoons anymore.

Finally I was over my attraction and need for the bar scene (even though the "bar scene" consisted of me, the only one over there most days), but as my drinking at the bar diminished, my drinking at home increased, and I was about to embark on my final months of serious drinking. I was beginning to notice how necessary that full glass of wine was becoming. It was security for me, and deep down I knew I didn't know how to live without it.

(Later) I honestly don't know what I would do without my daily meetings, but I know one thing, I probably wouldn't be back to writing. As it is that's just barely coming back. Oh, how I've beat up on myself this past year in recovery. They say that a day you don't drink whether you do anything else or not, is a successful day. That just wasn't good enough for me. My life was always in order when I drank. But that's why it was in order, so I could drink guilt free.

Problem was, I never knew how to have one drink. Once I had that first drink, it was a party! Maybe that's why I made sure everything was done first, then I could party with a clear conscience. The only consequences were mine alone, get too drunk, spend too much money, stay out too late and drag into work the next day, and sometimes not. Oh, but nobody else was affected.

By the time I was living with Gregory it was broken promises, no shows for dinner, late nights and apologies. I *always* had good intentions. I never meant to lie. I was going to be home to fix dinner, I just don't know what happened. Even when I quit with the late night stuff I was still rewarding myself with alcohol after a productive day, and when everyone you hang out with drinks like you do, you think it's normal.

(Evening) My sister just left. The two of us are so much alike, and we spent many of the wildest years of our drinking partying together. With us it was always, "Let's Party!" We talked about the fun we had, the risks, and the drugs we took, and how amazing it is that we survived at all. It scares me to look back at the self-destructive road I was on, especially since I thought I was on a spiritual path.

We shuddered when I reminded her of an incident that took place in the '70s. I had completely forgotten about it, and I was sure she had too. We nearly went off a cliff coming down from Scout Mountain in Idaho. We were, of course, wasted, and it was late. My sister's roommate's four year old was asleep in the back seat.

All I remember is coming down, and it's very winding. I don't know if I was going too fast, probably was, I must have missed a turn, and next thing you know we're heading off a cliff. I couldn't believe it. I put on the brake but it was no use, we were going too fast. I looked at my sister, and I'll never forget the look of shock on her face.

Then all of a sudden the car just stopped. Right on the edge of the cliff, which had we gone over, would have killed us. It was a miracle and we knew it. We had to get out of the car we were shaking so bad. Neither of us could believe we blocked that from our minds. I remember it so clearly now. In fact, thinking about what could have, should have, happened sends chills down my spine.

It was definitely intervention from a Higher Power, but it sure didn't have the same impact back then that it does today. I'm finding a lot of incidents like that, where I suddenly remember something I said or did when I was partying, and I remember not remembering it. Crazy.

Oh, recovery. It's a good thing I didn't know what it was going to be like, or I'm afraid I would have kept right on drinking! (I'm kidding.) Once I got over the shock of sobriety, I see that any amount of work I have to do is worth the peace and serenity that comes with living a sober life. For me, however, it's been a rocky road getting here, but I like the results, and the promises are coming true for me.

Nearly 15 months after I quit drinking, I feel empowered. I feel hopeful and encouraged. But only when I keep it simple, first things first, and easy does it, one day at a time. Those sayings didn't mean a thing to me in the beginning, but now they are handy reminders how to do my life.

For me, sobriety brought confusion, and disorganization. I could so easily "unravel," and for me, unravel meant panic, meant anger or despair, confusion, disability. I was trying so hard to get a grasp, but I couldn't. I didn't know how to cope without alcohol, I didn't know how to live without it, and I wasn't at all sure I wanted to. Although the crazy compulsion to drink left me early on, no one told me living sober would feel like this.

June 21, 1995

I've been so scared the past couple of days, thinking about the cliff incident. I've never been so scared thinking about what could have happened. It was my fault. I was driving. I screwed up and we went over a cliff! Dear God, you've saved me more than once!

I've just been talking to my wonderful husband for the past hour. He's so sweet. He just hasn't quite grasped the idea that I'm a changed person, that I don't think the way I used to, or react the way I used to. He's getting it though. I was telling him about our angel encounter on the cliff, and I found myself thinking how important my life really is. How, in spite of my own reckless ways and self-destructive behavior, there is a purpose for my life. I'm meant to do the things that are in my heart.

That's why I was given the memory of being saved from a fatal car accident. You just don't get a second chance with mistakes like that. Well, some of us do. It was a message, reassuring me that my life has meaning. All our lives have meaning.

At this point something incredible happened. I heard a reassuring voice speak to me, and I began writing what I heard as fast as I could. It felt like a gift, a blessing, and I cried as I transcribed what I was hearing.

"See, I'm not going to let you die. You have important work to do and you can do it. Your fears have kept you afraid to live, but you don't have to be afraid. I saved you from driving off a cliff, I will protect you from everything. Don't be afraid to do the things you like to do. Don't feel guilty because you're lucky enough to work at home. Your work is important work. It's yours and yours alone. You don't have to make excuses to anyone for what you're doing with your life. You're recovering! You're healing. You were very, very sick and you could have died, but I saved you then too. You have to be patient with yourself. You can't be as sick as you were and get better in a month. Fourteen months may seem like a long time to you, but it is such a small amount compared to the time you spent in your illness. You'll need to look at the things you did, they are significant to your growth, even if you didn't know it at the time."

This is such an incredible time of healing for me. I can't believe I was so reckless! I was obsessive, carefree, and careless. I wanted more, more, and more. No, I wanted it all! Oh, how did I survive? This fourth step work can be emotionally draining. Things that happened twenty years ago are just now having a powerful impact.

I'm not going to worry about confronting anything uncomfortable. I trust my Higher Power. Being reminded of the cliff incident, as traumatic as that memory feels to me right now, was a blessing. I see the purpose for it, and I thank God for the lesson in it. It was really an impact as far as my inventory goes. I need to have powerful reminders of where I was and why it had to change. And you know where I was that reckless night? I was exactly where I was for years and years and years. I was in "Party!" mode: no cares, no worries, no limits! I felt indestructible and immune to disaster. Live in the moment and get as high as you can.

Nothing was important, except what I was doing and who I was doing it with. As long as everybody was as fucked up as I was, we were doing fine! The times I not only drove a car (yeah, off a cliff!) all wasted, but the hundreds of times I partied while driving! Before you could get into the bars, cars were the next best thing! We'd cruise the strip, smoking joints and drinking Bacardi 151. Luckily, not long after that my sister moved out with a girlfriend and we didn't drink and drive anymore!

A couple of guys lived upstairs, my sister lived downstairs, and we were a party unit! The next day you'd find bodies passed out everywhere. People's feet in other people's faces, empty beer bottles and fifths strewn about, and the smell of cigarettes was stale in the air. Oh, such a pretty sight on a hangover!

There were many nights I should have died from alcohol poisoning, no doubt about it. We had contests to see who could drink the most shots and then passed out on the way to the bathroom. We played guzzling games and Passout, collected empty whiskey bottles and lined the ledge around the entire apartment—and we were proud of it! It was "Our Bottle Collection!"

Luckily I was too busy partying to be having a lot of sex, but I was too young to be doing either. The sex would come later, when I got my own place! Then I was back to drinking and driving, and boy, did I do a lot of that. I was definitely addicted to the bar scene from the time I could get in. I lived on the edge of town (I lived on the edge all right), so there were many late night, wasted drives home from the bar. Or even if it wasn't late, because it was a work night, I just got drunker earlier, then went home to pass out by 9:00 p.m. or 10:00 p.m. Sometimes I'd even pass out by 8:00 p.m., depending on what we were celebrating; or trying to forget.

This was the most reckless time for me. It was wild nights and gorgeous men! "No," was not in my vocabulary. I always drank too much and was much too eager to hop into bed with practically every cute stranger I met. Drinking, partying and having sex went together. I did it all and had no reservations about any of it (while I was doing it). I proclaimed moderation in all things, as I went about over-indulging in everything. I criticized people for doing things I did, because I didn't approve of such behavior! How stupid I must have looked. A rebel without a clue!

What I'm mostly feeling today is gratitude. I am so thankful to be alive! Surprised to be alive. And you know, it makes today seem really special. I could have wasted it away, but I was saved. I have a second chance, and that feels like the greatest gift I've ever been given. Today is a gratitude day, and it feels good!

June 22, 1995

(Mom & Dad's 39th Anniversary) - I've been thinking about my sister, and the relationship we have. We think so much alike, and we laugh a lot. I can't seem to quit thinking about the cliff incident. We almost died together. I was telling a friend about it and she couldn't understand why I was upset about something that "almost" happened so long ago. I guess because I just remembered it, it seems like it happened yesterday.

But I feel so good today. So glad to be alive, so glad to have my sister. A thing like that would have ruined my parents. Where would our family be if Kristie & I had been killed in the '70s? But we weren't and I feel so humble. I also feel tired today.

I seem to be getting into the simple things in life much more these days. I used to think I always did, but I didn't. My life was going way too fast for me to see and appreciate the things I do now. I take time today to enjoy simple pleasures.

But later that same day I was reacting in anger and had amends to make. It amazes me still, how I could feel so many different ways in one day. This was the uncertainty of recovery. I never knew from one minute to the next how I would feel. I could lose my serenity in an instant. I hadn't yet learned how to hold onto it. Lessons in humility were coming left and right.

Losing my temper and raging at people didn't feel the same as it used to. Now I felt like shit. Now I had to make amends. I didn't want to, but I needed to. I lost it at someone who asked me to do something for them, since I had nothing better to do. I was learning to defend my writing, to the extreme, and now actually carried a resentment against everyone who never took me seriously. I had to let all that go. This is what I wrote...

Well, I feel like a penny waiting for change, so I called and made a sloppy amends, and then really felt like an idiot. I guess I needed to see that I'm still vulnerable to reacting out of anger and resentment, and that doesn't feel good to me today. I'm sorry about it, and hopefully it won't happen again. Perhaps I'm just a tiny bit sensitive about my writing?

I can stand behind it without feeling a need to justify it to anyone. I'm doing the work I need to be doing, and that's all I need to know. What anybody else thinks is none of my business. I'm going to remember that. Why do I always try to make life so difficult? It's not meant to be a struggle, you know?

By this time I was going to a meeting at a women's treatment center once a week, one I still attend. Once I started going there I never again questioned whether or not I belonged in recovery. Listening to those women, most of whom don't even have thirty days clean time, reminds me where I came from. But the best thing that happens is I'm reminded of how far I've come, that I've made it through early recovery, where they are, and I can share my experience, strength, and hope with them.

As I've become friends with women from all walks of life, I've learned unconditional love and acceptance for all people, from the alcoholic housewife to the heroine addict living on the streets. We are all the same. We have recovery in common. What got us here is of little importance. I consider it twelfth step work, and we're all doing it.

June 23, 1995

Greg's putting the boat in the lake, where we hope to leave it all weekend. He & his brother hope to do a lot of fishing. I'm resisting big time going to the lake, the Bay, the beach, or even on the boat. I've always had reservations about doing "sun" things. It was nearly impossible for me as a kid. They didn't have sunscreen, and there was more than once growing up that I was deathly ill after a horrible sunburn.

Now there's sunscreen, and I can always wear a hat. Last year and the year before, I probably spent more time on the boat, but I always resisted at first. I guess I would rather stay at home. I love being on the boat, and I always have fun, but I'm always anxious to come back in too. This year I didn't even want to go over to the beach, and swim? Forget about it. I've been isolating, but the truth is I want to be writing.

When Gregory suggested getting a camp spot this weekend I was all for it, because I knew I could find a shady place and write. But, the bottom line is I'm resisting getting out of the house much, and I probably need to take a look at that. Maybe it's just the controlling alcoholic still in me. I just want everything I do to be my idea. I don't want surprise invitations to go swimming or out on the lake. I guess I need some work on spontaneity. I'm not spontaneous at all. Maybe that's the whole thing right there. I resist anything that hasn't been planned. Boy, I have a lot of work to do. But this is good, this is something that can be changed.

I sure have been tired lately. It comes on all of a sudden and I could just lay my head down and sleep. Most of the time I fight it, but sometimes I just can't.

At this point I'm progressing, however slowly it seemed. I was finally writing, so that felt really, really good. But I was so tired most of the time. I couldn't figure it out, it was nearly debilitating. I would get up, take a shower, eat breakfast, take my vitamin, and want to go back to sleep. It was horrible, and I didn't know if it would ever go away. I dragged myself to meetings, and talked about it, and read more about recovery, anything, to tell me this was normal.

I read a pamphlet I received in my newcomer's packet that said some alcoholics are tired for a year or two after they quit drinking. Still, my body was healing. I'd been through a lot. I'd been running hard for a long time. It's about time I was tired.

My relationship with Gregory was only getting better, the same with Megan, but it was increasingly stressful dealing with all the alcoholics and codependents in my life. Greg and I were both having a hard time dealing with "the families" and I was trying to let go of my own codependent behavior with them. We weren't very good at it and relationships were strained for awhile. I was learning to detach with love, but I had a lot of anger work to do first.

Chapter 14

ANGER

I found myself arguing or fighting with practically everyone around me. I heard a couple of things early on that stuck in my mind regarding anger. If I was mad about something for longer than a day, it was old stuff. That was good for me to hear, because I was used to nursing a grudge for days, even weeks. I knew how to stay mad.

Now, I wouldn't be able to justify staying angry for long periods, and I certainly wasn't going to be able to keep blaming it on other people. The other thing I heard was that if you find yourself fighting with more than two people, it's your stuff, not theirs. Ouch.

If I have anger work to do, I'm going to find myself confronted with every angry person out there. I can pretend it's about them, but if it keeps happening, I have to look at me. If I don't, I'll keep running into them. I didn't want to hear any of this. I wanted to be mad because of what *you* were doing. I didn't want to take any responsibility for my anger. If it weren't for all these people I kept running into, I wouldn't have anything to be angry about. Wrong. I was about to enter a phase of owning and confronting my anger, so I could continue to heal.

As I read over what I wrote at that time, I'm amazed how anger was just spewing out all over the place. I was pissed about everything—and nothing. When I finally knew I had to take a look at my anger, I started writing about what I was pissed off about, and I kept writing and writing. At this same time I was also talking about anger at meetings, a lot. No one wanted to talk about it, but everybody did.

I remember a few meetings where the subject was anger, thanks to me. A friend in the program came in late, so she hadn't heard the topic. It didn't take long to figure it out. When she spoke, she looked at me and said, "I take it we're talking about anger." I felt a twinge of guilt or something, but only briefly, because she immediately began talking about anger, right where she was at the time.

I look back now at the healing process, and I can see it as exactly that. But I remember how desperate I felt at the time, how pissed off I was, and had always been, but was in denial about it. It didn't feel like this before. I was pissed off about that. I was pissed off because I was having to do so much work to get better. I was pissed off I was so sick.

I thought I was angrier than I'd ever been in my life. That had to mean I was getting worse, not better. But the fact I was getting healthy enough to see how angry I'd always been is what made it seem worse. I could finally see it. Writing about it was out of self-defense. I was so pissed, and murder wasn't an option. I decided to DIG, and find out what the hell my problem was.

Have you ever been motivated like that by anger? I remember I could clean house real good or do some major physical activity and hardly notice, because I was so angry. My actions were literally fueled by my anger. I didn't see a thing wrong with that. I thought that was how you handled anger. What I didn't know was how much energy it takes to be in that space, how difficult it is to be there. I used to justify my anger, defend it, but now I wanted to be rid of it, however impossible that seemed at the time.

The anger work was the catalyst for codependent work, because half the reason I was pissed off all the time was because nobody was doing things the way I thought they should. I had my nose so far into other people's business, it's embarrassing now. But as I look back over the process, I see how much I learned, how much healing I did through all of that. And it wouldn't have had the impact without a huge dose of humility!

Tension had been building between my friend Cindy and me. She and I met years ago, and used to drink together. We hadn't seen each other for years, until she walked into a meeting. We were both surprised, yet not, to see each other. Things began to unravel early on, as we both had a tendency to work other people's programs.

She was going through a lot in her life, and was angry. I was sure she could be handling things differently. She wanted my advice, but didn't take it. We were friends until I said anything she didn't want to hear. I felt the need to point out how angry she still was (I cringe). We argued after a meeting and left without making amends.

June 27, 1995

"Anger." Well, I'm almost sure I must have been exercising my own will, for how screwed up things seem. I was just shaking after the meeting. I see now it was there that my anger began boiling just under the surface, anger I thought I didn't have anymore. Ooh. And after I quit shaking so bad I had to hold back tears. Yes, those angry tears I used to get (I haven't missed them!). Then I felt I wanted to run.

So, I made this out to be about Cindy and it's about me (although I do believe God killed two birds with one stone by putting us together so we can both confront our anger). I see how logical it is for God to point out my anger and my working other people's program, by putting someone in my face doing the same thing. Well, I'm embarrassed. But happy too, because what seemed like a confusing and awful day, has turned into a learning day, and those days are a blessing in disguise. Sometimes we have to make a fool of ourselves before we get it.

The confrontation continued over the phone, a couple of times. The last time I was angrier than when I started.

Once again I was shaking and upset, angry and confused. But getting smart enough to ask, what's going on with my program? Then totally at that moment, I recognized that this was my stuff, all about me, and that boy, these lessons can be really fucked.

So I chilled out and began replaying the events in my mind, searching for the meaning in each one. And of course I had no doubt what the "topic" was, what the main lesson had to be about, anger. The very thing I felt such a strong need to point out in Cindy. Yeah, like you're not taking a look at your anger, and it's pissing me off! Oh, the humility is so painful. But back to the issue I've probably been avoiding. What am I still angry about?

Well, I guess I'm angry that I still bite my fingernails, that I have to wear fake ones or I chew them to the quick, that I'm still nervous. I'm angry that I perceive certain people around me as nonsupporting of my writing. (What other people think of me is none of my business, what other people think of me is none of my business.) So what else might I be angry about?

Well, I've been angry for another incident where I'm working someone else's program, this time Susie. I've been building anger and resentment toward her because I feel she's not working her program good enough. How's that for judgmental, controlling and unacceptable behavior? It seems my ego has been under attack lately, and my reaction to hurt is going to be anger, because that's always been easier.

Let's see, what else? Am I angry about being an alcoholic? Probably. In fact, definitely. As grateful as I am for my recovery, this is hard! If I weren't an alcoholic I wouldn't be going through this. But then I wouldn't be learning how to do life in a healthy way. I don't need to drink today. I don't want to drink today, and I don't want to smoke. But on days I want to run away, I do. Oh yes, I sure do.

Let's see, the house. I guess I'm really angry about that. I'm angry I don't have a closet or a bathroom upstairs. I'm angry that I don't have an office. I'm angry that we always seem to be running on empty. I'm sick of feeling poor, and angry at myself for doing it. I'm angry that my parents suffer financially, that I can't help them, and that my dad has to work so hard. Boy, I guess I'm angry about a lot of things.

I'm really angry that I've been trying to work other people's program, when I know how important it is, and how much better it feels to work my own. Keep it simple, easy does it, first things first. How can I get out of that when it happens? I let go! I DON'T CARE WHAT ANYBODY ELSE IS DOING!! I only have to be present for me. I can't change anybody else, I don't want to change anybody else! God bless them all for what they're dealing with. Especially Cindy for having to deal with me! And also bless her with her anger too, that we might both heal from this.

I want to try to make amends again, but I'm afraid I'd be pushing it. I do want her to know, however, that it really was about me. I can see that now, and I guess I better do the work that needs to be done in my own yard, before I start criticizing the neighbor's yard! Don't you just hate eating humble pie?

(Later) Well, that humble pie tasted pretty good actually. I called and made amends. I told her how sorry I was for attacking her, and that this was all about me, no one else but me. How good that felt! I'm amazed. If you'd have told me a couple of hours ago that this was going to be all about me and my anger, I would have said you were nuts! Turns out I'm the crazy one! But I feel so much better now.

I don't have to work anyone's program but my own. I don't feel angry, judgmental, or resentful. I no longer feel a need to control. Oh, thank God! What a wonderful day! What a learning day. What a process to enlightenment. It was hard for me to remember step three today when it wasn't even my will I was worrying about! I'll tell you how I spell relief; Surrender!

I realized I was angry today. I acted out on it, recognized it, and made amends for it, which healed it. For today. I'm sure I'll be angry again, but hopefully I'll recognize it sooner next time. Relationships are so fragile, yet so strong. I'm learning with this program that I can move on from yesterday and be present today. I'm so grateful. I'm exhausted!

June 28, 1995

I'm angry that my Grandma Sue died when I was 15. I'm really angry that 22 years after her death I still haven't read a single word she wrote. Copies of her writings have been promised to me all this time, one disappointment after another. She was a writer. I'm a writer. They say I have her hands; dad says it's haunting. We're kindred spirits, and I've longed to read something, anything she wrote. The only thing that has kept me from feeling as hopeless and angry as I want to feel, is her own words. She always said, "Nothing is lost in the Kingdom of God. Everything is where it's supposed to be." I've tried to trust, but I've been angry.

I'm angry about the church. I'm sad that I've felt so guilty all these years for doing the things I had to do to be who I am. I never wanted to hurt my family, especially about the church. But I realize now it never has been about them. They would not judge me no matter what, but disappoint them, perhaps. So I've hid that part of my life from them and felt guilty for having found my own way. Guilt. What a terrible waste of good energy.

I always felt guilty about my drinking, and drank more to silence it. I had to drink, so I made up reasons. Any reason would do. I drank when I was having a good day, I drank if I was sad about something, I drank because my workday was over, I drank because it was the weekend, I drank on my birthday and your birthday, and after the dentist. But if I was angry, I got drunk. If I was angry I'd get the "fuck-its" and it was self-destruction, kill the pain, run away.

It was out of anger that I'd go charge something, then drink to justify it. How's that for insanity? It was out of anger that I did my most destructive drinking. It seemed to be the only thing that could make me not mad anymore. Getting drunk was the reward for having something piss me off. So I guess you know, the Jeremy years provided for a lot of angry drinking.

As the years passed by I continued to search for the fun it was in the beginning, the relief it was the first time I used it to kill the pain. But it wasn't that way for long. I continued to search for serenity, but instead found frustration, disappointment, helplessness, fear, nausea, vomiting, and guilt. Sounds like fun to me! Oh, what guilt trips I've put myself on over the years. Guilt, I believe that grew into anger.

Yes, anger that my solution had consequences, like hangovers and spending too much money, embarrassment over my actions, and memory lapses. But not in tune enough with my true feelings to see what was happening. It became a vicious cycle in which I became trapped. Drinking made me forget the guilt. Let me get this straight. Was this the guilt over drinking? Oh God, what insanity. No wonder I was pissed.

Anger. This seems to be what I'm learning lately. I guess I wasn't going to be able to skip by the anger thing quite so easily. And to think I thought I was done with anger, but what I was doing was "controlled" anger, and we all know how that control thing works, don't we?

So I guess I should be grateful this is happening now, because I didn't know I was still so angry. But oh, it's painful, and I go from wanting to cry, to being angry, and then that pisses me off! I don't want to be angry anymore! I guess I'll just keep writing about it and talking about it until it somehow makes sense.

All I know today is I want to have more of the peace and serenity I've experienced already in this program, and when I feel angry it's gone. The anger doesn't feel good anymore. It brings back my anxiety attacks too, and I really don't miss them! So my prayer for today is that

I will be in tune with my feelings and with my program so that I recognize the things I need to work on, in myself instead of attacking others for it.

I liked it when it didn't bother me what other people said or did. (That brief moment awhile ago). I liked it when I only cared about what I was doing, even when I wasn't quite sure what that was. I liked that feeling of surrender and release. I felt free, instead of bound by anxiety. Tomorrow's got to be better.

I need to detach my program from Susie's. I realize that whenever I'm trying to control someone, I get mad at *them*. Now that makes about no sense at all, but that's what's happening. The first thing I can do is stop judging. I can stop sharing where I'm at with her, and save it for meetings, if I don't feel she supports me. I can keep my nose in my own life, and *ignore* what others are doing. I can love them unconditionally, where they are and for who they are. I can pray for them. What's right for me is probably not what's right for them. Oh, I feel better already. God, help me in this moment. First things first. Keep it simple.

June 29, 1995

8:00 a.m. I was just in deep thought, thinking about all the gifts I've been given in life, and now I'm finally learning how to use them. This isn't about anyone but me. Everything that happens in my life, all the people in my life, happen for a reason, and the experience is for all of us. The only thing I have to worry about is me, my experiences, and how I deal with each one.

I watched a documentary about a wonderful woman whose name I didn't catch. She was a writer. The interview, prior to her death, showed what a remarkable woman she was. The main thing I caught from her philosophy on life was being in the present moment. She said once it's no longer the present moment, it's none of my business. Why would I want to stay in something that's over and done with and can't be changed? So it's important to stay in the present moment.

She also said if you want the good death you have to live the good life, because the two worlds are really one. She died peacefully at the age of 90. Everything she said made so much sense to me. She said it's so important to communicate, honestly, to state at every moment, with everyone you're with, the truth of the moment. She said she & her husband were having a discussion when a friend commented on how well the two got along. She responded, are you kidding? We were having one of our biggest fights, without all the resentments and stuffed feelings, and all the other things that happen if we're not truly honest with ourselves and each other.

I love that so much. I believe it's possible to live life free of fighting and misunderstandings. I believe we can learn to live together as one, with love and kindness for each other. I see it happening. I never run into mean people. I run into wounded people, and I've yet to have someone not smile back at me. The world is full of wonderful people.

I realize that anytime I see otherwise, anytime I encounter the negative, it's about me. Isn't that crazy? And pretty hard for me to swallow right at first. But I've tried it, and I know it's true. The sooner I admit it the sooner I can grow from the experience. It's amazing.

This has not been easy, coming to terms with my own anger, which has made me not a very nice person, in spite of what I thought. And I guess I thought that being nice when I was in a good mood, or had to be to keep up my positive image, would make up for the times I was a bitch. So basically what I've done all my life is think I know all about thinking positive and living a good life, because I was thinking the right thoughts, but what was I doing? My words and my actions were two different things. What I believed in my heart and what I wanted to believe were also two different things.

So now I find that other person in me, is leaving, piece by piece she's fading away. Or should I say layer by layer, like the proverbial onion. I'm finally getting down to the core of who I am. It wasn't going to come pain free. I'm learning patience for the first time in my life, or should I say I'm learning acceptance. I heard the most helpful thing at a meeting; with acceptance there is no need for patience. I loved it!

I'm finally learning how to trust. It's painful for me lately. It's hard taking responsibility for my own life, thoughts and actions. But it's necessary. It's a must if I'm to get healthy. As tired as I get, and as frustrated as I may be, I know it's worth all the work I have to do.

July 1, 1995

Wow, this program is so incredible. All the people in my world are mirrors, as I love myself, I can love them. I've had to do a lot of anger work, and hopefully so have all the other angry people who crossed my path while I was doing it! Today I can see a bigger picture.

At the meeting today the reading was about some of us being sicker than others, and how we need to treat those sicker ones the same way we'd treat any loved one with a serious disease, with love and compassion, patience and understanding. But it's hard. This recovery thing is the hardest, yet most rewarding thing I've ever done. I still had anger on my face once yesterday, and then again today, so I know I'm not done yet. But I'm not as resistant today.

July 2, 1995

Today I am again. Well, maybe not resistant, but let's say I'm leery, cautious. I'm still angry and I don't like to admit it. I've got to confront it, because I don't want to be like this anymore. I've been this way most of my life, and I'm ready to let it go. The day before yesterday I jumped right back into reactive behavior and anger all because my husband was doing anger. I couldn't get him to let it go, so I joined in! It totally amazed me how quickly I went back to that place. It let me know that I'm a lot more comfortable there than I want to admit. I don't like it there, but it's comfortable. Sick.

Then yesterday when someone said something about how I'd handled something in the past (poorly), I found myself in anger again. And when I was discussing it with my sister and she pointed out more of my anger, I didn't like it at all, and again was feeling the need to jump back in!

So I really have to take a look at this. Especially because it's just right there. It's just beneath the surface, and many things still trigger it. Sometimes I'm aware of it and sometimes I'm not. But it seems lately, I'm aware of every bit of it, and this really sucks! I'm also afraid. Extremely afraid.

July 3, 1995

It's about 3:00 on Monday afternoon, the day before fourth of July. There will be a 9:30 a.m. AA meeting tomorrow because it's a holiday, and you know how we alcoholics get when there's cause for celebration! Anyway, I'm feeling much better than I have since last night, and earlier today. Last night was a trigger for my anger that was so trivial I couldn't believe I was so pissed. I couldn't believe how much energy it took to be in that place, and how much of my life I spent there.

I'm beginning to believe that all the pain in my neck and shoulders is irritated by my anger. Because it's been giving me fits this past week, and especially when I'm writing about this stuff. I just tense up and freeze up, and it's incredible. There are many reasons why I need to work on this old anger, or I guess maybe it's rage, because it won't be eliminated, but I know it can be dealt with in a healthy manner.

The way I've always "done anger," and the way I'm still having it flare up, does not feel healthy, and that's why I want to work to change it. Maybe I just learned how to be angry by watching my father, and he from watching his. My dad is the nicest guy you'd ever want to meet, but he had an explosive temper. He was always fun loving when we were growing up, joking with us and the neighborhood kids, they loved him, everyone did.

He was always busy, always hyper, always willing to help everybody out. He never started anything he didn't finish, he was always productive. He was a hard working and happy person. He always worked hard, still does. He had to because he got married when he was a teenager, and had three kids in four years. He's had hard labor jobs his whole life.

Little things could piss my dad off, and boy it didn't matter what it was about, when he was pissed, he was pissed, and shit would hit the fan. It was quick, it was explosive, and it was over. Mom always dealt with everything by crying. Any confrontation, any uncomfortable situation, anything wrong at all, mom cried. Didn't talk about it, never verbalized her feelings, just go to her bedroom crying.

So I guess I never did learn a healthy way to do anger. I couldn't very well go around crying all the time, but I could go around pissed off all the time, and basically that's what I did. It's easy not to cry when you're pissed off. Although there's always been a fine line for me between being pissed off, and crying because I'm so pissed, and then that really pisses me off! Just like it used to piss my dad off when mom cried at the least conflict. He said that was her answer to everything.

So, not only did I learn an unhealthy way to do anger, so did they, and those before them. Since temper tantrums as an adult are not acceptable, and crying was out, I just didn't know what the hell to do with my anger, so I stuffed it and kept it at a slow simmer, in control as best I could. But boy, what a stressful place to be. I'm so grateful that I'm learning new ways to acknowledge and express my emotions, healthy ways. But those old tapes sure are hard to erase.

I guess that's my work for today. Take a look at the unhealthy way I've dealt with life, my expectations of other people, and my need to control and have things go my way. I just want to be able to let go. I don't want to live with rage simmering just beneath the surface. I don't want to have triggers ignite my reactive behavior. I want to relax, breathe freely, and have some fun. I don't want to take myself and everything around me so seriously.

I need to let go of the angry person I've always been. There's nothing nice about her. She's unpredictable and explosive and she makes it hard for her loved ones to trust her behavior. I want to be able to smile, feel serene, and trust my life. I don't want to know all the answers anymore. I don't want to fix anybody else. I don't want to worry and fret over how somebody else is conducting their life. Why should that concern me?! Can I change it? No.

If I don't stay in my own program I get angry. Or should I rephrase that by saying every time I'm working other people's program I am that angry person. I go right back to the old me that always knew what was best for everyone else and was always frustrated, irritated, and impatient with people, places and things. God help me.

I was beginning to realize I was guilty of everything that bothered me in other people. Edgar Cayce is quoted in Elsie Sechrist's book, *Dreams: Your Magic Mirror*, as saying, "The thing that irritates you the most in others is found in self. Else why would it bother you?" Dreams are interpreted only through personal associations, and the people in our dreams represent aspects of ourselves.

The study of dreams helps me in my recovery, because it's an easier way for me to start recognizing the defects I notice in others as my own. It teaches me to look at my thoughts about others and ask, "What does this say about *me?*" I don't like it most of the time, but being able to do that both in the real world and the dream world, helps me to learn more about me. The more I know about me, the more I can experience who I am.

Elsie Sechrist goes on to say, "Honesty in the analysis of one's dreams is essential, and this is precisely where difficulty lies. We have a tendency to place all the blame on the faults of others, because we can't admit to bad qualities in ourselves."

July 4, 1995. I awoke to a horrible dream. I couldn't imagine what it meant. I got up and went for coffee. I was still in shock at what I'd done in my dream. By the time I was stirring my coffee I was crying at the thought of what I had dreamed. I couldn't even tell Gregory about it. I didn't want to say it out loud.

There were five Gizzies (my cat). I was putting them all to sleep with a BB gun. I was shooting them in the head. I was trying to find the best spot so I wouldn't hurt her and she would die fast. I was on the last one, there were four laying dead up on a cement platform.

This is too horrible to my awake self. I remember shooting a couple of them. It sounded like a tranquilizer gun, and when I put the gun to her head and fired, she slowly laid her head down and closed her eyes, looking at me with trusting eyes to the very end.

The thought of it just sends me into tears. But the last one wouldn't die. It was hard for me to do this, and I struggled with the length of the gun and where to put it on her head. By the last one I was losing my nerve. I couldn't seem to get to her forehead. She kept moving. I shot her once or twice but she didn't die.

I shot a third one between her eyes and she finally laid her head down and closed her eyes. But she was still breathing and suddenly I felt horrible and devastated by what I'd done. I thought, "I've made a mistake! Now it's too late. Can I get her to a vet or have I done too much damage? Oh my God!"

I woke up and couldn't believe what I'd seen. It was too horrible to think about, let alone talk about. Now that I've written it out, I feel better. I've been able to make some sense of it, and one thing I know for sure it did, is open a flood gate to some unfamiliar tears. Well, familiar, but it's been a long time. That dream stirred in me some bottled up emotions I didn't even know were bottled up. The parts of the dream I can interpret stir up the same emotion.

I had to ask myself what Gizzie means to me or what she might represent in my dream. Since people in our dreams represent aspects of ourselves, maybe it's the same with pets. I think of Gizzie as stuck up and stand-offish. She keeps to herself, has a "Don't bug me" air about her. She gives Cali a look that says, "Don't mess with me!" and Cali runs the other way.

When you pick up Gizzie and try to give her loves, she straightens out both front legs, and plants her paws firmly on your chest. That's as close as you're going to get. Well, my, my, my, who does that describe? So, I know what the dream's about. The killing part, I'm sure, is the "killing off" parts of myself, or transition from old self to new self, which is surely taking place with the anger work I've been doing.

I've come a long way, and I have to remember that, but I feel like I have so much anger to deal with, and I'm already tired! But, hey, nobody said it was going to be easy. Nobody ever promised it wouldn't hurt. I'm to the point now where I'm going to muster up the courage it takes to face up to these painful character defects, to look something as scary as anger straight in the face, and say, "Why are you here?" And then be able to say, "Now go away. I don't want you around anymore."

So is that what's happening in the dream? Did I kill the anti-social part of myself; the standoffish, snobbish, or recluse? What about the unloving side that is Gizmo? She doesn't show a lot of affection, but that's just who she is. Did I kill off the part that says, "Leave me alone?"

What could the other Gizzie represent? Let's see. She's also overweight and lazy. All she does is eat, sleep, and go outside so she can lay on the porch and sleep some more. In a word, she's unmotivated. Oh, please let that be one of the parts I put out of its misery.

Gizzie eats too much if you don't watch her, and so do I. Boy, I never knew Gizzie and I were so much alike. Maybe that's why the dramatic symbolism of killing off five Gizzies (the last one of course resisting). I don't have to ask which was the last Gizzie. Without a doubt it was the one that resists being hugged. It's the one that resists letting anyone love me.

I can't for the life of me see how that side of me has served me at all. All it did was keep my kids at arms length, everybody actually, except maybe my husband, and now, I see I was even holding back from him, although he has definitely been safer for me than most. So, the guard, the protective and cautious person I thought I was being, for my own good, was not helping me.

What on earth was I guarding? Why the gates around my heart? When was I hurt so badly that I decided to protect my heart by only loving a little, by only allowing myself to receive a little bit of love, not as much as I wanted, and certainly not never-ending, unconditional love. I guess what I'm discovering is that it's not all about me withholding my love from my kids and others, like I've always beat myself up for doing, but instead, it's about the love I was keeping out, the love I withheld from myself. I was withholding all right, but not in the way I always thought.

I guess the dream had to be that dramatic to get me to cry like I did. With all the anger I've been weeding through lately, it felt good to cry and let it out, instead of hanging on to it. It seems that every day I'm realizing more and more things I've been angry about. This anger work really has me working. Courage is taking on a whole new meaning.

So, about two anger realizations a day? Is that how we're working it? Whatever. I feel better, that's all I know. I need to remember first things first. Whatever I need to work on will be there. Boy will it!

July 6, 1995

Today I guess I've been dealing with impatience or maybe it's anger in disguise. Anyway, I feel good today. I'm still in a learning space, so I feel a little exhausted, but I feel hopeful. Anger is still coming up today, or should I say I'm still getting triggered, but I'm aware of it now, and ready to take a look at why I still react the way I do, especially since the things I get so angry about are trivial, petty, insignificant. But it's still happening, and I have to take a look at that.

Today the topic at the meeting was fear, and it ended up being fear and anger. Fear is a big part of what I feel when I think of letting go of anger. Then there's a bigger fear that I won't be able to let it go, that I'm doomed to be a bitch. Say it isn't so!

I'm doing the work, and one day at a time I'm going to practice getting it. I'm never alone. I never have to be alone. I can always find a room full of wonderful people who genuinely care about what I have to say, and how I feel, especially if I'm struggling. I have my wonderful husband, who becomes more supportive every day. Today I feel empowered, and not quite as vulnerable. I'm also asking for guidance today because I found a lump in my breast. I'll do whatever I need to do. Oh, life.

July 7, 1995

Today I'm still learning. Learning about anger, learning about me. I want so much to be rid of the old me, the side of me that wants to medicate, and wants to be angry about the fact I can't. But I'm much more comfortable being sober, as uncomfortable as that can be at times, than I was in my drinking days. I guess each day I get a little more willing and a little more determined to face my demons. I don't want to be angry anymore, I don't want to be irritable and impatient, judgmental, critical, and full of expectation.

I want all the help I can get, and I know it's not going to be easy. It hasn't been a walk in the park so far, but I'm just tired of the stress of that old way of thinking. I guess I'm feeling impatient. I want everything to be fixed right now. I feel so tired. I know what it feels like to have peace and serenity, so how come I can't just stay there? Why do I have to look at this stuff? Why does it have to be there at all? I'm going to make it through. I've never not made it yet.

July 9, 1995

Life is good for me today. I'm scared of a lot of things, but I know that's okay. Being afraid today is not like being afraid in my drinking days.

For the next month or so I struggled. I see now it was because I was still running. I was indulging in everything I could so that I didn't have to look at myself. I was still concerned about other people's lives, and thought I knew what was best for them. I couldn't take care of myself, but I could tell you what you were doing wrong. I wrote a couple of angry letters to unsuspecting loved ones, and felt terrible afterwards.

I was vulnerable to everything in my life. I felt insecure and threatened by the kids' birth mother, even though I knew it was ridiculous. Nothing I was doing seemed to be working. Anger was coming out every which way and I was fighting with just about everyone around me. It seemed things were getting worse.

July 25, 1995

It's been a learning week for me, and I've felt more like an addict than ever before. I've cried a lot this week, and if I wasn't crying I felt like crying, or drinking, or smoking, and a few of the days I felt it was just too hard. I quit sharing at meetings and that's a bad sign for me. I get so much out of just listening, but if I don't share where I'm at, how I'm feeling, pretty soon I start feeling like what I have to say isn't important, that I'm not worthy of taking up precious meeting time, that is better reserved for those who really need to talk.

I made myself share yesterday, and I ended up crying in front of everyone, but it felt good. Today I was scared, shaky and very vulnerable, and I shared that. I need to do that and I know it. I felt so much better afterwards. I don't feel quite so much like I'm white knuckling it this afternoon. I think I'm going to make it.

The next couple of weeks were troubling. At times I was angrier than I'd ever been, but it was because I was sick of being in that space. I was acting out in anger over that! So, my writings for the next couple of weeks are angry, hopeless, and all about everybody else!

It's clear that anything and everything only added to my anger. I was so intolerant at the time. I wrote about being outraged by something I heard on the radio. They were talking about a man on death row who was found slumped over in his cell. He was revived and taken to the hospital, before being released to be put to death by lethal injection. I wrote:

"Now give me a break. Am I crazy here? What the hell is going on?! So while I'm at it, let's get pissed off about....."

Then I proceeded to write about how so-and-so doesn't know how to be a parent, and so-and-so doesn't take care of themselves, and every other injustice I could think of....all the while avoiding working my own program. After getting it all out, it was clear....the most important thing for me to remember is I can't be responsible for other people, places, or things. When I start building a resentment, it takes me to a really dangerous place.

August 5, 1995. Boy, what crazy dreams I had last night. I was in a yard with a friend when suddenly we were chased by a hippopotamus. We got on a motorcycle to get away, but it jumped on our backs. I was driving wildly and really fast trying to get it to fly off, but it wouldn't. My friend was more worried about us wrecking on the bike, and I was scared too, but I was more freaked about this animal on our backs. Then we were in the yard again and I ran into the house, with the hippo following, and locked the door. Then an Indian woman came in the back door, behind her Juan Valdez on his donkey.

The hippopotamus represents vast strength, hidden danger, and how I relate to my power. It seems overpowering to me. I'm afraid of it. It appears I'm trying to get away from it, like it's something bad. I've always been afraid of my power, but I guess I didn't realize how much I'm still running from it.

The Indian woman represents natural wisdom. Where in my life do I want more freedom from control? Wow. And the donkey represents simplicity, sturdiness. Where can I express my power more directly? It's all about understanding my power and utilizing my strengths.

At this point in my recovery I was struggling to work through my codependent issues. I'd been around the tables long enough to see people come in and out of the program. People I'd grown close to were relapsing. I didn't know how I felt about it. I didn't want it to affect my recovery, but it felt like it did. I was learning to let go of what other people were doing with their lives. I was also learning about healthy boundaries.

August 6, 1995. I dreamed that my husband called to tell me that a guy in the program, Dave, was drinking. Then Dave and his brother, Jim, were in my living room. Dave was drinking a beer, which he set down. He took a drink from a flask he was carrying. He was being mean and verbally abusive, unlike his usual self. There were young girls in my house, too young, and they had been having a party. They had trashed my house.

I was so upset that Dave had relapsed. I was trying to clean my kitchen and get dinner in the oven, which was already late. Dave was sitting in the dining room, drinking a beer. He looked at me and said, "Do you like your life?" I said, "Yes, I do."

The girls were making me mad. One of them hit me in the head with something, and I grabbed her by the hair and arm and literally threw her out the back door. Then the second girl started in. I threw her out the same way. Then I pretended to call 911 and asked them to send someone out.

I was trying to clear up the counter and there was a big bud of pot, skunk bud, all sticky and really good quality I could tell. There was a couple of film canisters, one had pills in it and one I opened and saw what was left of cocaine. I wanted to taste it. I knew there was just enough in there for one line, but before I could do any of it another girl, this one nice and apologetic for the others, came up and began helping me clean. She took the film canister. I was bummed. I told her where to get the baggies for the pot and she took that too. The cocaine was the only thing I was tempted to do.

This dream speaks to me of boundaries and temptation. I didn't quite know how to handle the fact that people were trashing my house, were relapsing in front of me, and bringing drugs and alcohol into my home. The aggression I showed toward the girls was a bit extreme, just like I've always dealt with boundaries. Either I had none, and everyone walked all over me, or I lashed out inappropriately. At this point I'm learning to recognize what makes me uncomfortable and that I don't have to tolerate it. I'm also reminded to "clean my house," and rid myself of temptations that are still there for me. The cocaine tells me that I'm still tempted to "speed," warning of the need to slow down even more.

August 22, 1995. I dreamed I was in a big two-story house, lots of people around. There were several people from AA, as well as a friend of mine who is still drinking. It was a party, but no drinking or drugs. It was good, clean fun. Then I was outside walking with two friends, one who is still drinking. She started in with her defense of her drinking and denial of her problem and I lost it.

I attacked her and threw her to the ground, choking her and slamming her body against the ground. She passed out and was making choking noises when I stopped. I looked at the friend and said let's go, and said I hoped I hadn't killed her, and for a second I felt really scared, because that was not what I meant to do. I just wanted to "beat some sense into her."

We went back inside and there was a bunch of electrical stuff all in a corner. Too many TVs, stereos, lamps and everything all hooked up. Wires everywhere. Someone tried to fix it, but now when I tried to change the channel the light would go on, everything was all mixed up. I told Gregory about it and wanted him to see if he could fix it. He couldn't believe how everything was so mixed up.

Then in burst a friend from my childhood, one I'd gone to church with. She was as loud and disruptive as she always could be. She gave me a hug but didn't seem surprised to see me. She sat down and was still loud when she realized others were praying around her. One girl got up and shut the TV off and they continued praying. Then more girls from the church began arriving and it was clear to me that we were being invaded by surprise guests. I wanted to get out of there.

Then there were several girls sitting around a table, including the friend I'd tried to choke. I gave her a hug and told her I was so sorry for what I had done. She said, "I hope you don't ever forget that last vision of me choking on the ground." The girls around the table looked at me in judgment. I went to the phone to call Susie and she said to come over. We were eating pizza and I told her all about my "dreams."

Clearly there is too much going on in my "house." It's a very busy place, and in one room (the TV, stereo, lamps), there was too much power going to too many things, so nothing was working properly. Every aspect of myself appeared in the dream; the "recovering" side (people from AA), the drunk or sick side, (the one I tried to knock some sense into), my angry side, the side I've completely rejected (the church), and the side I embrace (Gregory), all were represented in the dream. The loud and disruptive side (my childhood friend), the side that searches for serenity (the prayers), and the side that wants to get better, represented by calling a friend for help.

Everyone was there and too much was going on. I need to clean my house and relieve all the confusion at the main power center. I'm trying to run too much off one circuit, so nothing is working properly. It's all mixed up and confused. This dream sums me up perfectly.

Chapter 15

GETTING TO KNOW ME

*A*ugust 25, 1995. I dreamed I was home. My sister was here, and my mom was in the kitchen, cooking. The toilet and the sink had milky water sitting in them. My sister said they had been this way for about an hour. I knew I couldn't use the bathroom, yet I really had to go. Just then, the drain gurgled and all the water sucked down. I could hear the kitchen sink do the same thing. It was like, wow, it fixed itself. I felt good. The problem was solved.

This dream, like others, related to cleansing and release. My mom cooking in the kitchen relates to nurturing and nourishment. The milky water relates to maternal love and sustenance; the cooking, nourishment. This dream was encouraging, because while things were clogged in the beginning, everything cleared up and the way was made free for cleansing and release. The motherly images relate to loving myself and learning to nurture myself, which feels good.

August 26, 1995. Whew! More wild dreams. In the first dream I was in a small, private plane. Susie was flying it. I was in the back seat and an unknown person was in the passenger seat. Susie had never flown a plane before, but she was confident that she could fly it. The guy in the tower was going to guide her. She got to the end of the runway and started speeding up (I was a little afraid). Then she said on the radio, "Are we clear for takeoff?" He cleared her and then told her what to do. She fol-

lowed his instructions and up we went, but we were tilting way to the right and we couldn't keep it in the air.

We hit the ground but didn't "crash." Susie knew she could do it and turned the plane around and headed to the start of the runway again. We picked up speed, raced down the runway, the guy in the tower cleared us, and this time up we went! We flew around for awhile. I was a little concerned about the landing, but before I knew it, we had already landed safely on the ground. Then we were up in the air again, flying around, then on the ground again.

This dream clearly describes my recovery. Planes represent movement across great distances. Am I in a hurry for change? Apparently, since the plane is being flown by an inexperienced person. Susie still showing up in my dreams represents the side of me that is still running, doesn't want to do the work (sure, I've never flown a plane before, but I can do it).

The unknown person represents unacknowledged parts of myself, which tells me I still have more to learn about me. The plane taking off, flying around, landing, taking off again, and back and forth clearly describes recovery to me: lots of ups and downs with reassurance that I won't crash.

Next I was in a house. The upstairs room was decorated with Christmas stuff. It looked beautiful. I was showing it to some people, then we went downstairs. My sister was with me in the living room. I looked outside and the whole street was decorated for Christmas. Then a beautiful and detailed Christmas float went by. I ran out on the porch to see it. I called my sister to come and look. We could see another beautiful Christmas float on the next street. It was a Christmas parade!

Then I was back in the living room. There was an unknown woman sitting in a rocking chair, no other furniture was in the room. I was standing back and a "zombie" kept coming in, trying to get us. I ducked out in the hallway and managed to evade this guy, but it was very scary.

Then we were walking into the house and the unknown woman was carrying her newborn baby. I was close behind, being protective, still afraid of the zombie. The guy was unlocking the door, and another man was with him. I recognized them as the "zombies," only they looked pretty normal, but I knew it was just a cover-up. We laid the baby on the

couch and uncovered her. Then she was a little girl and wanted to know
where her two "friends" were (the zombies). I told her they weren't really
her friends, but she disagreed.

Breaking this dream into symbols and interpreting each one paints a
picture of my recovery, my new life, my discovering myself, what I need to
take a look at, and what I'm afraid of. Christmas represents celebration,
reunion. What am I celebrating? What do I wish to reunite with? The parade
relates to fanciful displays, options. What part of me wants to be seen? The
porch relates to outside of self. Where do I want to be more approachable?

All of these questions are running through my head as I progress in
recovery. I want to be more approachable, especially to my children. I want
to reunite with my higher self, and I'm learning that I have choices. I've also
had to ask myself what part of me wants to be seen, and how much do I still
want to hide? When I'm feeling strong I want to reveal everything. When I'm
feeling vulnerable I want to hide it all.

The zombie clearly represents living death. What am I afraid to look at?
Hiding out in the hallway shows I'm in transition, but not ready to face all
my demons. I still want to stay in my safety zone at times. The newborn represents my infant self, a rebirth, trust. What is being re-born in me? What do
I trust? The baby who turns into a child represents innocence, the new self
seeking to develop. Where in my life am I developing? What part of my
nature is childlike? Um, do angry outbursts and temper tantrums count?

Overall I think the dream spoke to me of nurturing, mothering, celebration, and fear. I think that about sums up my recovery to this point. I'm
finally learning how to take care of myself, recognizing my strengths as well
as what I need to work on. Alas, I'm growing up (scary).

August 28, 1995

I just feel so scared sometimes. When it comes to my purpose in life,
my true source of joy and fulfillment, my writing, that's where I feel the
most fear. I must be so afraid of failing, I've decided to do nothing,
thereby risking nothing. Even success. Can't risk it! It's so crazy. I'm
suffering here. I don't know what it is.

Why am I so afraid about my writing? Am I more afraid of success
than failure? If so, why? How do I get over it? What am I going to do

with me? It's the crazy me at work here. I can sure as hell see it in every-body else, like Susie. She continues to show up in my dreams, but do you think I'll get the significance? It took a dream book, turning up mysteriously, to make me think about it.

I couldn't seem to let go of Susie, and a sick attachment to taking her inventory. Night after night she appeared in my dreams. I knew that the people in our dreams represent a part of ourselves, so I knew I had to try to understand what the significance of her in my dreams was all about. I found the dream book in a box in the basement, it wasn't mine. I practically turned right to a part that said something along the line of, an individual who has character defects that he refuses to recognize will have dreams about a person with irritating characteristics, in my case, Susie.

So I had to ask myself, what do I think about her? As I started thinking it became painfully clear why she keeps showing up. I'm guilty of everything I accuse her of. This is how I still see her. She's still as busy as she ever was, still not allowing herself time to just be alone. She's always got to be going somewhere, doing something, buying something or going out to eat. She still talks too much and too fast, and she doesn't listen any better now than she did when she drank. She won't slow down long enough to feel what's really going on inside. She's still medicating, but now it's with simple pleasures.

What does all this say about me? If this is how I feel about where Susie is in her program, what's that really saying about me? How much of those old, unwanted behaviors are still there in me, and I just can't see them? I need to take a look at this. I want to keep recovering, keep progressing, but it's hard to look at something you can't see.

I see now that this was a turning point in my recovery. I didn't have a sponsor. I was going to need one if I was going to really work the steps and do a thorough fourth step. It was becoming clear I needed to do one. Susie was my first sponsor and the one I took my first fifth step with. I don't know what I would have done without her my first year in recovery.

We used each other as sponsors, and not a day went by we didn't talk on the phone or see each other. I would call crying, out of my mind over noth-ing, and somehow I'd feel better. On a day I was doing pretty good, she'd show up in tears. We were there for each other. Everybody needs that kind of support, especially in the beginning.

As we both continued in recovery, the mirror image stuff became too painful, I think. All of a sudden neither of us felt safe to be who we were with the other. The phone calls were fewer, the visits were stressed. We were pushing each other's buttons and didn't know why. We backed away from each other. She found another sponsor and I struggled. Here's what I wrote:

> I don't seem to want to get another sponsor, I don't want other people pointing out my character defects. I'd rather let them gently present themselves to me as my Higher Power seems fit. But I know it takes longer that way, because we hang on to our defects longer than we like to admit. It makes no sense, it's part of how the disease works I suppose.
>
> Not a whole lot about alcoholism does make sense, and it's very complex, but there's a map available to anyone who wants it bad enough. To everyone whose suffered enough. I did, and have, but I sure like to make myself go through more it seems! Always got to make it more complicated than it is, always expecting more from myself. I should be stronger I say to myself, I should be able to fix it, make it better. But I haven't been able to.

August 29, 1995
Well, I shared at the meeting today about my fear of writing, of life, of sobriety, and how I just don't seem to know how to do it some days. I'm so afraid a lot of the time, but I've been too afraid to admit it! I don't want to be so busy in my head or in my life that I can't feel the moment, that I miss what's going on around me right now.

It sure scares me when I'm not doing anything. I'm so afraid just to BE. Or to go to the word processor and write, or pray or meditate. Yeah, right, I'm supposed to meditate when it was always easier to medicate. I never realized those two words have only one letter difference. Crazy, one is a temporary fix, the other has the power to heal.

I'm afraid of getting in touch with that part of me, so afraid of surrendering to a power greater than myself. So ready to run. I'm tired of running, I really am. I've *got* to stop. Painful as it may be, I want to get better. I want to start accomplishing more of my goals. I want to start living more, doing more, being more.

September 1, 1995. Seventeen months after I quit drinking, I had my first drinking dream. Susie and I were on Mackinac Island. Gregory couldn't go (it's a trip we really have planned for next weekend). I was in the bathroom. I had to go really bad. All the stalls were full, but no one was waiting. Then all the bathrooms became free at the same time; but a crowd of people came into the bathroom at once and everyone went into the bathrooms ahead of us. I was mad. We had been first, and I really had to go. This happened twice.

Then, we went into a very crowded restaurant to have dinner. The next thing I know it's the next day and Susie is saying she can't believe we drank. I said, "What? We drank?" I realized it was true, because I couldn't remember anything. I felt so terrible, like I'd thrown everything I'd worked so hard for away.

I was also afraid that I'd spent my money and was trying to find my purse, which I did. We were getting ready to go somewhere and I noticed my wallet wasn't in my purse. Then I found it under a table. I opened it. I saw a fifty, a twenty, a ten, and a one, I thought. "Well, I still have money. It wasn't that bad." I wanted to pretend the relapse hadn't happened, but Susie said, "Oh well, we start over." I was mad and said, "You mean I have to start all over from today? No way! I can't do that."

Then we were riding our bikes to the gift store. I saw a couple of boys I'd gone to junior high with. One reached out and touched my butt as I went by. Then our clothes were wet for some reason. They felt really yukky. I wanted to change clothes before we went anywhere. I started putting on dry clothes, but when I got dry pants on I realized my white lace panties were laying on the floor. I was embarrassed, but decided I wouldn't need them. So I picked them up and put them in my purse.

I have many books on dreams, but my favorite, and the one that seems to be most helpful to me, is by Alice Anne Parker, titled, *Understand Your Dreams*. Her interpretations are followed by questions. I like that. The above dream told me several things. First of all, I was beginning to dream more and more about having to go to the bathroom. I was blown away when I read the associations: release, usually of emotion, anger, and embarrassment at emotional release. What feelings am I clearing? Am I pissed off?

That's amazing. The bathroom represents a place of cleansing and release, and bathrooms were beginning to show up a lot in my dreams. Not being able to get a stall tells me that other people are getting in the way of my emotional release. It tells of codependent work I'm going to need to do, as well as learning to set healthy boundaries. The restaurant represents choices; a crowded restaurant, lots of choices, and nourishment. In other words, having lots of choices about what's good for me.

The purse and the money relate to what I value, which appears is my sobriety. I was horrified that I drank. I think the dream happened so I can take a look at two things. One, I'm reminded that the choice to drink is always there, and two, I know how terrible I would feel about it (the loss of something valuable).

But then I found my purse under a table (place of activity, work), and there was more money in it than I would normally have. To me that represents security in my work, as long as I value it.

Bikes represent self-propulsion, recreation. Do I have enough strength to make it? Will it be fun? I see that again I'm questioning whether or not I can do this thing, the writing, recovery, life. But riding to the gift store relates to recognition and appreciation, so it tells me that's where I'm headed.

Clothing represents identity, image, an exploration of new roles or a rejection of old ones. Since water represents emotion, the wet and yukky clothes tell me I'm drenched in emotion. The water being unpleasant relates to overwhelming (saturated) emotions and indicates change, represented by changing into dry clothes. The panties represent my feminine, private self, my sexual identity. What are my hidden feelings? What am I ready to expose?

Apparently not much, since I was embarrassed about the panties and put them in my purse, thinking I wouldn't need them. I obviously think they're valuable, I just want to keep them private. This dream also told me that there are still things I don't want to deal with, private things, and that if I don't, there is a risk of staying sick (relapsing).

Chapter 16

WHEN THE STUDENT
IS READY

September 2, 1995 - I dreamed I was in a school. I was going there. It was a new building and I was familiarizing myself with it. I walked down the empty, new halls and found myself remembering what it was like when I was in school. It was exciting. It felt good. It was like the hope for a future filled with new things to learn.

Then, I was at a desk in the hall, where a teacher sat. He was helping other students with directions. I was having trouble carrying everything, which not only included books, but also stacks of clothing. I couldn't seem to keep my hair out of my face, and I was unusually concerned about how I looked and how others would perceive me (I wanted to look my best).

A young man was headed to a nearby classroom. He stopped to talk with me. He was cute. He asked me if I'd seen his jacket. I said no, then realized I had it. I threw it on a chair and looked in the classroom to tell him. He was out in the hall again and had borrowed my pen, but now it was gone. He felt bad and went down the hall to the bookstore to get me a new one. I told him not to worry about it, but he was already gone.

I looked in the classroom and saw him in there. I asked someone if there were two of him (was he a twin?). They said yes. I knew I was running late for class, but I didn't know where to go. I was getting stressed. He came back and handed me a new blue pen. I was setting all my stuff on the stairs to find my class schedule (my hair was still giving me fits, falling in my eyes). Much to my relief, I found my schedule but still didn't know where the classroom was located.

A friend from early childhood came out and told me our first class was Italian, and showed me where to go. I walked in and all of the desks and chairs were in a circle. Half of them were a bright, vivid orange with matching desks, and the other half were brilliant turquoise. There were a couple of empty chairs of each color right where they met. I wasn't sure if I was supposed to sit in a certain color.

I really wanted to sit in the turquoise chairs, but felt that I shouldn't. So I sat in the very first orange one, next to an empty, turquoise chair. As I did, I looked at my friend sitting in the turquoise section, as if to ask if I was supposed to sit somewhere specific. She nodded, like it didn't matter. I could see her, another friend from childhood, and an unfamiliar girl sitting at the table. I remember thinking it was great to see them again. They were sitting on a higher row of chairs than I was.

It was then I realized we were in college, having come back to school after many years. I wondered why the three girls were there, because I knew they were already teachers.

I looked to my left and saw a young couple dressed in wedding clothes. It was like they were doing a demonstration, speaking in Italian. She went first and spoke fluent Italian. We all laughed when she said something funny, even though we didn't understand the language. It was as if we couldn't intellectualize the language, but we understood. Then he spoke and it was the same thing. We laughed when we were supposed to, intuitively knowing he had said something funny. I was enjoying listening to the language and thought how fun it was that I would be learning it.

My hair was still bothering me. I didn't have a barrette to keep it out of my eyes and was using my sunglasses to hold my hair on top of my head, but pieces kept falling out. I took the glasses off and got a brush out of my bag. I brushed the hair up (hoping I wouldn't get in trouble for brushing my hair in class), and then put the sunglasses on to hold the hair up. Then the sunglasses broke in the middle. Of course, they weren't any good at all now for keeping my hair up. I reached in my purse, hoping to find a barrette but was quite sure I didn't have one with me. Much to my surprise and delight, I found one. I was so relieved. I stood up to go to the bathroom, so I could fix this darn hair once and for all.

Next I was walking down a long roadway. I was going somewhere specific, maybe even to school, but I was walking instead of driving or taking a bus. I carried books or something in my left arm. In my right hand I held a golf club I'd found along the way. The golf club seemed to be a safety device. I held it casually, almost like a cane or a walking stick. It was my security, like a warning to potential attackers or whomever that I could defend myself if I needed to. At first it was a golf club, then it became a fireplace poker. I met and smiled at a few nice people along the way, but didn't stop my journey. It was the same on my way back down this same road.

As I continue to learn the language of dreams, I'm amazed at the many messages each one brings. Dreams have a very special language, understood fully only by the dreamer. Every "symbol" represents something different to each person. A snake may represent energy and sexuality to one person, while representing fear to another. It takes time to look at a dream and to analyze its messages, but as I learn the language of my dreams, the meanings become clear.

That's why it's important to write them down. I'm so grateful I did. It made it possible for me to take each symbol and ask myself what it means to me, what it makes me think about. All the symbols relate to each other. I've never found a time they didn't. This is how I'm learning the language, and the more I do it, the easier it becomes. I'm able to interpret my dreams, as if I were reading a letter.

In analyzing the above dream I found myself in a school, and that's how I feel in sobriety, like I'm in school, a place of learning. The building is new, so that tells me everything I'm learning is new (sure enough). The halls are empty, and everything is exciting and new. Pretty clear.

The desk represents organization, getting down to business. What am I ready to accomplish? It's a simple message since my own work is done at a desk. I'm ready to get down to business. Being in the hallway represents transition, change. (If I got down to business it would be a change all right.)

Trying to carry too much stuff tells me it's getting difficult carrying the load. I'm going to have to get rid of some of it. The clothing represents my self-image, my identity, and speaks to me about my fear surrounding my image. I'm not wearing the clothes. I'm carrying them, and having a hard time at that. In other words I'm not comfortable in my own clothes. The dream also tells me that I'm still concerned with my looks and what people think of me. That too, is getting in the way.

At this phase of my recovery it was becoming clearer all the time how amazing denial can be. I was finding I wasn't as honest as I thought I was, represented by saying I didn't have the jacket and then finding that I did. The blue pen I take to represent my writing, showing me that it's not as important to me as it ought to be. The color blue represents harmony, inner peace, and devotion.

Again, I was running late and didn't know where to go. That clearly describes me. I always beat myself up for being where I am. I always think I should be further ahead (running late). In this new adventure of recovery and possibilities with the writing, I'm afraid. I don't know where I'm going. I'm afraid I won't know where I'm supposed to be. It's because I'm still trying to control, still having to know everything, and that creates stress.

The whole experience of being in school is stressful. I still have a need to be prepared, to know everything, to have all the supplies. I set my stuff down on the stairs to find my schedule, my hair represents my thinking, and says that I need to straighten it out. It's interfering with my vision.

The part about being in an Italian class was interesting to me. Why Italian? I have no idea, but it's foreign, indicating distant, strange, exotic, and may refer to a desire to spruce up my life. The orange chairs represent emotions and healing; the turquoise, spiritual healing. It felt to me that the orange ones were for learning and the turquoise ones were for teaching, since three teachers were sitting on that side, and that's where I wanted to be, but didn't feel I was ready.

The wedding couple symbolizes spiritual integration, and an ability to understand something I don't understand (finally let go of needing to know everything). In other words, it may not be a language that can be understood with the head but it can be felt with the heart. It was a sign I was learning to trust and have faith in the unknown. The feeling of excitement I had listening to this new language, and the anticipation of learning it, is how I'm beginning to see my recovery, my life.

The hair thing again, symbolized my feeling unattractive. Hair in the eyes and sunglasses relate to vision and insecurity, followed by reassurance (find the barrette, leaving to fix the hair).

The last part of the dream, walking down the road to school, and carrying my books, as well as a club for protection, tells me I'm learning to take care of myself, and that I'm capable. The fact I'm walking instead of driving or riding a bus affirms I have everything I need to get where I want to go. Plus, I meet a lot of nice people along the way.

September 3, 1995 - I dreamed we were walking across the street to a park from my childhood. There was a black bear walking toward us on a leash with some kids walking him. I was afraid of the bear and he seemed to want to come toward me. I tried to get away but he came after me and wrapped his mouth around my arm. I was so scared he was really going to hurt me. Then the zoo keeper was there and tried to distract him, and the bear began mauling him and I was afraid the bear would kill him.

I went across the street to the parking lot where my mom and other family members were in a trailer. I told them about the bear incident and showed them my arm, where there were a couple of blisters and a red mark. It was very scary I told them, but they didn't seem to think it was any big deal.

This dream related to my fear of my own power, fear of the changes taking place, the transition from old to new. The childhood park represented the old. Bears represent power, the untamed self; and black is a transition color, representing boundary, separation, introspection. I feel I was being shown how I would need to detach from the family as far as what I'm doing (recovery, etc.), because they wouldn't understand. In other words, they wouldn't see it as a big deal. The leash represented control and relates to the restraints I've always put on my power, myself.

This was so important to me, because I needed to learn that not everyone is as excited about the things I am. I always felt I had to tell the world what I was doing with my life. I'm learning that my experiences are personal, and mostly private. I know what I'm doing and God knows what I'm doing. That's got to be enough.

The mouth represents nourishment, new attitudes. The arm, strength and preparedness. The injury to my arm in the dream tells me I'm afraid I won't be strong enough to get healthy, to learn new attitudes. I'm afraid I won't be prepared when I get where I'm going. Since red represents energy, vigor, and passion, I feel that the red mark on my arm represented my passions, which others saw as no big deal.

September 4, 1995 - I dreamed there was a guy standing in a hallway and my husband was shooting all around him, scaring him. With one shot to the forehead, the man fell over backward and was dead. I was shocked that my husband would murder this man for no apparent reason.

I only remember bits and pieces, but a guy I knew had killed himself. I was surprised that he did this, even more surprised to find out that his middle name was "masturbation." What kind of a parent would give a child the middle name of masturbation? No wonder he killed himself I thought. The woman who was telling me all of this was the head of the school. She wrote his full name on the blackboard, saying that when he came to her she was given only the middle name of "Master" and she underlined that part of the word masturbation twice.

Then I was to get up in front of the room or something and found myself in the middle of it. Two people stood on a platform above me, and one or perhaps two to my right. There was something scary going on, but now I can't remember what it was. I wanted to get out of there. I was wearing a skirt and wanted to change. I slipped on my favorite and most comfortable shorts under my skirt and was headed to my room to finish changing. I was taking my slip off as I entered my bedroom. It got hooked on my high heels and I was losing my balance.

An old boss of mine was there, along with several others, having a party. He caught me and thought the predicament I found myself in was real funny (with my slip caught on my shoe). I went to the closet, trying to find something to wear. He followed close behind me. I thumbed through several shirts, but they weren't my shirts.

On several hangers were long skirt after long skirt, with panty hose thrown over the middle of them. I knew they weren't my skirts. I said, "These are not my clothes." I knew the skirts belonged to a relative of mine. He reached into one of the hangers and said, "These are my socks." He was surprised and curious that his socks were in my closet.

Then I was on a bicycle, still in a skirt with my shorts underneath. I was headed somewhere, I don't remember where. My mom was in the yard of a house doing some yard work or something. She asked me if I wanted to go to lunch or something. I said I couldn't because I was headed some-where else. She got on her bicycle and rode down to where an old lady was trying to get on a bicycle, one Mom had sold her. She helped the old lady and then began riding down the road. I started riding down the same road, only a bit behind her. I could see her up ahead.

The first part of the dream, with my husband shooting the stranger, has to do with killing off unidentified aspects of self. The forehead represents the intellect and relates to my desire to "get out of my head." The death relates to the end of a cycle: I'm ready to do feelings.

The suicide has to do with giving up a part of self. Masturbation relates to self-love. What am I ready to accept and love in myself? The underlining of "master" tells me the importance of mastering self-love. The people stand-ing all around, some on platforms, relate to different stages of my journey. The platform represents position, stage, thus the feeling of fear.

Skirts represent the lower self, passions. I'm uncomfortable in them. Shorts, however represent comfort and freedom. Since I left the skirt on, it indicates my desire to get comfortable with my passions. The slip represents my private self, the inner me, and relates to what I'm ready (or not ready) to show the world. High heels represent glamour and restriction. Catching my slip on my heel relates to my difficulty integrating parts of myself (the two together cause me to lose my balance).

I believe the old boss represents old ways. The closet has to do with stor-age of ideas and identity. Shirts represent the upper self, emotions, but they're not mine. Again, skirts represent passions. The fact they belong to my relative who is lazy, keeps a messy house, and doesn't want to work, tells me that I'm lazy about my passions.

The fact that they aren't my clothes tells me that I'm not being true to my own desires or passions. "There's someone else's clothes in my closet," and they are those of a lazy person.

Again, riding a bicycle has to do with self-propulsion. My mom in the dream was doing things very uncharacteristic of her. She doesn't ride a bike, doesn't do yard work, and doesn't sell bicycles. I feel this dream relates to my fear about being able to live this new way and think this new way. It's all very uncharacteristic of me. I believe my mom represents the part of me that feels unworthy and is afraid to live.

September 5, 1995 - I awoke from a disturbing dream, one of those when you wake up and realize it was just a dream, it's a big relief. Gregory and I were going to murder a guy by beating him on the head with a flashlight. And we did. I have no idea why we thought we had to murder this poor guy, but Gregory beat him while I kept watch.

Suddenly, I noticed a policeman climbing onto the boat or barge that we were on. I told Gregory we had to go NOW, or we were going to be caught red-handed. We managed to slip off the side before the policeman turned toward us. We were walking across the street and I remember thinking, "Could we really get away with this? Do some people really get away with murder?" Then I thought, "No way."

That frightened me, thinking that we might get caught for what we'd just done. Again I thought, "Everybody gets caught. Besides, what's the likelihood that NO ONE saw Gregory killing this guy?" So I was afraid, worried that we'd get caught, but also upset about why we had to kill this poor guy in the first place, and the hope that maybe he would survive.

The biggest feeling I had was guilt. I couldn't believe I was going to have to live with this kind of thing on my conscious for the rest of my life. Even if we never got caught, I couldn't live with myself and that kind of heavy burden. Here my life was going so good, so honest; how could I let something like this happen?

Then I was at the women's treatment center for a meeting, only it wasn't going to start for over an hour, even though everyone was already there. I didn't want to hang around for it to start, so I headed home. A couple of the girls shared their concern about one of the girls they thought wasn't dealing with her issues. She was in la la land (the pink clouds) and wasn't "getting it." I assured them that she would get it, believe me, and that it would be in her own time and there was nothing any of us could do to help the process along. "Don't worry," I assured them, "she'll get it."

I got home and went up to my bedroom. I saw that something was wrong with the window. The wind was strong and had knocked out part of the window. I feared it was broken or perhaps the lamp on the nightstand had blown over and broke. The lamp was fine and although the window was blown mostly out, it hadn't fallen to the ground. It was still hanging on one side and wasn't broken. It was in about three sections, I carefully removed each one, being careful not to lose one out the window or to break a section.

I couldn't figure out how to get it back together so I went to find Gregory. He was talking to someone outside or something and after waiting for a long time for him I finally said, "Honey, I need you to fix the window." He said, "Okay," and came with me.

Then we were in the bedroom and he pulled out a brand new car battery. I was immediately suspicious and wanted to know where he had gotten it. I was afraid he had stolen it, which I was totally against. He just smiled and indicated he had just "got it" that's all.

I was quite upset. I told him, "You know, nothing is free. It's going to cost us a lot more than the price of a battery. It's Karma, you know. And it's going to come back on us. Nothing is free." I was very upset about it. I wanted him to understand "the law" the way I do. I want my life to be completely honest, no betrayal, no deceit, no breaking any laws, total freedom and honesty. I was frustrated at the situation I found myself in.

Again, murdering someone has to do with killing off aspects of self. The policeman represented order and control. My fear and guilt over killing the "poor guy," indicates my feelings about giving up parts of myself, guilt about what I'm doing, because I'm unsure of what's right or wrong. It also shows that I'm beginning to value my new-found honesty.

The part in the treatment center shows my tendency to work other people's programs, represented by the girls' concern that one of them isn't dealing with her issues, and the other part relates to the progress I'm making with my codependence; don't worry, she'll get it.

The window represents vision, the lamp illumination and vision, and the wind has to do with sensory overload; where do I feel overwhelmed? A car represents personal power, ego, and a battery powers it. The fact that I thought it had been stolen relates to lack, need, judgment; what do I fear I don't deserve? What am I afraid of losing?

September 5, 1995

Today is Tuesday, after a four day weekend with my husband and the girls. The weather was perfect and we had the boat out on the lake all weekend. We went tubing and just had a great time. I can't believe how much better I'm getting about getting out and doing things. I never realized how much I isolated, but boy did I. I didn't like to socialize, unless of course it was a party, then I was anxious and primed for it. But to go out on the boat, or go to the beach, I always had an excuse.

I see now that the only thing that was important to me when I was drinking was creating a safe little haven for myself where I knew my surroundings and what to expect. I had to be in complete control at all times with no surprises, and spontaneity, well forget about it! That hasn't been any better in sobriety, at least not until lately.

I guess the promise that says fear of people will leave us, is true, and it feels good. It used to be if anyone asked me to do something I wasn't planning on, my first response was always no. Only because I wasn't expecting it, it wasn't part of my plan, and we can't screw with the plan! Little by little I find myself more open. The more I let go, the easier it gets. Since I quit expecting so much, it seems I'm much more comfortable with the unexpected. It feels wonderful.

I'm still having a problem with feeling useless though. I felt lost after the meeting today. I wandered around the house thinking I should just go upstairs and write, but that still feels uncomfortable for me. I know why too. My dreams have been pointing out to me for a long time now that I'm running away from my own creativity, my passion, myself. I want to be writing, but I'm so afraid, and yet I can't figure out why.

There's still such a big part of me that doesn't know how to live without alcohol. It motivated everything I did for so many years, it's like I don't know how to do life without it. I'm learning how, and it feels good most of the time, but I can't deny there's a huge part of me that's afraid of reality, of choices, of life in general, so I can certainly see why I medicated for so many years.

But, my dreams are talking loud & clear to me, whether I understand them all or not, and little by little the message is getting through to me, "just write." That's all I have to do. I don't have to write something specific, I don't have to finish anything, I just have to re-familiarize myself with that chair in my office. I have to re-introduce myself to the part of me I've been running from ever since I got sober.

Chapter 17

PROGRESS NOT PERFECTION

*S*eptember 6, 1995 - I dreamed I was on a bus with a few other people. My mom was sitting right behind me. I was worried because
the roads were really bad and the driver didn't seem too sure of
himself. I thought he was going too fast because it was raining. What if
we rolled the bus? I knew I would be okay, but could my mom handle it?
Then we made a sharp turn and headed down a steep road on the right.

This dream pointed out my codependence, how I worry too much
about other people "making it." My mom represents my fearful side, my feelings of unworthiness, and it is that part of me I'm afraid won't make it, while
another part of me knows I'll be okay. I'm learning to trust...a little.

September 6, 1995

Whoever would have dreamed recovery would be like this, feel like
this. I was so sick and didn't even know it. *So* sick. Still am. Today happens to be a day where I'm grateful to be an alcoholic, grateful to be in
recovery because of what a trip it is. Amazing. Every day I'm grateful to
be sober, thankful that finally I'm free from the bonds of alcoholism,
free from that damn drink that I just couldn't stop picking up.

It's funny when I think about it now, but it was damn serious business, getting this controlled drinking thing down, and for years I was
just sure I could do it. I didn't have long periods of off and on drinking
like some do, I was just going to stop one day and be done with it.
Somehow I thought the day would just show up, and in the meantime

I gave into the strong urges I had for just one drink, just this one day, and days turned into months and months turned into years. Fifteen of them.

That's amazing to me. Especially knowing how absolutely sure I was that I could do it, by myself, just watch, I'll get it, no wait, let me try again. The sheer insanity of it makes me laugh. What a blessing that is. I haven't laughed like I've laughed in recovery, in sobriety. What a gift laughter is. And to find that in recovery, one of the hardest things in my life, my laughter returns. In fact, it's a wonderful defense mechanism. It sheds a different light on my circumstances, and softens the hard road I came in on.

Laughter was the one thing I had truly lost in my disease. My husband was the only one who could really make me laugh, and thank God for him, because the rest of my life just wasn't that funny. Oh, I thought I was having fun. I thought I had it all. I was tripping through life like it was one big party and all the while I was missing the main event. Whatever reason the God of my understanding had for helping me when He did (or not helping when He didn't) remains to be seen, but I think I have a slight clue already.

The lessons I'm finding in everything that's ever happened in my life, are staggering now that I can sit back and look at the whole picture. I can see that each thing happened for a reason. It's all falling together for me now. It's painful. There's a lot of stuff I really don't want to look at. But suddenly I have a reason for all the crazy things I do. It's beginning to make sense. I'm having a pretty easy time recognizing a lot of my character defects, but *changing* them is the part that requires so much work.

It's hard. I want to change. I recognize that I was a maniac. I can see how controlling and manipulative I was. I know that everything had to be my way and I had to have control of everything around me. I knew what was best for everybody's life and if everyone would just listen to me I'd fix you right up. And I believed it! I thought it was that easy. I didn't have a clue. I was blind to real life. I had my head so far in the clouds I was literally missing out on my own life. I guess I'm feeling extremely reflective right now. It's good for my recovery. I have to remember how it used to be. It's the only way I can see how far I've come.

September 11, 1995 - I dreamed I was in my house and heard some commotion out back. I looked out and could see there had been an accident at the bar. It looked really congested in the alley. I could see a police car. I knew that someone had come out of the bar drunk and had an accident. When I looked closer I could see the bartender was involved. In fact, he was drunk and was the one driving.

I could see that his black pickup truck (he doesn't really have one) had crashed into and was sitting on top of our pickup. Our truck was crushed. I could see two guys trying to carry the bartender around the side of our house. I told my sister to duck down in the dining room with me so they wouldn't see us. I thought they were just walking by, but they came to the front door. I told my sister to hide with me in the dining room.

I felt bad for ignoring them. I knew the bartender was not only drunk, but that he was also hurt from the accident and needed help. I didn't want to help them because they were drunk. I felt guilty about that. When I went outside to see how bad our truck was wrecked, it was gone. I saw it on the side street, being towed away. I was very upset because no one came to tell me that there had been an accident involving our truck, and now they were taking it away. It was totaled. The cab was scrunched down and so was the back end.

This dream reveals the difficulty I'm having separating myself from the drinkers in my life. I'm not healthy enough to be around them. I want to hide from them. The trucks represent an ability to carry the load. Can I carry the responsibility? The wreck relates to violent destruction, a barrier to progress. What is trying to stop me? Black is a transition color, and shows the difficulty I'm having adjusting to my new life and establishing healthy boundaries for myself. The very nature of the disease of alcoholism, represented by the drunk bartender, could very well get in the way of my progress if I'm not careful. I don't want to let them in, but perhaps hiding isn't the answer either (I felt bad about it).

September 11, 1995

I've learned that everything that bothered me about Susie is something I need to look at in myself. I know (especially in my drinking days), I didn't listen to anyone. I thought I was listening, but I was more into what I had to bring to you, how I could help you improve your life and how important what I had to say was. Boy, the feelings I had to have hurt, the people I had to have invalidated by lack of interest in anything they had to say or what was going on in their lives.

I sure hope that insensitive side of me is gone, or at least not in charge anymore. I know there's been a big change in me. It's only through, as the promises say, losing interest in selfish things and gaining interest in my fellows, that I've been able to even recognize that I was that way in the first place! What? I don't know what's best for everyone? Hell, I don't even know how to run my own life, without alcohol or drugs, or food, cigarettes, etc.

I needed something in order to run my life. I could not do it alone. Ouch. Once I was willing to accept the possibility that I didn't know it all and was no longer in charge, things began getting clearer, making sense, feeling e a s i e r. But what a blow to the old ego, what a slap in the face humility is. But it somehow feels good. It's unknown territory, new, unexplored or unfamiliar feelings, and I don't know what to expect, but somehow it's been the softer way, and maybe when life gets tough as it always will, I won't run away.

Maybe I'll just feel this new feeling for awhile instead of medicating it away. And if I think I'm going to die, I can always go back to my old ways. No one is forcing me to be in recovery, I'm here because I've made a choice to be, and whether I like it or not (my ego hates it some days), I've made the commitment, in my heart, to do things different for a change, to see what this new way has to offer me that drug and alcohol addiction couldn't give me. Taking a gamble that, maybe, just maybe, this unknown territory might be the path to whatever it is I've been searching in a bottle for all these years.

And so, as part of my recovery for this day, in September, 1995, my challenges include realizing that my winter pants somehow "shrunk" over the summer. I'm getting the message that I haven't been paying attention. I have a lot of work to do, but I've come a long way from where I was. I don't have to fix everything today. First things first they say, and it's progress, not perfection. What a relief!

Chapter 18

ACCEPTANCE

September 12, 1995. Well, I'm in quite a good place today. Quiet, peaceful, serene, it feels good. I guess what feels the best is that I feel teachable today. I don't feel resistance, I feel surrender. I feel humble and willing. I realize I need to surround myself with people who make me feel good about myself.

September 13, 1995

Oh boy. Life. Recovery. It's so cool though, it's just that when I get reflective, which I've been doing a lot lately, it seems like a wonderful story being told, and I've been embracing that part of me lately (in my mind). I feel patience, love and understanding with my past, and some of the things I've done. I don't like it. I haven't begun to look at it all, but I'm not so afraid today.

I've felt incredibly humble the past couple of days, yesterday in particular, but today feels pretty much the same. I guess I'm in awe of this new way of life. I'm in shock that somehow I found myself smack in the middle of it, and that I like it! And it wasn't my idea?!

For the first time in my life it's a comfort to find myself in a place where I'm not the one in control, and wonderful things are happening all around me. To stand back and be able to see a different plan unfolding, perfectly, as it always has, hard knocks and all. Today I'm feeling like I wouldn't change a single thing I've been through, although I shudder to think of EVER repeating any of it. But I wouldn't be where I am today if it weren't for where I've been.

The healthier I get and the stronger I feel, the more convinced I am that my life has special meaning. I believe all of our lives do. My experiences are uniquely my own, and for yesterday and today at least, I'm embracing them, with forgiveness in my heart, not only for myself, but for everyone and everything that's been a part of my journey. I guess it really feels like a journey today, and I feel the fun and excitement that goes along with any journey or vacation, and for today at least, I don't feel so much fear. Instead I feel a lot of faith.

Someone said in a meeting the other day that doubt was nothing more than the absence of faith. It helped to hear that. I believe it's true, that if I work Step 3, and have faith that my life will be okay, it will. I have to believe it, trust it, have faith in it, with no doubts, and it will happen for me. I believe that with all my heart. I've proven it to myself whenever I have trusted completely.

Doubt and fear have been a hard one for me to shake off in sobriety. I used to get my courage and zest for life out of a bottle, and when that was gone, I found I was more frightened, and more unsure of myself, than I'd ever been in my life. I didn't know what fear was. I wrote a whole chapter in the first book on it, but I didn't have a clue what it really was. If that's not a hoot! Thank God I can laugh at myself and the insanity of it all. I was going so fast. I was running so hard to get away from myself, I was going to end up dead. No wonder I needed to drink and medicate, my life was too crazy, too fast. If I didn't have something to take the edge off, how was I ever going to keep up?

September 17, 1995
Some old ways and old behaviors are creeping back in. I have to keep right on my toes in this recovery thing or I'm back trying to control things again, and we just can't have that!

Then there's my daughter. A mirror image of myself. Some days I have trouble with that, some days I'm accepting and patient. Hopefully, by watching me change the way I've always been, and taught her to be, she can change too. She won't have to be as frustrated and crazy as I was in her adult life, wasting precious energy trying to control everything and everyone around her, like I taught her to do.

Now I see how hard it is to be in that space. No wonder she seems irritable, impatient, and most of the time has a grumpy look on her face, one I'm sure she doesn't realize is there anymore than I realized how I looked. I need to keep talking to her and share the journey I'm on, where I've come from, and the mistakes I've made. She'll be able to identify with what she needs to for herself, and we'll both continue on our way to recovery.

I've got to be there for her, and I haven't wanted to this past week. I've been impatient with how she is, and frustrated at having to take a look at myself in her. Oh, God, help me in this moment. I have a lot to take a look at. I have a lot of work to do, but hey, what else have I got planned?

September 18, 1995

I've been thinking a lot about how I used to be, so different from today. Ever since I was a little girl I was a neat freak. My bed was made before I hit the floor, my room was always spotless. I was a perfectionist. This carried over into every area of my life, and it takes a very busy person to maintain all that, especially if you're the kind of busy I was, busy running away from myself. It shouldn't have surprised me to hear that most alcoholics/addicts are perfectionists. We're the over-achievers, we're doctors, lawyers, workaholics, and parents. We're busy, busy, busy. And we drink.

And I wonder why I drank? It makes sense to me now. Alcohol made it all go away. Alcohol was an escape from my busy head, my busy life. How hard I fought to keep it all under control, work, house, kids, husband, myself. I thought my life was perfectly manageable. I knew I was powerless over alcohol, but no way was my life unmanageable.

But oh, how wrong I was. My life was totally unmanageable, and I was spinning out of control, and didn't even know it. It was about to unravel, I'm afraid, and I was blind to what was happening. It's scary to look back sometimes, because I was so careless. I was losing a battle with an illness I didn't even know I had.

The first time I heard that alcoholism was a fatal disease, a shock ran through my body. Somewhere I'd heard that, and believed it, for some people anyway. After all, my uncle died as a result of this disease, and millions of people have died alcohol related deaths, I guess I did-n't realize that *every* case of alcoholism is fatal if not treated.

The lucky ones get into some kind of treatment program, and stay sober one day at a time. But we are the minority. Only a group of us escape this disease, but with any luck at all, we can learn how to live a fulfilling and successful life without alcohol. The odds are improving.

I learned that alcoholism is a progressive disease, and for me at least, this had been true. I progressed to the point that no amount of alcohol seemed to be enough. It was taking a lot more to do the trick. My old buddy alcohol was failing me for the first time. I was scared. I didn't know what getting to this stage meant, or what stage would fol-low, but instinctively I knew it was a bad sign when my consumption increased.

In early recovery it was a struggle just to stay sober. That feeling of total desperation, drowning was how one recovering alcoholic described it, and that's how it felt to me. I was barely hanging on in early sobriety, *barely* hanging on. I felt like I was going to fly out of my body, or that my whole body was going to fly into pieces, and it was tak-ing every bit of strength I had to hold myself together. I have never been so scared, and I have NEVER felt such rage.

I was committed to not picking up the first drink, but by God, I wasn't sure I could do anything else, and for many 24 hours I did noth-ing else. I functioned best I could with the family. I remember how dif-ficult it was to go to the grocery store. It took everything I had to plan meals and go shopping. I remember a couple of times wanting to run out of the store. Going down isles that seemed a mile long, thinking I was never going to get through this, thinking I had to get out of there, then forcing myself to get it together and do what I had to do.

Simple things. Ha! What's that? Suddenly nothing was simple to this alcoholic. Everything seemed complicated, too big, too difficult, too much! And then I was told to keep it simple, first things first, and easy does it, and the sayings, although I'd heard them many times, began making sense to me, and in fact, became life lines during trying times.

There were a lot of trying times. Heck, life for me at this point was extremely trying. I didn't have a clue how to live without alcohol. Many times I really didn't think I was going to be able to do it, but then I didn't know what in the hell I thought I would do instead. Drinking wasn't an option for me at this point. Just the thought it might be was scary, and created a tremendous amount of frustration, fear, anger and rage. I didn't ask for this burden. Why me? Why now? Please God, help me! I will never forget the day it all exploded.

I was so enraged about a fight Gregory & I had. It was the way of the moment it would seem, me not handling sobriety very well, and Gregory not handling me very well. He stormed out and I fell to my knees, screaming at the top of my lungs at God that I DIDN'T WANT TO BE AN ALCOHOLIC!! I'd come far enough to know I didn't want to drink again, but I sure as hell didn't want to be going through what I was going through, *feeling* everything I was feeling.

I went to a meeting and before it was over I was coming down with a migraine headache. I was out of commission for the rest of the day, and the next. It became very clear to me that nothing was worth getting that mad over. It was a turning point in my recovery, a blessing in disguise. I haven't screamed in anger like that since that day, (haven't had a migraine since then either).

I didn't know surrendering my will would feel like this. It was a feeling I was going to have to get used to, learn to live with, as I slowly started over. Every time I was afraid I wasn't going to be able to make it, I remembered how hard it was in my drinking days. A lifestyle that was getting very hard to maintain.

The days were dragging by slowly during this period. Many times I felt caught between a rock and a hard place. I couldn't move backward, but I didn't have the strength to move ahead. I read the promises over and over again, trying to believe.

September 20, 1995 - I dreamed that Susie and I were in a vehicle. She was driving. We turned onto a winding, uphill road. I knew Gregory was supposed to be following us. I kept looking back but he wasn't there. We figured he would be coming, so she kept driving. I was worried and wanted to make sure he was behind us, even though I knew he knew the way to where we were going.

We drove on this unsafe, narrow, winding dirt road with ruts and stuff in it. We were going uphill. I was nervous because of the road and wor-

ried that Gregory might not be following us. Finally, when I looked back, we saw a vehicle coming. I was relieved he was coming—then I realized it was an off-white van.

I wanted to turn around and find Gregory. I thought Susie was going to try to pull off to the side as best she could and let the van go by (I didn't think there was room). Somehow she made a three-point turn and we were facing the other direction, heading back down the hill. The van went off on another road below us. I was so relieved not to be headed up the hill without Gregory.

Another vague part of my dream also included Gregory. We were trying to get through some sort of basement building, someplace where there were downed wires and water and stuff. It was hard getting over and under all the debris, but because I was with Gregory, I felt totally safe. Although a few times I was a little spooked about what might be around the next corner.

This dream relates to my fears and the rough and winding road I feel I've been on lately; and how much safer I feel when Gregory is with me. I don't want to climb this mountain without him. The same with the basement dream. Basements represent the lower or buried dimensions of the consciousness. It appears there are a lot of obstacles and danger there, which I relate to fourth step work I need to do. But, again, as long as Gregory is with me I feel safe.

September 25, 1995

I feel so disorganized, out of control and frustrated. While I was back into writing, it seems that's all I did. When am I ever going to find the balance I seemed to have when I was drinking? Of course I know it was a false security, and it was in fact falling apart, but all I know at this point, is when I was drinking my house was spotless, the laundry was done, I was writing, I "seemed" to have it all together. Of course I was running 200 miles an hour, probably stressed to the breaking point, but my outsides looked good! I know I can find the balance again.

I wish I knew what I wanted. I wish I knew how to ask for it. I wish I could stay in the moment and just do what's in front of me. I want to. Oh, it's such a roller coaster ride! But at least now I know better how to hold on. I know better how to try to make it a fun ride. I'm learning how to stay and deal with it rather than running away all the time. Today I'm trying not to run.

September 27, 1995

I was really being tested earlier. I couldn't find a paper I needed to take to my doctor appointment. I was so mad, frustrated, and I just wouldn't let it go. I haven't done that in a long time, it felt horrible. I guess if nothing else, it was a good reminder of how powerless I am over situations in my life. I have to learn to trust more, I have to let go of my need to know everything, control everything.

In my frustration, I not only got uptight, which I don't need to be doing, but now my neck and shoulders and back are causing me pain. It just wasn't worth it. And I still didn't find the damn paper! Oh, God help me, I'm so sick. But I'm getting better, and I'm so much better than I was even a year ago. I'm probably worried about the tests I'm having done.

Megan & I had a wonderful hour long talk when she got home from Youth group tonight. She said she'd had a wonderful spiritual experience. She was touched to tears, and said she couldn't believe how good she felt. I was excited for her, and it opened the door for a conversation I've been waiting to have, one about God, about our spiritual journey, about being guided in our lives by a power greater than we are, and about trust.

I was even able to "lovingly" bring up some of her character defects, the ones I so carefully instilled in her as a child. At first, in typical me fashion, she wanted to defend herself, and justify her actions and explain to me why she does it (worry about everyone else's lives, get frustrated and judge and criticize the choices people make), but I was able to steer her out of defense mode into one that was lighter, happier, more hopeful, and she was rather receptive to the concept of laughing at ourselves for it, instead of beating up on ourselves.

It was really great, and I know she's going to start the process in her own life of changing unhealthy behaviors. She's been much more stressed than she needs to be, when life at 15 is stressful enough. I really hated to see her all wound up over things that are out of her control.

I mentioned the Serenity Prayer and told her she'd be hearing that a lot, and would probably have to remind me once in awhile, but that's okay. We're all just learning and growing. It's all progress, there is no failure. All in all it turned out to be a wonderful evening. I love how it works!

I went to the doctor, not only for the lump in my breast, but for some other symptoms as well. I couldn't believe that everything that was going on with me was part of my healing. I was just sure something was wrong. Besides the lump, I'd been experiencing what I thought was low blood sugar or something. I couldn't get the least bit hungry or I was sick to my stomach, weak.

My upper back was out and had been for years, but seemed much worse. I'd experienced a lot of leg aches as a kid, and throughout my life, but now they hurt all the time. I was just sure something was wrong, I was afraid, I was tired, and I wasn't doing my recovery very well. I stayed sober, and continued going to meetings, but I was distracted, I had other things to worry about. I couldn't take a look at myself, I couldn't possibly do a fourth step until I learned if I was to live or die!

I laugh now, but at the time it wasn't funny. I was really scared. I figured with all the abuse I'd given my poor body, it was probably going to fail me now that I'm learning to live a healthy life. Long story short, I went through every test you can imagine. It cost a whole bunch of money for a whole bunch of tests that all came back negative.

The only good thing to come of it was the physical therapy suggested for my back, which to this day doesn't bother me as long as I do my exercises. Well, that's not the only good thing. I got peace of mind. I got a clean bill of health. I had to look at me. I had to look at what was really going on with me. I started drinking aloe vera juice and all my symptoms disappeared. Yoga helped my leg aches and my back.

I soon came to refer to my time with illness as the "distraction," since that's exactly what it was for me. As long as I was going to focus on my outer body, I didn't have to look at my inner self. It was back on the road to recovery for me, no more fooling around.

Chapter 19

LETTING GO

October 14, 1995 - I dreamed I was at a theatre to watch a movie. I had my typewriter and all of my work with me. Susie asked if I could help her with some of her medical transcription work because she was overloaded. I set the stuff down by one of the seats in the theatre, then went to find the bathroom, because I had to go really bad.

I found the door to the basement, where the bathrooms were. The stairs were old and crooked. They were made of cement, and were wet and treacherous. I slipped on the first one and caught myself, but hurt my hip. I carefully got to the bottom, but it was very dangerous. I thought, "I need to tell management about this. This is not good."

There were two doors at the bottom of the dimly-lit stairs. I found the women's and opened the door, only to find the bathroom in a disgusting mess. There were two toilets, but they were mismatched. They were up on pedestals, with no room for your feet. I opened the lid—both were a mess. The water was up to the top and it was yellow, clearly urine and toilet paper. They were backed up and wouldn't flush. The toilet seats were all wet, and since there was no room for your feet on the pedestal, it was impossible to even stand over the bowl and pee without sitting down. I really had to go bad.

Then I saw the bathtub. It was wet and yukky too, but I could at least find a dry spot to stand and squat down and pee down the drain, which I did. But it was still disgusting and dirty. If I hadn't needed to go so badly I wouldn't have used the facilities, but I had no choice. I was really drowsy. I couldn't think straight.

I knew I'd been gone a long time and was missing the movie. Besides, I knew I wasn't going to have enough time after the meeting to get all the transcription work done. I had my own work to do after that. I was so drowsy though, and thought if I could sit down on the toilet for a moment (it was clean now), I could go back to the movie later.

I opened my eyes. It was hard to focus. I was so drowsy. My daughter was standing there. She was telling me where she was going or something. I hugged her and we headed back upstairs. I told her to be careful on the steps. She said she had already slipped. I told her I had too.

At the top of the stairs was a large woman. She was blocking the doorway. She was on the second or third step. I told her she probably didn't want to walk down these dangerous stairs. She said, "I suppose you want out." She backed up the stairs and went back to work behind the concession stand. I knew she worked there, so I told them they should do something about those stairs, otherwise they were going to have a lawsuit on their hands.

This dream speaks to me of the need to do a fourth step, to clean up the past and wade through the emotional issues I've buried for so long. The basement represents the lower dimensions of self. The bathroom represents a place of cleansing and release. It's apparent what I think about those lower dimensions; they're a mess.

The urine has to do with emotional release, even anger (backed up). The difficulty in relieving myself indicates the fear I have about that, but also the necessity for cleansing. The bathtub represents the need for physical cleansing, and speaks to me of my need for a complete overhaul of body, mind, and soul.

At this stage of my recovery, it was clear I needed to do a complete and thorough fourth step, although it would be another six months before I actually did it. Still I was beginning to accept the idea, and I began doing a fourth step "in my head." My recovery was at a stand still. I kept hitting a brick wall. I was not progressing.

I'd experienced a lot of peace and serenity amidst the turmoil, enough to know it's possible, enough to want more. I'd been writing a little here and there, and was beginning to function in sobriety; for the first time it seemed. But now I was backsliding. Now the core issues were coming up and I was running like crazy.

October 17, 1995

Well, I haven't been here for awhile, and I don't know what's going on with me AGAIN. I'm not accomplishing anything around here. Things are still a mess, I'm unmotivated, I don't know what to do. I feel pretty good about life, but something is missing. I'm tired of the mess I guess. I've got to write more. I'm isolating (from myself) again. It's time to get back in touch.

October 19, 1995

Well, one thing I'm finding, if I talk about what's bothering me, it doesn't bother me anymore.

October 24, 1995 - Man! What a wild dream. I'll relate it the best I can remember. A bunch of us were on a ship, a big ship. The weather was terrible. At one point there was a huge tidal wave that came up and threatened to overturn the ship. Then there was a tornado headed our way. Everyone was screaming and shouting. I looked up and saw it coming from some clouds, then it disappeared. I could see something like an invisible funnel, a waviness of the air, swirling and heading toward us.

Everyone braced themselves as it came right at us. I closed my eyes and held onto the side of the ship as it passed by me. High winds nearly blew me off, but then it passed and it was calm again. My daughter and niece were somewhere on the ship too. I was not only worried and concerned that we were all going to be killed, but I was especially concerned for their safety. I felt responsible, as a parent, for taking care of them.

I remember trying to get from one deck to another. It was so intense, and very frightening. The gigantic waves and the roughness of the water was terrifying for all of us on the ship. I had to go to the bathroom and someone was in there. My niece was waiting too, and tried the door. It was locked, but she forced it, thinking no one was in there. I could see someone was in there, even though the light was off. I stopped her from going in. Then I realized Susie was missing and began looking for her.

I found Susie all right. The pressure and the fear of the situation we were in was too much for her. She was on the ground trying to get up. I helped her and could see she was drunk. I couldn't believe it. She was dis-

gusted too and was acting mad at me. She wanted me to leave her alone. She had done what she had and that was that. Just leave her alone.

I was so amazed and disappointed that the pressure was too much for her. She figured we were going to die anyway, so she might as well get drunk, I felt there was nothing that would make me drink. I didn't believe we were going to die, even as frightened as I was.

There was something about my purse, and trying to keep track of it and other stuff of mine, especially with the boat bouncing around on the rough water. Then we were safe on shore or something, more like at a dock. We were gathering our stuff and getting off. I grabbed my purse and could tell it was really light. I thought my wallet was gone, but when I looked I could see it in there. It was just flat, light, so I knew someone had stolen all the money out of it. I couldn't believe someone would do that when we had been in the situation we were in.

I remember stairwells on the ship, in between decks. We would try to pass from one to another on the rocking ship, holding onto the rails and falling into the walls or each other, trying to get to the bathroom. Everyone was terrified. The whole dream seemed intense and life threatening, surreal. I actually woke up during it and couldn't believe what I had been dreaming. That huge tidal wave was so intense and frightening. It hit and we got wet. The ship almost tipped over, but we survived it and the tornado too.

Whew! That dream was very powerful for me. The meaning was pretty clear. It's all about emotions overflowing and out of control; and fear. The ship represents movement across the depths of feeling. The storm represents tumultuous change. What forces are struggling within me? The tidal wave represents overwhelming emotion; the tornado, a violent force of destruction. What dramatic change can I see approaching? Since the tornado was transparent, I relate that to subtle but powerful changes.

Again, I have to go to the bathroom. I'm beginning to realize this represents my dire need to do a fourth step (I need cleansing and release). My fear about the safety of my loved ones and the whereabouts of my friend reveal that I still worry too much about other people. I still want to take care of them, or more importantly, I don't think they can take care of themselves. More work on codependence.

Finding Susie drunk represents the side of myself that is prone to relapse when the going gets tough. The part of me that doesn't want any help is represented by Susie saying, "Leave me alone." Trying to find my purse and stuff indicates my need for security, and the money being stolen relates to my fear of losing something valuable. After all was said and done, we were back on dry land, safe, which tells me that no matter what storms I may go through, I will always return safely to dry land.

October 24, 1995
Well, I'm in my "stuff" today. I'm doing feelings, and it doesn't feel too good. I guess I'm just sad. I went to a meeting today and talked about it even though I didn't feel like talking, and I felt better when I left. I'm over-sensitive right now. I'm pissed about a lot of things, and I don't know why. There's really no reason for it.

Life is good for me today. I'm grateful to be sober, especially that, and I'm grateful for my house, my family, my job, my life. I don't know what's the matter with me. I guess it's just an off day. Good day for two meetings. I know I'll feel better after my step meeting. I'm not sure what step we're on, probably eleven; Sought through prayer and meditation to improve my conscious contact with God. Now there's an idea.

October 27, 1995
My life is so.....heavy. I've been out of sorts all morning. I'm doing much better than I give myself credit for. It'll get better. It always gets better. I know this. I've done this. A lot. The faith of knowing it will pass makes it easier to get through, but it's still a struggle. I felt like I was unraveling, just on the edge of being really pissed off about something. It's too hard to be there. It takes more energy than I've got at this point.

I do feel better though. I relaxed, did some readings and before I knew it I was sitting back reflecting on life, how intense it is sometimes, and how crazy recovery is. This "reflecting" thing is a good sign, I only do that when I'm in a grateful mood, when I'm finally out of myself.

November 7, 1995
I feel so at peace in this moment. Right now, I get it. I know I've been afraid to express myself, to do all that I'm capable of doing. I've been

so afraid. But right now I'm not. I've had so much fear all my life. I think all human beings feel the same at one time or another. Aside from a few delusional people here and there, most of us feel inadequate, insecure, less than. I know I have.

It's been hard to learn to be myself when I've never quite been sure who that is. Today I feel like I'm okay just the way I am. I don't feel like I have to fix anything or anyone. It's such a relief! I don't feel like being hard on myself today. I guess you would say I'm feeling a spiritual connection.

Today I know I'm worthy. I never fail, I don't make mistakes, I never do anything wrong, I'm simply learning. Oh, the pressures off! Now if I can just remember this. If I can just stay in the moment, and trust.

November 14, 1995

Boy, how can I stray so far from where I was a week ago? Goes to show you I have to keep on my toes every moment. I can't afford to stop trying. I haven't been going to as many meetings. I totally lost my temper this morning and threw things! I just lost it for a moment and threw anything I could get my hands on, as Gregory retreated to safety. I picked up the garbage can and flung it across the room, banana peels and cigarette butts flying everywhere, it was gross.

I picked up the phone and threw it into the entertainment center! I have no idea how it kept from smashing through the TV. Gregory & I went from two people in total love and committed to each other, to two people screaming at each other, one packing (him not me), and the other begging him to stay. All over a comment I made (harmless I thought) which pissed him off, which in turn pissed me off, and the rest is reaction history.

So, we're both exhausted, but we're back where we need to be, wondering what went wrong and feeling guilty that we haven't learned better by now. I have a headache. I'm tired, and I feel useless and full of myself. I know I need to get back to meetings.

If I put on anymore weight I won't be able to wear my jeans, honest. This is the worst it's been in over 10 years. I'm going back to one of my oldest addictions, food. I'm using it and abusing it like I haven't done in so long, and I'm paying the consequences.

I'm eating when I'm not hungry and too much even when I am. It's old behavior for sure, the only thing I'm not doing is throwing up, but I've been tempted a time or two. It's all back. I have more work to do than I thought I did. I need to get to the bottom of "what's eating me." I'm still okay, I'm going to make it. I feel better just getting it off my chest. It's not the end of the world.

Gregory & I are fine and that's the most important part. I can turn this mood around. I can quit eating crazy and the weight will come off. It's a beautiful day outside. The bay is so blue, so is the sky. It's colder than heck out, but it sure looks nice. Oh, life. It's so crazy sometimes. Never boring though!

November 17, 1995

Well, I can't run anymore. I can't deny what's going on, not to myself, not to anyone. I've been isolating, not going to meetings, all the things they say not to do. I've been so afraid, and the more I keep to myself, the more frightened I become. I'm getting so I'm not doing anything.

November 18, 1995

I better start talking about what's really going on with me these days, and I better talk until I make sure I understand, because I've been doing just about all the running, hiding, isolating and denying I can stand. I'm falling apart here, yet I think I'm so clever, so smart. Like it's not really happening. And things keep getting worse, or should I say better. I've learned that much. But I'm running so hard from something. I wish I knew what it was.

I'm doing old behaviors and using food. I can't fit into my jeans. Do you hear that, Lori Jean?! You can't fit into your jeans and you've really been craving cigarettes, bad. Almost smoked one last week. Oh, but nothing's going on. I'm handling everything just fine.

Yeah, like the rage attack I had last week. Where did that come from? I didn't think I was still capable of such blind rage. I didn't know I had it in me. The closer I was getting to revealing the next thing I needed to deal with, in other words, when I started getting too close to something I've been protecting, the more I backed away. Defense mode kicked in and I quit reaching out to anybody, especially my Higher

Power, my writing, my prayer and meditation time, myself. I've been busier than hell, doing absolutely nothing.

I can't run from myself any longer. I can't hide anymore, I'm tired of hiding. I want to feel free to be me. I want to quit being so scared, so protective of my inner self, my potential, my gifts. Am I ever going to escape the bonds of self?

That was the last entry in that notebook, until five months later when I finally did the thorough housecleaning I needed to do. What I did in the five months, it seems, is struggle. In my mind at least, I was trying to prepare to do a fourth step. I was beginning to want to, and my dreams were telling me I would have to. This is what I wrote in my dream journal:

December 5, 1995
With all that I've been going through in my recovery lately, recognizing that I'm trying to run again, that I must be getting too close to some emotional pain or something, I see how my pattern has always been to run at this point. I've come far enough to know this is what's going on, even if I didn't recognize it right away. I feel I'm ready to at least try and take a look at the pain, try to work through it, so it was no real surprise to me when I dreamed what I did last night.

I was at a narrow foot bridge and I was pulling a cart stacked full of lots of neatly packed little boxes. I was not going to be able to cross the bridge with all this "stuff." Then I saw a sign above the bridge which said, "CAUTION: BRIDGE MAY BE ICY." I looked down and saw that there was a sheet of ice across the bridge floor. Then I heard very clearly, "DON'T SLIP."

This dream was profound. In dreams bridges represent transition, going from one place to another; a connection, overcoming problems, overcoming troubled waters. This dream told me very clearly that there was no way I was going to cross this bridge with all that baggage. I was going to have to go through them and get rid of everything I no longer needed to carry. It also told me that if I tried to cross the bridge with all my stuff, I would surely slip.

To slip is to drink. A slip is very dangerous to a recovering alcoholic. This dream helped me visualize the process of unpacking the boxes and taking a look at what's inside. I needed some help with this. I didn't know how to discover what I didn't know was there. How could I bring back something my conscious mind had forgotten? The dream helped.

The very next evening I opened up one of the "boxes." I remembered how deeply my Grandma Sue's death had affected me. I had stuffed all the pain I felt when she died. It was too traumatic. It was too unfair. It was too final. I see now that I didn't care what happened. I was discouraged. I couldn't trust anything anymore. I went wild.

I drank whatever was in front of me, took whatever pill I could get my hands on. No drug was off limits. I tried them all; everything except heroine and morphine. I never used needles. Those things were not around. No one I knew did it, but who's to say I wouldn't have if given the opportunity?

I had a motto, "The only time I say no is when they ask me if I've had enough," and "Born to be Wild" was my self-appointed theme song. I even wanted it put on my headstone. Only now I think I'll put "Born to be wild for awhile." Anyway, it became very clear how Grandma Sue's death affected me, and I was surprised to see the past twenty years in this new light.

Then I began remembering all the losses in my life, starting with my great Grandpa Hall when I was five years old. It seemed to never stop, even with years in between. Each loss was hard, each one different, yet the same; so much hurt, so much sadness, so much loss and grief.

That was what was revealed. Grief. I've never done my grief work. I haven't allowed myself to go through the whole process. I always cut it short. It was too painful. With that I'm afraid came loss of trust and a fear of losing someone or something else I loved.

I was afraid to live because I didn't know how to process the painful parts of life, the sadness and loss that is so much a part of it. I'm just now learning how to use these emotions of mine properly. I guess if I don't fully look at an event and process it completely I'm never free of it. In other words, I carry it around with me in boxes!

Well, I've got to unload some boxes, and not just a select few. I want to completely clear off my cart so that I can walk across this bridge in front of me with a lighter load, free of the past so that I can move on through the future, full of joy, and sadness, yet with a freedom that makes it all okay. For the first time in my life I feel how heavy my load has been, how much "stuff" I still carry; and the importance of ridding myself of everything I no longer need.

Chapter 20

SPIRITUAL AWAKENING

April 6, 1996. I've continued to dream about my cousin, either she's just there and doesn't really have anything to do with the dream, or she's up on a mountain, over across the way, and I can't get to her. It's been so frustrating, and I've been so afraid. Last night was the worst. I woke up crying and told my husband that she's going to die.

It was how she looked in the dream, a mere skeleton. She was so frail, skinny, and sick. I held her, hugged her, and cried as I tried to talk to her about getting help. I knew when I hugged her there was barely anything left. I was losing her.

She had a drink in her hand. I asked her to come in the bedroom with me and talk. I told her she could bring her drink because I knew she wouldn't go anywhere without it. She seemed to kind of listen, but when I mentioned AA, she backed off and didn't want to hear another word. I knew it was too late for her. I hugged her again and said good-bye. I let go of her, knowing I had lost her.

I've cried all morning. I feel like I'm watching her die from 2000 miles away.

April 11, 1996

Oh, if I don't quit dreaming about my cousin! Every night for the past 4 nights I have dreamed of her. It's heartbreaking, it's all consuming, I know it's what's making me tired every day. I can't rest at night because I'm spending all my time with her, and I'm sad. I love her so much, and whatever is going on in her life right now, it's not good.

In last night's dream I watched her lose her daughter because of her drinking. At least she looked good in this dream, but I still felt she was lost to me, to us. The night before I dreamed she was at the treatment center, but kept coming to my house and raging at me. They had to keep coming to get her. I knew she was never going to stay there, never going to make it. I was hiding from her but she kept finding me. I'm tormented. I know she is.

This dream could mean one of two things. It could be that I'm having a psychic dream, that it is literally about her, and that she is going to die. I've talked to family members who say she is, in fact, a skeleton and looks very sick. She's been drinking vodka in the morning for over ten years.

The other possibility is that it's a normal dream, where she represents an aspect of myself. In other words, the alcoholic in me is dying. It's probably a combination of both. At any rate, it got my attention, and I decided to get real serious about my own recovery. I was finally ready to "go to any lengths" to get better.

It took me a few weeks to finish my fourth step, but once it was done I made an appointment for my fifth step, and I felt healed at depth. Never in a million years did I think I could actually be freed from my past, free from the guilt and shame and remorse. Free. But I was. Finally I loved myself enough to let it go, enough to forgive myself and get on with my life.

I heard forgiveness described this way, and it helped me see it differently. Forgiveness is like acceptance, it doesn't mean I have to like what happened, it means I choose to let it be and get on with my life. Finally the promise which says we will not regret the past nor wish to shut the door on it, had come true for me. I began to have a spiritual awakening.

June 3, 1996

Life. It's all so perfect. Everything has a purpose and there is a time for everything. That seemed crystal clear to me this morning. Everywhere I looked I saw divine order. Even amongst all the mess and disorder around me right now with remodeling in process, but that's what was so clear to me, it's all a p r o c e s s! I feel like I'm seeing with clear eyes, with hopeful eyes, with *trusting* eyes.

Everything is just okay. No one but God & I know what a transformation has taken place. It's a miracle. At the risk of sounding ridiculously religious, I feel like I've been saved. I feel like I was a person trying all my life to stay afloat, drowning all the while. Now I feel as if I've been plucked from the rapids just before going over the falls.

There is no doubt in my mind that is how close I came to death on more than one occasion throughout my years as a reckless and dangerous alcoholic and addict. It's frightening looking back, especially having finished a thorough fourth step, and a very special fifth step, where I looked at, and shared *everything*.

But instead of regret I feel, or any remaining guilt at all, I feel peace, and acceptance. I feel blessed. How about that?! No more guilt, no more regret, just overwhelming gratitude. I'm going to try to make life a little easier on my guardian angel. Although I'm sure angel's rewards for saving lives go without saying, my angel earned her wings!

In an instant today, this morning, I look around and see the world through different eyes, clearer eyes. I believe I've had myself a spiritual awakening! It seems today I'm able to see the bigger picture. Greg & I are better than we've ever been, taking our relationship, like recovery, one day at a time. We love each other as much as we can, whenever we're together, always being the best we can in the moment.

When the goal is to love and take care of the one who's loving and taking care of you, it's the most rewarding and fulfilling kind of love. It's what we believe relationships were meant to be. When we do that, it's pretty easy. No expectations, no worries about the future, just life right now. Today I will lovingly detach where I need to with family and friends.

I was just thinking about how we adults are when we're watching small children perform. Aren't we just as proud as we can be of our children when they're in a play or a sports event? It doesn't matter to us if they blow their lines or lose the game, we encourage them, point out the good they did, and minimize the faults.

We show loving acceptance and praise for their efforts. The fact they tried at all is good enough for us. With really small children we're even more accepting, noticing how the mistakes make it more endearing. It's always a huge success no matter how bad it was. We know they are learning. We know they're growing and that they'll make mistakes along the way, but we encourage them to move ahead, try again, don't give up. We forgive them their mistakes and encourage them to try again.

Sounds like a good way to be with all of God's children, young and old. In fact, if we all learned to see each other through the eyes of a loving parent, what a wonderful world we would live in. I can try to do that. I can have love and acceptance in my heart for every human being that struggles through this life. I begin to see my children, not as mine, but as having the same loving creator I have, with the same wisdom and guidance available to them.

I can only take care of me, and by doing that, I'm teaching those around me how to take care of themselves, and we all have room to grow. I guess I'm not feeling like beating up on myself anymore for how I'm recovering. I can see that it's all just perfect. Even the infirmity. Even the fears, the anger. It's all a part of getting better, even when it feels like I'm worse.

This awakening came at a good time because I've been in another slump the past couple of weeks, feeling really sleepy and tired all the time, never really waking up fully all day. Sleep a full night, wake up tired. Drink coffee, shake & yawn. It's easy for me to get overwhelmed with the work left on the house, impatient at the time it takes. But today I feel different. The awakening I believe started with my dream the night before last.

It was already clear to me that something was still wrong, not just because I was so tired, but that too. I felt so much freer having done steps four and five, and I'm grateful for being relieved of so much guilt and shame I've carried around, but still I felt stuck. Still I felt frozen, afraid to move, afraid to change anything. I was staying where I felt safe. And then I had the dream.

I was standing in front of a huge cement wall. It was very high, with some writing on it. But I couldn't see what it said. I was surprised it was such a big "block." I'd imagined maybe a fence or some rough terrain, but a cement wall?! It was if to say, " There's no getting around this one."

Then I was at some kind of retreat or something. I've had two similar dreams before, but the surroundings were different. In the first two dreams I was leaving early, and almost left when I was suddenly panicked. I remembered I'd left all my stuff! I went back in time, thank God, but I was dismayed when I saw how much I had to gather up. I wasn't packed or anything and I had stuff everywhere. Plus I wasn't going to be able to carry everything over to catch the boat. I was running late.

I had the first two dreams before I did my fourth step, this one after. I was leaving a retreat early. There were people around but no one I knew. I got to the front door and almost left when I panicked, as I remembered I'd almost left all my stuff! I went back to my room and again realized I had too much to gather. But I started pulling stuff from under the bed any-way. It was dusty and dirty under there, like it had been there for years.

I pulled out a dirty, old, and battered suitcase. Even though it was empty, I had to bring it with me. I also stacked an empty, old, broken-down, and filthy cardboard box on top of the suitcase—and an old, empty purse. Junk! Dirty, yukky, ready for the trash. I just had to bring it all with me. It was my stuff.

Then I was at the front door looking down. It seemed the cottage was on a dirt hill or something, and it was rutted all the way down. There did not appear to be a road. I could see my car at the bottom, my old Maverick. I was trying to go down the left side (the car was to the right), and thought I could come around and be able to drive the car up to get my stuff.

But on the way down a black panther passed me going up the hill. He was pulling a couple of horses behind him. I was surprised to see this wild animal. Then he turned, as if to attack. He growled and snarled at me, ready to jump at any moment. I tried to move away but he followed. I stopped. Then, as I heard a voice say, "Don't Run!" I ran. The panther bolted after me, but I stopped and I didn't get attacked.

Well, the cement wall told me I still have a big block somewhere, and I knew that. I find that just having the awareness helps me be open to reveal-ing what it is. The dreams about leaving my stuff tell me that I'm still much too concerned about what I carry with me (can't leave it behind!). The one after I did a fourth step tells me that although I've emptied out most of my boxes and suitcases, I still feel the need to carry the old empties around. In other words, for some reason I think I need to take the "containers" with me. Maybe that's because I don't know how to feel without any baggage to carry.

The panther represents wild beauty, grace; what force do I fear or wish to release? The horses represent power, and they are being pulled by the panther. In other words, grace brings about power. The attack warns of the danger of running. If I stop running, I won't get attacked.

June 10, 1996

It seems more & more I'm getting spiritual awakenings as a result of working the steps, especially the fourth. I'm sure my willingness has helped. I've been saying the Grace Prayer intensely, focusing on the "reveal what needs to be revealed," so I can "heal what needs to be healed," and what am I finding? The answer is in what I find myself doing; surrendering, practicing non-resistance, and acceptance. I'm incredibly grateful. I feel free.

I'm slowly allowing myself to be okay just where I am, the house, just where it is, and all the people in my life just where they are. I've had to do some praying for clarity about my role in my life right now. I feel a bit overwhelmed, with working on the house, trying to write, and trying to work a recovery program.

I don't want to miss my meetings either, and sometimes I need to if I'm going to get into a detailed project like stripping the oak panels. So I have to learn what's best for me. If I go to a meeting am I going to feel it's an interruption? If I don't go to a meeting am I going to worry what I missed?

One thing I know for sure. Things have been going so well, it's no time to change anything. This is not a program where you get healthy enough not to need meetings. If anything, going to meetings even when it didn't seem like it was working, is exactly why finally it is.

Now I know why they say keep coming back. I think I've got a good schedule worked out for myself which consists of a meeting every day, and it's got me this far, I'm not going to change anything now. I spent a lot more than an hour a day on my addiction. Besides, I need some extra help right now with my "codependency tendency," which I've come to recognize is my way of taking the focus off me, and I can't afford to do that today.

I'm not going to run anymore. I've done my 4th & 5th steps, and now I've got to quit putting off step 9, and make amends. Everything else will follow. I need to work the steps. I'm on 9 now, no time to stall. I'm almost there. Maybe that's why I've been a little too concerned about my friends and how they're working their programs.

I've also got to give my sponsor a call. I know that's a block I've got to get over. But I'm making progress. I know that now. Before I didn't believe that, couldn't trust it. Now I do. I'm continually improving. I'm learning that it's okay not to do it all right now. It's okay that I will never be perfect, never "arrive," but I can be guaranteed joy, and adventure along the way.

I can know pain and sadness as well, but that's a part of being alive, of living life, and the promise is that I can always know more joy, more love, more peace, than all the pain and sadness I'll know. I trust that today. I have faith and an inner knowing. It's always been there, but it's a part of me today more than ever before.

Chapter 21

THE CEMENT WALL

I went to a meeting and someone was talking about going through old pictures (photo therapy). I went home with that in the back of my mind. I was out of sorts and found myself at the word processor. Here's what I wrote:

June 12, 1996
Boy, I don't know what kind of mood I'm in! It's not bad, but it's not particularly comfortable either. It feels like a sadness somewhere, a loss of some kind. I want to cry and I don't know why, or maybe I do. Megan left for Idaho this morning, and I cried all the way home. Not so much because she'll be gone for 2 weeks, but more because she's almost "gone" already. I'm feeling what many parents have felt, the empty nest syndrome, and that's the only way I can describe how I feel.

I'm sad that my baby girl is almost grown. I'm sad that my 3-year-old daughter (when I got her), is 16 now and has a drivers license. God has been so great to me with Megan. She *is* my daughter, in every way but one. What a gift she is, and while I'm incredibly grateful for her, I'm sad for the years I wasted. Sad that I didn't see those two little people for who they were, and how cute and innocent they were, and how hard I was on them.

—Break—

Well, I just had one of the best cries I've had in a long, long time.

I was overwhelmed with sadness about the years gone by. I sobbed with regret, and had to get out the picture albums from those first days, and I cried some more. How could I have been so mean? How could I have been entrusted with these beautiful children when I was going to run them like little soldiers.

How I wish I could have seen my own children through the eyes of unconditional love like I see every child in my path today. Oh, God forgive me. I was given a job and I blew it. I loved them so much, I really did, I just didn't know that I wasn't doing it right. And I feel so sad about that. I feel incredibly sad that Jeremy is in prison right now, exactly where his path has been taking him, and for the first time I hurt about that.

Before I've always been mad, thought, "Fine, he'll get what he deserves," and I'd be pissed when the system failed again and again by letting him slide, even though he had developed a pattern of behavior from early on, which warranted attention. They just kept giving him more rope. While we were at the end of ours.

I realize I've been so angry for so many years, that I haven't been able to pray for him, to wish good things for him, and especially to ever want him back home again. I guess part of me wanted him to keep getting in trouble so I wouldn't have to deal with him now that he's 18, and although I thought I wanted him to get better, I didn't trust him, I couldn't believe it might happen.

So I stayed mad because I'd tried love and devotion for eight years while we battled schools, courts, counselors, doctors, and lawyers. Nothing worked during that time. Then when he went back to his mother's when he was 15, and continued to get in more, and increasingly more serious trouble, I'd had it.

He was in and out of school, court, jail, and halfway houses over the next 2 years, and even added one to his list, psychiatric hospital when he took an overdose of his prescription medication to "get high," and they thought he was trying to kill himself (only Jeremy knows for sure). That one cost our insurance company over twenty thousand dollars, before they quit paying after 18 days and Jeremy was promptly "cured" and released.

I continued back in Michigan to be 1), grateful he was in Idaho, and 2), pissed off at him. I look back now and I realize I've been pissed off at that kid for about 12 years. I've had so much anger and resentment built up in me from him, that I wasn't aware was there. I've been getting so much healing with this. For some reason lately, since Jeremy's been in the hard core prison system, right along with the murderers and rapists, I've begun to forgive, and mend my angry heart toward him.

It's taken me a long, long time though, and the sadness I feel not just for Megan's, but Jeremy's lost childhood, is something I never expected to feel. I never saw Jeremy as a child. I loved him, but he was a thorn in my side, a sneaky, sly, and conniving trouble maker who was out to ruin people's lives by demanding incredible attention. I never saw him the way I saw him a minute ago, looking at old pictures. I had two small children, whose lives I didn't cherish, because I was too busy with my own life while drinking.

I guess what got things started this time, is like every time, Megan going to visit her birth mother, a real trigger for me. I always feel threatened, insecure, scared when she goes. It's then that I realize what I've got. It's always been that way for me with the kids. I always knew how much I loved them, and was grateful for them when they were away. I always remembered cute things they did or said to tell our friends when the kids weren't around, but I didn't see it when I was dealing with them. I just hope I wasn't a total step-monster, and that I showed them some love and acceptance.

I think that's the hardest part of all for me to deal with now, I simply wasn't *there* for my children. I was there physically, whatever state of intoxication I was in, but I see now that I was never there emotionally for them. I feel like I am there with Megan today, but I've had some guards up still with her, and maybe this is it.

Maybe I'm just feeling pain about her childhood and that has kept me from letting her get real close. I think she feels closer than I feel like I've let her. It's taken a lot of work on my part, to let her feel safe with me when I didn't feel safe with me.

I guess I've always been sorry for how strict I was with her and Jeremy, especially her because she was never an ounce of trouble, but you wouldn't have known it by me back then. I made something out of nothing. I looked for things, and I punished for "kid" stuff, like getting dirty, or having too many toys out. They didn't leave the table until their plate was clean, even if they didn't like what we were having.

I was hurried and rushed and so busy, I didn't even see the little children in front of me. I'm so sad about that. I know other parents feel sad because our kids grow up so fast, and it's a loss of the little person they used to be, but I feel my loss is different. I mourn that part for sure, I thought about my young lady at 16, just this morning, and I do miss the little girl she used to be, but I have remorse on top of empty nest syndrome.

I'm sure I'm not the only parent ever to be so caught up in their own life that their children grew up while they weren't looking, but ouch. I wish someone would have told me it would feel this way. I just wish I would have allowed them to be children and feel safe in doing so. I'm sure my kids didn't feel safe to just be, I know they watched their every move with me, Jeremy rebelled, Megan was a "Stepford" child. And I was a wreck. A nervous, hyper, controlling, overbearing, talked too much, never listened, kind of person who had to have everything my way.

I controlled everyone and everything I could around me, and how they all put up with me I'll never know. Megan was too young to know any better, that's why she still defends me. I say I was strict and very mean, and she says, "no you weren't." She loves me. I don't know how and I don't know why but she does. And so does Jeremy. He calls me "Ma" in his letters, and signs them "your son." It means the world to me. It makes me cry.

I guess I didn't do so bad after all it seems, but I know that I have amends to make to my children, and many more to my husband. I think I see now that this is an answer to my grace prayer and request to "reveal that which needs to be revealed," that "something" I knew was still there, but couldn't see. It's there all right, and it's painful. I didn't touch near enough on it with my fourth step, I thought I did, but I see now I wasn't quite ready to feel the pain. I wasn't ready to deal with the regret and remorse.

Megan being gone again to Idaho (my trigger for 8 years now), really brought it into the light for me, and I'm so grateful. It's about my kids! It's about something only as minor as parenthood and lost years with one's children, that can never be retrieved. It's about exactly what the topic of the meeting was today, the one I cringed when it was mentioned; grieving. I talked about knowing I had grief work to do. I also remembered something else about the cement wall dream, the writing on it. It was a headstone. The dream's message was even clearer than I thought.

I've realized something else. I never thought I wanted children, so I set myself up with that belief. I knew for sure I never wanted to bear children, so when I "inherited" my kids, I guess I never allowed my mind set to change. I didn't enjoy them while I had them, because I never expected to have them. I didn't know about living in the moment a day at a time, damn it. I didn't know how to love a child, the way I do today.

I'd give anything if I could have been different with my own, if I could have given them more of me. But clearly, I couldn't. I have to say I did the best I knew how, even though I don't think it was good enough. Obviously it's the best I could do because it's what I did. I can't change any of that now, I can only change how I relate to them today.

June 13, 1996

Well, I'd made it through the first photo albums yesterday and felt sadness and remorse for how mean I was to the kids, and I prayed that I had at least in some way let them know I loved them. Gregory was so wonderful with me last night and let me cry. I told him how sorry I was for all the years with the kids, his kids, and it was hard because we talked about how frustrated he got at times and how bad he felt for the kids, and how none of that mattered to me. After that he made me laugh a lot, so it was a very healing day. But I knew I wasn't done yet. I knew I still had two more photo albums to go through.

As I started looking through the next album I got my reassurance about whether or not I showed the kids I loved them. There was picture after picture of me with the kids, Megan always hugging me, or sitting on my lap. Jeremy with his hand on my shoulder. It made me cry because it was what I needed to see. There were some good times all through those years, and my kids knew I loved them. Hard as I was, it appeared I wasn't a total liability.

What I didn't expect as I continued through the pictures, was that a whole different issue would come up that I haven't dealt with, turns out none of us have. It's more grief. This time over the loss of Jeremy from our family.

I ran across a picture of the four of us on the deck in the backyard of the house in Idaho. It was probably 1984-85. I remember when the picture was taken. We used the timer on Greg's camera and he ran around and got in the picture. Suddenly it hit me like a flood, our family, the *four* of us. It was who we were for eight years. It was a loss, like losing a branch off the family tree. A person missing from the family photograph, one that's been missing for the past 5 years, yet we went on like nothing changed.

July 9, 1996

Well, you can see some time has passed since last I wrote. I've had a lot to process, a lot has happened. I was overwhelmed at the revelation I had about mourning the loss of Jeremy. And it occurred to me that since we've been remodeling the house, about three years now, all of our family pictures have been stored away. Where there used to be a whole wall of family pictures, Jeremy in most of them, there has been nothing.

So, not only did we put Jeremy "out of sight out of mind" after he left (we were tired and angry), but then with all our pictures out of sight, we had nothing to remind us of our son. His calls during the past few years have been few and far between, especially if he wasn't in some kind of lock up, then we never heard from him at all, and didn't know where to get a hold of him.

I guess it was easy for us to stuff our feelings about Jeremy. They've been stuffed long enough. I've been so mad for so long, I haven't allowed myself to cherish and remember the good times we had raising the kids. Dysfunctional or not, we were a family and we loved each other, and up until 1991, we stuck together.

I know I still have more forgiving of Jeremy to do, I'm not all better, that was revealed to me the other night when he called. I could tell it was one of his undesirable calls, where he blames everybody but himself for his life. I got the same old pit in my stomach and didn't want to talk to him. I got in the shower so I wouldn't have to. I let Gregory deal with him. But I had to look at why I did that.

I've been trying not to react in old ways to something that came up the other day. I found out Jeremy wrote in a letter to his mother how she had always been there for him, and how much that means since, "dad doesn't care." The old me wants to write a nasty letter.

The old me wants to be filled with anxiety and frustration. The old me is trying really hard to feel that way, the new me is trying harder not to. It's been a struggle. I guess it was a test of sorts. So, how'd I do? I haven't written any nasty letters, and I'm not going to. I'm not going to dial an argument either. And when I'm ready, I will write the letter I've been going to write to Jeremy for weeks now, the encouraging one. But I can't bring myself to do it just yet. I'm hurt.

Nobody tried harder than Greg & I did, and nobody was more frustrated. I don't know why I think I have to defend us. We know what we did, how we tried, and how it hurt when nothing we did worked. Nobody spent more time and energy trying to help Jeremy than we did.

That's the kind of resentments I struggle with most. Injustices. I hate when that happens. But I've also learned it isn't worth it. Nothing for me today is worth fear, anxiety, anger. Nothing. I've found serenity, I know peace, and that requires letting go. God help me let this thing go.

I still have work to do. Jeremy called and I didn't want to talk to him. I was mad. Maybe only a little, no burning rage in the pit of my stomach, but I couldn't deal with talking to him. Red flag! Still need to do some work, still need to forgive, and really need to LET IT GO!!!

I find that I still have a low tolerance for him when he acts out. In other words I'm sorry to discover, my love for him is still conditional. I have a hard time not shutting off when he's up to his old bull. Boy, I sure opened a can of worms when I opened those photo albums didn't I? But I'm thankful. I'm so grateful that I've been shown what I need to pay attention to. I knew there was something but didn't have a clue, now I know. I'm grateful for the knowledge, even if it requires some work on my part.

After all was said and done with the grieving about the kids, I felt incredible relief. I shared the experience with Megan and made amends to her again, she in turn wrote Jeremy a letter and told him what I'd said. I wrote him a letter as well. As sad as I was, I processed it and let it go. After all, I can't go back and do it again. Amidst the pain and the tears, I also discovered everything that was good during those years, and it's that I'll carry with me.

Chapter 22

HUMILITY

J uly 24, 1996. Humility. Sucks. Just kidding. It sure hurts sometimes though. Only good thing is it feels so darn good after the lesson is clear! I've been learning a lot lately. I'm pretty vulnerable and fragile at this point. I've been kicking myself around again, then beating myself up afterwards. Only problem is, there are always others I seem to kick around in the process. That's the part that really drives the point home I think.

And those damn amends. I hate having to do it. But you know, it seems to get easier, and it feels so good just as soon as I do it. Especially when, like earlier tonight, I don't want to make amends! I don't want to admit once again that I was wrong. Once again take the blame for a situation that had many players.

In fact, by God, I wasn't going to, not this time. Yet that felt horrible! What was I going to do?! The phone rings. It's my victim. Before he can say anything, I'm crying, and I say I'm sorry, and that I just don't know how to keep my big mouth shut. How I still haven't learned to mind my own business and stay out of everybody else's, family or not! Especially family. I was forgiven. I'm learning.

But when will I learn the easy way? When will I just stay out of things that don't concern me? When will I learn how to say what I'm feeling without attacking someone else? Bottom line, I have a hard time expressing myself. I'm tired of being in other people's business. I'm tired of gossiping about other people, and how they're living their lives.

I don't want to judge, I want to allow everyone to work their own program, but when people do things I don't approve of, or when I think I know a better way, I have a hard time keeping my big mouth shut, can't seem to just stay out of it. So, what I need to be able to do is simply say, I really don't care to hear about this, or this is none of my business.

Instead, I let it get to me, I make judgments, and then I spout off at the mouth inappropriately. I think I'm learning. In fact I know I am. Those lessons sure smart sometimes. It had to happen though, I see that now. I step in way over my head, completely cross other people's boundaries, and end up humbled. For me, it takes those kinds of lessons. It has to be intense it seems, for me to get it. But I thank God for those lessons. I thank God for the humility and the pain. I've learned a great deal.

This morning I woke up remembering a dream I had. I don't remember much, except that there was "rubble" everywhere. There were broken buildings, ruins, all around.

I woke with the word on my mind. In my dream book it said, "What do I wish to restore to wholeness?" That about says it, doesn't it? I want to be restored to wholeness. I want to stop leaving debris in my wake.

I'm sorry for a comment I made during that last conflict. I yelled, "Go have another drink." Just what a practicing alcoholic, after having several drinks already and reeking of alcohol, needs to hear. I guess the alcoholic in me knew that one would hurt, and I was surprised and upset at myself for still being capable of purposely inflicting that kind of pain. I did exactly what he's doing for nearly twenty years. I really had room to talk, didn't I? As if I'm any better now just because I've escaped the alcohol trap myself. I never want to be that kind of recovering person.

August 7, 1996

Well, this is what's happening with me. I don't know how to do my work. I don't know what I'm supposed to be doing. I want to write but I'm so damn afraid. Why? It makes no sense. It's totally out of my control and I just have to say that. Being right here, right now, writing this, is something I did not want to do. I tried to avoid it, like I always do, but today I decided enough already.

Today I'm really getting pissed off at myself for not doing the things I want to be doing. I DON'T UNDERSTAND WHAT THE PROBLEM SEEMS TO BE. I'm in recovery, is that the problem? No way. But I was writing when I was drinking. Well, that's a lie too. I *was* writing, all my life I've written, but honestly, the last year is all I did was drink.

Did I think that was going to change? Did I think it was going to get better? Did I really think that writing, and not drinking, would once again be an important part of who I am? I was only fooling myself and it hurts to acknowledge that. I'm just so damn afraid. I'm sad, and I'm frightened. Sad that I don't think I'm worthy of expressing the gifts God gave me, and frightened it might be true.

I'm a recovering alcoholic and I'm barely touching the surface of the healing work I have to do, and since I've done a lot of work already, I guess part of me just isn't sure I'm up for any more.

I almost wrote, "I can't seem to do it," meaning my writing, but instead found myself writing that I've stopped myself. *I've* stopped me. I've held myself back. Just saying that is so freeing. Since I've sat down to write, I feel so much better. My hands have been going a mile a minute from the time I sat down, yet I didn't think I wanted to write? I'm crazy I tell ya! I slide into the fear, and before I know it I've forgotten why I'm here, what I'm supposed to be doing.

Next come thoughts of using some kind of mood altering substance as a way of avoiding life. And why would I want to avoid my life?! What is it about life that scares me so much? What is it about me that scares me so much? I'M DESPERATE!!! I want to get out of this! I want to get on with my life.

Fear. It's incredible. I guess that's what drugs and alcohol do for a person, make you fearless. Feeling-less is more like it. I think what the deal really is with this writing thing, is I don't even know where to begin telling my story. I guess because I wrote the book once already, I'm not quite sure how to go about this enlightened version.

How to deal with the humiliation regarding the first book, and my arrogance in thinking I had it all figured out. Bottom line, I wrote a book called *Recovering From Life*, all the while a practicing, everyday drinking, alcoholic. Go figure. No wonder it didn't get published, there was no honesty to it. Well, I shouldn't say that. I'm sure there's some good stuff in there, but I've been too afraid to even pick it up.

I'm so afraid of what I wrote. So afraid of how I'm going to sound to myself. I guess I'm afraid to see how much I've grown and healed, or should I say I'm afraid to see how sick I used to be!

Most of my story was written in my fourth step, some of it I still have, some of it I burned! All I know today is I am so grateful that I'm sober, and being in recovery has saved my soul! Not to mention my life.

August 10, 1996

Wow! What a dream! First let me say that we're camping; last night was our first night here. Can you believe that I forgot my notebook and pen on this trip? Hello? What was I thinking? But one good thing has come of it; I've had an incredible urge to write since we got here, something lost to me lately. About the dream....

I was flying (more like floating), at a high rate of speed. I was racing through the air, above a slightly winding, paved road. The area and parts of the road were snow-covered, with high, thick banks on both sides. I could see the snowplow guy, here and there and everywhere, clearing away the thick snow.

Then suddenly there was a thick patch (wall) of snow, a spot the snow plow had missed. I hit it. The impact flung me over and I came to a sudden halt, sitting on the ground with the road above me a bit. I'm reeling from the shock of sailing along one moment and suddenly being stopped.

On the road above me is a man in a wheelchair. He stopped, turned quickly to face me, stared right at me, and with a smile on his face, his eyes suddenly began to glow a beautiful green color. They opened wide. They were stars and moons. The glowing light could be seen from his ears and mouth as well. At first I wanted to run. I was frightened, but then I thought, "No, this is a supernatural event, something I've waited my whole life to experience." I decided to stay. I wasn't going to fear this thing.

As I experienced it, it was awesome! I was taken aback by the power

I felt and the humility of being blessed enough to witness such a thing, even though I didn't know what it meant. It was incredible.

Then I was standing at the doorway of a large tent. Inside people were sitting around in a circle. There were people standing outside, where I was too, watching what was going on inside. Inside there was some kind of spiritual experience happening. The people who were "getting it" were shaking uncontrollably, their entire bodies. There was a little girl being held by her mother, she was shaking and having the experience.

A couple of the people who were standing outside were affected too. I knew this was a place for people who'd had experiences like I'd had. I knew I belonged with this special group. I felt humbled and grateful. I leaned against the doorway and relaxed. I was open to whatever might happen next. I knew I'd been given a gift. I knew I was blessed.

Quite simply this dream says that I'm on a path, a good path—but I'm still going way too fast. I'm trying to race to a spiritual experience, and if I would just STOP, the spiritual experience would be right in front of me. Also, the experience may come in a form I don't expect, in fact, may even seem a bit frightening, but I still don't have to run.

The wheelchair represents the inability to run, to walk away, and signifies the importance of sitting still in order to experience what's in front of me. The dream also told me that there is a place to go for a spiritual experience. The tents represent the house of self (going within), and that not everyone "gets it" at the same time, and the importance of "becoming relaxed and open."

I found myself thinking, "Sure, it feels good to be on this spiritual path, but if I'm breezing along at high speed, I'm going to miss so much of the journey. I'm going to miss the important and awesome events along the way." This day is so beautiful. The water is so beautiful. I feel incredibly grateful, and full of peace and serenity. I feel like I belong out here, in nature, out in the midst of God's creations. I think I'll take a walk through the woods. I feel like thinking. I feel like praying.

August 12, 1996

I've been in fear mode, about writing. But at least it wasn't overwhelming, and it's getting easier for me to take the cure (sit down and start writing), but I get so confused about things I think I should be doing. Part of me knows what the answers are, but it's the questioning, it's the confusion at times. I don't trust myself yet.

Funny, during my drinking years I trusted no one but myself, thought I knew it all, for everybody. Then in early recovery I found that I knew absolutely nothing, didn't have a clue what's right for me, let alone anybody else, and had no choice but to depend on a Higher Power (I choose to call God).

Then, as recovery progresses I find I can trust myself a little more, or should I say trust the process, trust the tools I've been given, and therefore begin to trust my intuition. But there are still times when that old consciousness kicks in, the one of fear and doubt, and it's then I have a hard time following my inner guidance, I keep getting in the way. But, I feel okay now, just having said that. I'll go to a meeting and feel even better.

This morning I watched the most touching episode of Little House on the Prairie while I was ironing. I found this episode, or maybe just this morning, made me cry all the way through it! Charles had written his parents to come and live with them, something he did every year, something his mom longed to do, but his father refused.

Just after Charles' last letter arrived, mom died, never having seen her son one last time, or her grandchildren, let alone how and where they lived. I cried and cried and cried. I have to ask myself about all this crying business. Why do I cry so easily? Why do I feel like crying so much of the time?

They aren't tears of sadness or regret, but tears from having your heart touched, tears at the awesomeness of life, and how incredible the whole process really is. Why am I so touched? Why does it feel so deep to me?

(Later) I guess I need to confront myself on what's really going on with me. I haven't made myself accountable to anybody, and that's scary. Things are going really good actually. Sound marriage, loving partner, great kid, wonderful house, dependable vehicle, time for my writing (that's the best!), and courage to do the writing (that's even better).

I did miss meetings while my grandparents were here, and I was fine until toward the end. It's vague, I was way too cranky and yelled at Megan for having an attitude (mirror what?). Now it's been amended and we're on to new lessons. But the verdict's back, I need daily meetings, or at least five a week, Sundays I go to church. That seems to work for me.

Otherwise, I find myself just a little too interested in what other people are doing, I find myself a little too skeptical when my daughter asks me to go somewhere or spend the night somewhere. That's old behavior for me. Very old. So that's a red flag.

Then there's the food thing. I'm eating again. Too much. Too often. Eating for reasons other than the healthy ones, hunger. Thinking about food too much. Enjoying it too much. Feel good while eating, bad afterwards, yet still want to eat. Eat more, feel full and miserable, still want to eat more. Well, there's my eating disorder in a nutshell, right out of the 70s, but NOT NOW!!

Not in 1996, when I was just sure I was in recovery from that disorder. I guess it just goes to show you how complex and interweaving addiction and recovery are. The key is to head myself off as soon as I become aware I'm running, but that's so hard when denial is so strong. I've known I wasn't eating right for months now, and most of the time it's fine, I just have to work harder to keep it in control.

All of a sudden eating is not the normal, everyday necessity that it is for most people, all of a sudden I'm much too aware of it. I'm much too aware of food in general. In other words, it consumes my thoughts and my life. That's running! That's the cunning part of addiction. As long as I find some way to alter my mood, some way to defer my attention from myself and what I'm supposed to be doing, the longer I'm going to stay sick, the longer I'm going to suffer.

So that's it, I don't want to suffer anymore. I'm calling myself on every little disorder. I need to pray more, I need to meditate more, I need quiet time. I need to write when I feel like eating, so I can determine how I'm feeling, and why I want to eat.

All I know is that I'm at another crossroads. I'm at a place for more lessons, more growth. I need to surrender, or at least accept and trust. I want so much to get out of my own way, to be healthy, but I guess all things take time. In other words, I guess I'm rushing the process again.

I swear I'm my world's worst enemy when it comes to expectations. I think I should be so much further along than I am, and yet I'm so afraid at times, I know I keep myself back.

I don't know why I'm still running, why I'm still nervous, afraid. How can I take a look at what's really going on with me if I haven't got a clue what it could be? Impatient again, right? I need to quiet myself, I'm high strung again and I don't like it. I need to get back into my Yoga. Why do I always stop doing what's good for me?

I still have work to do with letting go of other people's expectations of me, in fact, opinions at all. What other people think of me is none of my business, and I have to remind myself of that every day. Every minute sometimes. That's been my struggle lately. Fighting with myself again. Letting the old ego creep back in.

August 23, 1996

Life feels so good to me today. It feels wonderful not to be fighting anything anymore. It feels good to trust, even in the midst of uncertain circumstances. But what I'm most excited about these days, is how I feel about my writing. It's been a long few years that I feel like I've been absent from the creative side of myself, and I feel I'm back now.

I was back into my old "useless" feeling for a few days, but now I'm finding time to write, I'm wanting to write more & more, and for the first time in over two years, I'm writing instead of doing "busy" things.

I've been so afraid, and I've been so hard on myself these first couple of years in recovery. It's been quite a journey, I'll say that, but it's been a necessary process that couldn't be rushed, and it's been perfect. I didn't always think so, but I know so today.

Chapter 23

THE CHILDREN

I live three doors down from a recovery house for women. Little did I know I would be so much a part of what goes on in that house. I was headed upstairs to write when I heard a child crying, screaming out on the sidewalk. She was hysterical, like she didn't want to be with whomever was behind her. Then I saw who it was. It was one of the women currently staying at the house.

I realized it was Saturday, most likely visitation day, and from the sounds of things it wasn't going very well. I know the woman. I was proud of how she handled the situation. She carried the crying and resistant child back to the house, holding her and loving her right where she was. I couldn't help but know that this could have been any one of us recovering mothers, and I reflected on the reality of what the children go through. How wide-spread and destructive this disease is.

The children. They are part of the miracle of recovery as well, and in fact the greatest one of all. I was reminded of my own situation, my own children. The fact they're not my biological children makes no difference. I raised one child from the time he was eight years old until he was going on sixteen, and another from age three, she's sixteen now.

I got sober when Megan was fourteen. Jeremy is nearly twenty-one and never saw me sober. I can make amends the best I can with my children, and the rest is about me. I have to take care of me, and everything else will take care of itself. I get to start all over and do it better this time. It's never too late to get healthy and influence my children positively. I think most of us seek approval from our parents for as long as we live. I don't believe our children ever stop watching us, stop learning from us.

I wish I would have sobered up when Megan was little. I've often felt I could have been more help to Jeremy had I been sober, but who am I to think this wasn't how it was supposed to be? The important thing is to do the best I can, and love the people in my life as much as I can today. That's all I have to do. I can be patient and loving with my daughter, and love my husband every moment I'm with him. I can make today as good as it can be, or I don't have to. But a moment at a time, just for today, I can do it. This recovery, it's wonderful!

I was just talking to my daughter, or should I say she was talking to me. Teen-agers have a lot to process. Everything is life or death to a sixteen year old. But she's healthy. I'm so grateful. I'm so proud of her. She's my daughter, but God didn't give her to me until she was three years old. She's been mine ever since. This may not always be a good thing.

One of the things that amazed me the most in early recovery was how much we pass on to our children. How much they learn from us that we don't know we're teaching them. It's scary, really. At least it was for me once I sobered up and looked at my life. I had this exact replica of myself. Some good things, thank God, but I was saddened to see that I had taught her how to be uptight, worried, needing to be in control of everything and sometimes everyone, and fear-based. That was the most frightening to me. Worried and afraid that there wouldn't be enough time to get everything done, always in a hurry, always uptight.

Children are so impressionable. I've found they are always watching us, and as we change, they change. I was told early on that I didn't have to worry about my daughter, all I had to do was take care of myself, and the rest would take care of itself. I was amazed how true it was. By sharing what I was going through and what I was learning, she was learning too.

She's better at this stuff than I am. She's still watching me, and she's finally getting from me what she needs. The behavior automatically improves (both of ours). But it takes time. These changes don't take place overnight, and my husband and my children aren't going to trust me just because I say I'm different.

I have to show them, and I have to be patient with them as they get to know the new me. As with the woman on the sidewalk, some of our children are going to be pretty angry. There are going to be explosions, as finally the children's feelings are being heard. The beauty of the program is that we can change behavior, we can make amends, and we can be forgiven.

I don't believe the word "taught" is the proper word in this case. I believe I showed my daughter all these things. She learned it by watching me. That's a scary thought. We may learn from books and teachers, but our primary instinct, I believe, is to learn by watching other humans, in most cases our parents, just like most of God's creatures learn about the world.

I've been especially surprised how the mannerisms are copied. Since Megan isn't my biological daughter, these character traits (defects?) couldn't have been inherited. I'm more aware than ever that it's like looking in a mirror when we look at our children.

It reminds me of when Greg and I were out at a restaurant. I'd been sober about a year. A family of five sat at the next table. Mom and dad were having a drink before dinner, and smoking. I watched the children watching them, and I realized that it didn't matter what the parents told their kids about drinking and smoking, they were teaching them how to do it.

When Megan was talking to me just now I could see how I must have appeared to people. No eye contact. I was uncomfortable looking people in the eye, so I always looked away. I would glance back, make quick eye contact, but then I looked off to the side or up. I watched her as she was talking to me, and it was apparent that she was doing what she learned by watching me. But then the miracle again, she doesn't do this all the time anymore. I notice that she's learning the new behavior by watching me.

I just about died one day when she said she had an amends call to make. I didn't really think I'd ever said anything to her about amends, although I've made amends to her so she's aware of how it works. After she made the call she came and told me about it and said how much better she felt. More and more I see her taking responsibility for herself, and being able to admit when she's wrong and say she's sorry. It's such a change from the way I always was, and the way I'd taught her to be. I'm so grateful for this little angel in my life, who is more of a help to me than she'll ever know.

She still gets too upset and angry about things sometimes, but she knows how to talk about it. She's learning that talking about it *first* is even better! It just gives me such hope for this new way to do life. I'm unable to justify my codependent ways with honorable intentions, or caring. It's codependence and that's all it is! The best way I can help those I care about is to help myself, take care of me, and be the best me I can be.

By doing that, I'm teaching my daughter how to take care of herself. In fact, everyone in close contact with a recovering person learns about taking care of themselves, and if they don't want to hear it (aren't willing to change), they usually flee your life, either that or it's constant conflict.

The way I used to think and the way I'm learning to think today, definitely clash. One is healthy and feels good, is empowering. The other one doesn't feel good, and usually drains me. I can feel the energy it takes to be in that space, and it's just too hard to be there. I can't believe I spent most of my life in that state. I'm so grateful that my daughter doesn't have to live her life full of anxiety until she's in her thirties, the way I did. She can learn an easier way now, and make the rest of her life less stressful.

I can give her the gift of learning to live life on life's terms. I believe the inability to do that is what makes a person turn to alcohol or drugs, food, whatever. I may be totally wrong, but I don't think she's going to be as prone to addiction as I was. She won't be trying to find a quick fix, a pain killer when life gets too complicated. We're learning how to do feelings, how to live a day at a time, and that's all a person can really do anyway. Somehow the future takes care of itself. What a concept!

Live in the moment, live in the day, do the best I can with what's in front of me, and love the people in my life while they're in my life. What a wonderful way to live. No time for expectations, no time for disappointments, although there are always those, but the good will always outweigh the bad as long as I focus on the good. I truly believe that. I see proof of it every day.

Living in the day, I'm able to see the beauty in each moment. I'm able to appreciate and enjoy my daughter, little children, a beautiful day or a gorgeous sunset, whatever is in front of me, I can see the beauty. All I have to do is look. I feel like my eyes are being opened for the first time and that my ears hear for the first time. It's incredible to have been asleep for twenty years and suddenly wake up. It's even more incredible to finally start growing up, and be aware of the process.

They say we stop growing emotionally when we begin medicating with drugs or alcohol, food, whatever. And when we stop, we start growing. I was a sixteen year old girl in a thirty-four year old woman's body. I'm still shocked and amazed at my age. Not that I think thirty-four is old, but I feel the same age as people who are young enough to be my children. I always think people are older than me, and am usually shocked to discover I'm several years older than they are.

I look in the mirror and I see me. I don't feel like a little girl or even a teen-ager, I feel twenty-something. I know this is part of the process, and I'll probably catch up to myself one of these days. I'll look around and realize I'm in the thirty-something crowd. Growing up this time around is better. It's easier when I'm in the solution instead of the problem.

I spent most of my life in the problem or fearing the problem. No wonder I was a bundle of nerves. It feels good to be in the solution, to feel the peace and serenity that comes from trusting life to turn out okay, believing that somehow I will always know what I'm supposed to do next. As long as I take care of myself, which for me means eating right, sleeping right, and thinking right. I do that by going to a lot of meetings, reading AA or other recovery material, and praying. I use the basic HALT system. I don't get too Hungry, Angry, Lonely or Tired. I find I feel like doing more and more that's good for me, and that's good for everyone around me.

Chapter 24

THE FAMILY

The healing of the family, in my case with my husband and daughter, has been a process all its own, it hasn't always been easy. It has, however, been worth all of the work we've had to do. There were conflicts, resistance, and hope as we tried to relate to each other in this new, healthy way. It didn't happen overnight. Here's what I wrote in May 1996, just over two years sober.

I have such a war that goes on inside, between the old me and the new, improving me. I've heard that most of us are controlling because we're afraid. I realized early in recovery how afraid I've always been, but masked it with anger. Now I've been able to see how controlling I was, with everyone, in every situation. I had to know what was going on, have a plan, follow a schedule, and by damn, everyone around me was going to follow it too. There was absolutely no bending.

It all hit home the other night, when my dear husband, who has been raised, surrounded by, and married to alcoholics his whole life, revealed how he has been affected. We had a situation we were trying to resolve. Our communication is improving in recovery, but we've got a ways to go. We've also come a long way.

What I realized was how I had never allowed him to have his own opinion, his own thoughts, ideas. They always had to be mine, and before me his father's. Never before has an awareness hit so hard (alcoholics do not allow those around them the freedom to think and feel their own feelings, let alone validate them), as when Greg & I were talking. He came back upstairs after an earlier conversation we had bothered him, something I'd said.

What he didn't realize he was doing was reacting to the old me, assuming that because I had a different opinion on this matter, it meant I was right, he was wrong (the way it used to be). We were trying to get to a point of understanding about what happened, where we started to fight. In other words, go back and find out where things went wrong.

I was trying to point out where I was coming from, when he, in turn, reacted in old behavior and said, "I'm wrong. I'll leave." He turned to leave like he'd always done, carrying with him all the resentments that go with such an injustice. Past history would have him angry and brooding about it for a day or two until things cooled down enough to forget about it (stuff it). We don't get to that point anymore.

I said, "stay!" and he stopped. His statement of "I'm wrong I'll leave," even though he knew he wasn't, painted such a clear picture of the frustration experienced by those living with (and loving) an alcoholic. And painted an even clearer picture of me, which I never would have believed. At least I didn't go into beating up on myself. It was a humble awareness.

I knew that I got my behavior from my parents, they from theirs, and Greg's family same thing. I can take responsibility for my behavior and my actions, and I can be patient with Gregory as we both learn and experience new ways of relating to each other. This time with loving acceptance of each other's thoughts and feelings. Again, what a concept!

It isn't safe to feel vulnerable with an alcoholic, and the alcoholic doesn't feel too safe himself, so we change the best we can, and try to be patient. Greg & I resolved the situation and felt loving again. We had successfully worked out a conflict, and nobody had to be right or wrong. We really are getting better at this!

A couple of months later I summed up "the marriage, the family," this way:

Wow. Where do I begin? So many things have changed. The whole dynamics of my marriage has been transformed, as well as my role as parent. It got a little ugly from time to time during the transformation, but everything seems to be thriving as we look at life and each other in a new way.

I was so controlling before I quit drinking. What I said went, and I manipulated things, or forced things, to go exactly like I wanted them to go. The fact that it didn't usually work out that way, and that I was struggling in vain, didn't seem to occur to me, or matter. I continued to try to force life and everyone in it, to do things my way, and I couldn't see how very tiring that was, is.

By the time I sobered up, Jeremy was 18 years old and had been living in Idaho for 3 years. Megan was about to turn 14. She was probably the most confused about my alcoholism. She didn't know anything was wrong. I got her when she was three years old, and at a time when I was drinking my heaviest. By the time she was six years old I had to shape up or lose everything. From 6 to 14 she experienced me as a "controlled" drinker, with periods now and then of "tipsiness" on the holidays or birthdays, but the times I was really partying, for whatever reason, a wedding, Christmas party, or special event, your birthday, my birthday, Friday, was usually when I wasn't going to have to deal with the children at all, then I could get really "happy."

It was pretty pitiful sometimes, but such is life. Toward the end of my drinking, especially once it progressed and I was really going through the wine, I hid it from Megan. Knee deep in denial, I was still aware that I could be seen with a glass of wine in my hand more and more.

I didn't want my daughter to always see me that way, so I began hiding it. If she went outside, I got a glass and took it upstairs. If I was drinking while in the kitchen baking or making dinner, I'd hide my glass behind a canister or something on the cupboard, and sneak a gulp when she was out of the room.

I laugh at this behavior now. I can't believe I did it, now. I didn't see the implications of it at all. Everything was justified, everything could be explained. But even then I think I had wine with dinner every night that last year. You see it's acceptable to have a glass of wine with dinner, but what used to be a once in awhile thing, became an every night ritual.

I knew even with hiding my drinking, my daughter was seeing me drink a lot. Still she was surprised when I told her I was going to meetings, and that I was, in fact, an alcoholic. You see, there have been many alcoholics in both my family and my husband's, not to mention her birth mother's, but nobody acknowledged it, most of us didn't understand it. I was learning.

Some of the things I was learning, I didn't want to know. Like the fact that I taught my daughter to be just like me, that alcoholic thinking had been passed down not only to my parents and to me, and my husband's down to him, but now to our children. I didn't want to be confronted with myself in my daughter. I didn't understand the concept of this being a "family disease." I didn't realize that "alcoholism" is passed down in families even if there isn't any drinking going on.

By watching my daughter I could see that it is a way of thinking, a way of life. It's complicated and I was confused, frustrated. Not only did I have to look at my own thinking and behavior, but now I was confronted with all she had learned by watching me. But, alas, I was told I didn't have to "fix" her, I only had to work on me. She's still watching me, learning from me, and as my behavior changed, so would hers.

That's been the greatest gift of this program. What they said was true, and I was grateful. It's easier for the children than it is for us. They don't have quite as many years of playing those old tapes. Their tapes are easier to erase, to replace. It was not an easy process, and it continues today, but I remind myself to keep it simple, and to only deal with what's right in front of me. I can't change yesterday, and I can't control tomorrow. I just have to relax in today, and make it the best I can.

During my drinking years I was so hard on the kids. I expected a certain behavior, and my disciplines were harsh. I see now that I scolded my kids for my behavior, though blind to it at the time. When I started recovering I found that while I was saddened to see myself in my daughter, I felt love and patience with her, clearly recognizing what was really going on. How she didn't have a chance of being any other way, she had learned by watching me. Never was that so clear as when I was healing enough to recognize my own misguided behavior.

I was amazed at the love and tolerance I had with her, when my history was to harshly reprimand her for her behavior. I had no one to blame but myself, and I guess the love I was beginning to feel for myself helped me to start loving her unconditionally. I saw myself in my father too, and was suddenly aware of where I had learned to be the way I was. I didn't blame him either. He didn't become this way by choice, he learned it from his parents, as I'm sure they learned from theirs. And we all did the best we knew how.

I guess the loving acceptance I feel when I see my dad, and when I look at my daughter, is a direct result of the loving acceptance I've been able to find for myself, because never was there a desire to blame. It's just the way it's always been. Until now. I really never knew how to be a parent. Oh, I knew about taking care of their physical needs, and in a lot of ways I was a good parent.

When Greg & I were raising the kids, we were always home with them. I made dinner every night and they had a regular bedtime. I was conscious of the food I cooked, making sure they got their vegetables, and I was moderate about sugar and snacks. We enjoyed family outings like camping, and I never missed a school play, teachers conference or sporting event. I'm grateful that I can say that. I'm glad I was there "physically" for my kids, but I'm saddened that I was never there emotionally for them, that I wasn't a safe person for them to share who they really were.

It was always what I expected them to be, demanded of them. But, we made it through and no one died! One of my kids is in prison, though, and it was a process coming to terms with my part in that. Bottom line, I can't change anything that has already happened. I can't take back the years I was strict and controlling, unforgiving and unloving. I can't take responsibility for Jeremy's behavior either, especially now that he's over 21.

I regret many of the things I did raising the kids, but I've still got one at home, and it's never too late to show my kids who I really am. It's never too late to guide them and be an example for them. The one I've really had to work to forgive, is me. I've done that now. I've made amends to both the kids, and to my husband. I've owned my behavior, and there are no secrets in my life. I can't change the years, but I can let my children know that if I had it to do again, I would have done things differently.

As for the way I did things? I can recommend counseling! The biggest thing that was missing was communication, feelings. They weren't allowed to have any. I didn't allow myself to have any. So now we're learning, and I've found it's never too late. I can't imagine what my daughter would be like right now if I were still drinking.

She's almost 17 and she's a wonderful young lady. She values education and is planning to go to college. She has a part time job and is saving for a car. She goes out with friends but is never out late, and she's quit worrying about how they're doing their lives. She's calmer now. I don't worry about her, and I trust her.

That's not to say she won't make mistakes, or get into trouble, but I guarantee she'd be searching "out there" somewhere if we didn't have the kind of open communication we have today. It's not always perfect. I have my days and she has hers. But we always come back to a place of understanding and forgiveness. It's a miracle.

My relationship with my husband has been transformed as well. Aside from the "ugly years" and all we went through at that time, I thought we had a very good marriage, a loving relationship and mutual respect. That's what we have now. That's not the way it was. I didn't allow myself to have feelings, how could I allow him to have them. I had to be in control of everything, I wore the pants in the family and what I said went, or pay the price. It's sad to look back and see the real me, especially with full knowledge of the me I thought I was, but humility has been gracious.

The awareness of how I was always comes once I've changed. It's not quite so hard to recognize the way I "used" to be. It's harder to confront it through the veil of denial. I didn't know how to listen to my husband. Hell, I didn't know how to listen to anybody! I knew all the answers, I had all the plans, you had to listen to me! Ugh!

Twelve years of active alcoholism and suddenly I want my husband to tell me how he's feeling? Are you kidding?! It was never a safe place to do that before, why should he think it is now? We had to learn. Both of us. I had to learn to listen, and he had to learn not to react to the old me. He didn't know I'd changed, how could he? It took time.

He didn't understand what was happening, and neither did I. All he knew was he'd finally learned how to deal with me, how to make our marriage work, and I go and change all the rules. He didn't like it. I wasn't sure I did either. The promise of a better life was there, but was the journey going to be worth the struggle? We took it a day at a time.

We stopped trying to communicate if all we did was fight. We took time outs, came back and tried again, learning for the first time how to validate each other. Me validating him for the first time, and he trying to allow me to have my feelings without thinking I was forcing them on him, as I'd always done. Never before in our marriage had it been okay for each to have his own opinion, thoughts, feelings, and it's not always easy for a person to receive validation when it's never been given before.

In the beginning my husband would stutter when trying to express his feelings. He was so used to being cut off, criticized, or ignored. He wasn't going to suddenly start speaking freely from his heart without trepidation. Out of self-defense he went to Al-anon. We came to terms with the fact that alcoholism is, in fact, a family disease, and that we were all "in recovery." Things began to slowly improve. He started feeling safe with me, a little at a time. He tested the waters slowly at first, expressing a feeling then waiting for the reaction. He got none. He shared more.

I watched the light inside him shine brighter, and my love for him grew. I was saddened to see how long he had been silenced, but grateful he was free at last. It took us both awhile to learn to validate the other's feelings without feeling attacked. Both of us were pretty good at being so busy being under attack, we weren't able to hear the other person.

Once we realized if we were busy listening, understanding, and validating each other (even if we didn't agree, *especially* if we didn't), we didn't have time to be under attack. And more importantly for me, I learned that by making it about me, feeling attacked and reacting to that, I didn't allow him his feelings. Right or wrong I've learned, we're all entitled to our feelings.

I still remember the first time we made it through an entire conversation (formerly known as a fight), until we got to the heart of what each of us was feeling. It got stressful in a few places, and a couple of times we threatened to run, but we stayed and worked it through, allowing each other to be where we were, and loved each other even though we differed. If we aren't allowed to feel our feelings, how can we process them?

I think that's a problem in a lot of marriages. It's not my job to make my husband *be* anything, he already *is*. My job is to love him where he's at. I thought I believed in live and let live, but what I really thought was live and let live as long as you live my way. With that realization I had to look at some other glaring character defects. I had to come to terms with the fact that I was a very judgmental and critical person, still can be. It wasn't okay for you to have your own thoughts and opinions if they didn't agree with mine. I judged you for that.

I criticized the way people led their lives, raised their children, treated their spouses. AS IF IT WERE ANY OF MY BUSINESS!! One of the things I'm most grateful for in recovery is the ability to lovingly accept others where they are, without thinking I know a better way. I don't. Today I believe that we all make the best possible choices we can in each moment, given the circumstances of our lives which other people cannot understand. I thought I always felt that way.

There is a section of the first book under "Judge Not," where I talked about the choices people make in their lives. I wrote: "I try to be a compassionate person so I don't judge anyone for the choices they've made, especially since I don't know all the circumstances surrounding the decision at the time. Regardless of how wrong it appears to most of us, and even to them years later, the decisions were still made with the best knowledge and information they had *at the time*.

"Life is very complicated, with events having a chain reaction link to everything else that has happened, is happening, and will happen. It would be totally unfair for a person to judge another for his actions without first having walked a mile in his shoes. It's not enough to assess a situation by the way it appears. Appearances are deceiving."

As I've read over the first book, I'm amazed at some of what I wrote. I'm amazed to find sections titled, "Fear, Hope, Freedom, Anger, Recovery and Forgiveness." I always said it wasn't me writing the book. My fingers would fly across the keyboard and I would write for hours, reading later what I'd written seemingly for the first time. It seems my "source" knew all about recovery. I even have one section titled, "One Day at a Time."

It's amazing to me now that I'm really in recovery. I wrote a book called *Recovering From Life*. I had the right idea. I was divinely inspired in many ways, yet I wasn't yet ready to "hear" the words that were given to me. I thought I wrote the book for you, but it seems it was meant for me. I'm listening now.

I'm especially grateful that I can listen in my relationships, and that it's important to me what my loved ones are thinking and feeling. Now that I'm busy living my own life and feeling my own feelings, it's nice to have healthy relationships where I can be validated as well. I get to feel what I'm feeling, be where I'm at, instead of worrying about where I think you should be. Whew! It only gets easier.

Chapter 25

GRATITUDE

Seeptember 6, 1996. Today I feel full of gratitude, amazed at life. I had the opportunity to spend seven days with an old friend who drinks like I used to. It was the most wonderful experience, and I remembered so much about myself, about this disease, and most importantly, about my recovery. My "spiritual condition" is much better than I give myself credit for, and maybe that was the most important lesson, or message, of all. I feel good about me.

I feel good about the choices I'm making in my life today. *My* life. Not yours, not my husband's, not my children's, not the alcoholics in my life, but my life. It's so simple. I'm amazed. Why did I insist on making my life complicated, all my life, all the while thinking I had everything running so smoothly? Who cares? That's the other thing I know today. It's not important what I did, what I used to be like, or who I was before I began to recover.

It's not important who you used to be, or what you did, or who you are now. The only thing that matters is who I am today, and who you are when we're together. I feel free from the past. Thanks to this incredible program of recovery, started by two men who wanted more for their lives than alcoholism/addiction could offer. Two men, 60 years ago, who believed what worked for one man, could work for all mankind. And they were right.

But it takes "rigorous honesty," and that's a hard one. Denial is an amazing thing, and for the life of me I didn't know I was as dishonest as I was. God knows I wasn't going to get any further in my recovery (a year and a half into it) if I didn't look a little closer at the guidelines of this program, then look a little closer at myself and how I was working my program, then get real about what's going on with me.

I was so good at running, and it's amazing how little a person can accomplish while keeping so busy. But I wasn't busy, I was just working real hard to make it look like I was busy. I was lying to myself and I believed it. Well, part of me, the part that's good at masking real feelings, and avoiding responsibility. But just the willingness to get honest starts the process.

Life used to catch me off guard, I would just say whatever came to my mind. With my children I always immediately said no, no matter what they were asking. There were times I quickly realized that maybe they could do it, but many times my pride wouldn't let me admit I was wrong.

Then I did "change my mind," and would say to the kids, well, I guess maybe that would be okay, and they would be so excited. I remember Megan was about four or five, and asked if a friend could spend the night. I said no, of course, and she was always so good to take the answer (as if fear of the wrath of me had nothing to do with that), then I went downstairs.

I thought about it, and decided, oh, why not? I was trying to soften up as a mother even then, I just wasn't very good at it for several more years. I came back upstairs and said, I guess she can stay over. Megan smiled big and turned to her friend and said, "I told you sometimes she changes her mind."

It made me smile, and I remember that was a turning point. It felt good to be nice. I didn't have to be so strict. I quit saying no right away. I wouldn't answer right at first. Then I was amazed at how often I could say yes to them. It made life much easier. I wish I could raise Megan & Jeremy over again, well, kind of. I love my life today. I love that my baby is 16 (after I cried over it), and that Greg & I are still young, and now we're free to do whatever we want to do.

I wouldn't change my life today for anything in the world. I know I'm right where I'm supposed to be. I guess if I were to say anything about the past, I can say I wish I would have known then what I know now, but I didn't. Thank God I do now, because the *rest* of my life is going to be different. And it's because I vowed to get honest. I had to entertain the idea that just maybe, I might have been wrong about a few things.

I educated myself on the disease of alcoholism (as did my then 14 year old daughter when she wrote a paper on it for school), and I researched the effects of alcohol on the human body, and quit lying to myself about the harm I was doing to myself. I threw out all the excuses and justification for drinking, and got down to the challenging task of figuring out why I was running. I'm still not clear on a lot of the whys, but I'm learning to recognize when I'm running and I can learn to stay where I'm at, and look at what's going on with me.

I have faith and trust like I've never known. Acceptance. I love that word, and that's what I have today. It makes life so much easier. I guess you could say I'm not a fighter anymore. I didn't know I was one, but boy, was I! I fought life. I fought change. I fought myself! All the while thinking I was in control, doing everything the best possible way it could be done, *my* way. Thank God those days are over!

Today especially, I feel full of gratitude, aware of the wonders of life, and happy to be alive in these times. As I rode back from my meeting along the bay, I stopped to look at the water. There were a few fishing boats out there, but mostly it was quiet and peaceful. It's the week after Labor Day and even the lifeguard has probably gone back to school. It was kind of an awareness that this beautiful weather, the warm breeze, and the ride to meetings on my bike, would soon end.

That's okay with me, I love all the seasons, that's why I live in the north, but we've had a different kind of summer, never very hot (extremely rare for Michigan), temperatures in the 70's, clear days with beautiful blue skies, I mean it just doesn't get any better than that. But winter was long, it began in November and ended in May, and spring was more like fall and lasted well into summer, and it just doesn't seem like it should be fall again so soon.

After spending a week with a drinker (I haven't had to smell booze in awhile-yuk), I feel pretty good about who I am. I'm stronger than I thought I was, and I'm doing better than I've given myself credit for.

My husband is out of town. I used to drink more when he was gone. I would never have admitted that, but it's true. I didn't have my "keeper" watching over me. I stayed out of the bar as much as possible that last year, except when I was working, but I drank a lot more at home than I would have if he were here.

That's pretty sad really, especially because I love him so much and didn't like it when he was away. But the alcoholic in me liked it. I guess I didn't think it mattered that my daughter was here, what was she going to say? Even when I didn't drink in front of her, didn't I think she could smell it?

I didn't think about that, never did. She was probably so used to my smell it was normal to her. Being around drinking again was a rude awakening, and thank God those days are gone for me. I must have smelled like a brewery most of the time, I don't know how my husband stood it. Well, I know how he stood it for awhile, he drank with me, but that only lasted a couple of years, and he never drank like I did. He usually had one, and then I think he just watched out for me. But once he quit drinking and I didn't, I don't know how he stood it.

That's another reason I feel so good about being sober. I can try to make it up to him for all the years of my drinking, and I know he forgives me. I also know he loves the new me. It was a little shaky for us in early recovery, but that's because he didn't know that alcoholism is a family disease, and that recovery is necessary for all members in an alcoholic home.

September 9, 1996

I was thinking about how we're probably all addicts. Whether our "drug of choice" is alcohol, food, relationships, work, shopping, busy-ness, whatever, the behavior of an addict is much the same, regardless of what we use to run away or numb the pain. I heard early on in meetings to look for the similarities not the differences. I've seen why that is so important.

Recovery is what we have in common, how we got here isn't nearly as important as what we do from now on. I remember a young girl in treatment who said she didn't really get anything out of AA because she's not an alcoholic. She said she gets more out of NA because drugs were her problem. She couldn't see that she & I were no different, that where I picked up alcohol (mostly) to numb the pain, she chose a different pain killer.

I used to watch her in AA meetings. She would roll her eyes, look restless, fidget in her seat, and generally looked bored. She wasn't listening, couldn't "relate." I couldn't help but feel that this young woman had a slim chance of staying in recovery. I had to be willing to take a look at the bare me, what I was left with after the drugs and alcohol were taken away. What I'd begun with before I ever picked up a drink.

It just so happened that alcohol was my primary drug of choice, but I obsessed over many things during those years. It's not important what drugs I did, how much alcohol I drank or for how many years, it's about my life and recovery *after* all of that. It's my recovery that's important to me today, not the pain that got me here. I had to go through the pain before I could get to where I am today, but now I can concentrate on my recovery.

I had to work the steps, I had to especially do a thorough fourth step. I was never going to get beyond the addiction if I didn't do the work, if I wasn't willing to take a look at my life, all of it, and then be willing to take responsibility, and make amends where possible.

It wasn't fun. I didn't want to go back to some of those places. I wanted to forget about a lot of things, but they weren't going to be forgotten. I was never really going to be free until I was willing to take the suggestions of a couple of boozers who wanted to get sober over 60 years ago. They lined it all out. They even wrote it in steps, clear cut directions to follow. "Here are the steps we took....."

It worked for them, and it's worked for thousands upon thousands since then. They claimed that *no one* would fail if they *thoroughly* followed their path. I wasn't willing to *thoroughly* follow their path for about the first year and a half. I thought I was, and I did real well looking back. I stayed sober and I continued to heal, although slowly.

I would move forward, fall back, move forward fall back, until finally I kept hitting a wall and could not move forward. I had to get serious, I had to get honest, I had to do a fourth step! Now that I have, I kick my butt for running for so long, and I've become somewhat of an advocate for working the steps, because it's impossible to move ahead with recovery and life until we do. Ultimately, I believe, we'll end up drinking or drugging again. That just isn't an option for me today.

September 10, 1996

The process of writing, re-writing, and putting together this book is an incredible experience. I've been overcome with emotion a lot lately. The gratitude I feel in my heart is incredible. I finally love myself enough to know I deserve a good life.

Chapter 26

A WAY OF LIFE

O ctober 5, 1996. (Women's Retreat) - I've heard everything I needed to hear. I feel so good about who I am, where I am, and where I'm going. I don't know how I could doubt all the things I've doubted, how I could fear all I've feared. I'm filled with such hope for my life, my writing. I feel so blessed.

It seems that all the doubts and fears I've had in the past month are no longer there. Nothing has changed and everything has changed. I'm not worried about our finances, Christmas, groceries, or Gregory's job. I trust. I don't feel pressured or obligated to get a job (other than the ones I have as writer, mother, wife, homemaker and friend). I feel free.

I'm sitting on the dock, overlooking a little lake. It's a beautiful fall day. The sun is shining, the water is beautiful and the birds are singing. I have my jacket with me, but I don't need it. The sun feels warm on my face, the breeze is slight, and while not warm, it's not cold either. It's like me today, it just is.

The trees surrounding the lake are just beginning to show a slight change in color, but most of them are still lush and green. The sun shining through scattered clouds paint a picture in the sky that could be framed. The gentle flow of water beneath the dock, creates a calm inside me and a peace I've searched my whole life for.

How could I have dulled my senses all those years, with the delusion I was enhancing them? I wouldn't trade this feeling or this day for all the riches in the world. This feeling of peace in my soul is what I searched in the bottle for all those years.

I thought I could find what I was looking for, create what I thought I wanted my life to be, and yet I was never going to find it until I quit searching "out there." It's been "in here" all along, and all my years of abuses with drugs and alcohol, food, work, and relationships, only prolonged the discovery.

I will quiet the voice in me that questions, that doubts, that fears, and nurture the one that knows. I know I'll be afraid again, I'm sure I'll feel unworthy, but I'm not going to let it stop me again. I don't have to do everything today. I can take baby steps when necessary and leaps when I'm able, and I will always know I'm where I need to be.

I've done the work I needed to do to love myself enough to do it. At least for today, and hopefully again tomorrow, I'm going to live in the moment, and leave the past in the past, and the future up ahead. It doesn't feel so scary that way. It isn't. It seems so simple when I'm aware. Help me stay aware!

November 3, 1996- I dreamed I was with my sister. We were on an island or something, and there were lots of people. She was very angry and unapproachable, like I used to be. She was mad because she didn't have any pot to smoke. She was taking it out on me, on everybody. She was so angry.

Next she's on a bicycle, riding away from me. I can't keep up with her. I'm running after her, trying to catch her; but she's so far ahead. I feel abandoned and left out. I know she's making plans for dinner and stuff with other people, but I'm not included. I feel really panicked at one point. I want to cry and feel sorry for myself because she's leaving me behind.

Then I'm walking in a ditch filled with branches and all sorts of debris. It is hard to get through. It's also very dark and I can't see where I'm going. There are people walking in the ditch toward me. I can feel a small child at my legs. I help him get around me, as I try to get out of the ditch and back onto the road where I can try again to catch up to my sister.

Then I'm in the room I'm staying in. There are three kittens, but I can't enjoy them, because I'm too upset about being left out. Susie is around and she too is making plans that don't include me. I feel so lost and afraid in this apartment. The kittens make me smile, but I have an overwhelming sense of fear at being left alone.

Then Susie kind of indicates that maybe I can go with her and her date, at least to dinner. We decide to ride bikes because it's easier than trying to drive the car in this busy tourist town. I'm in the bathroom, getting ready. My hair is cut short, but I didn't seem to be shocked by this. I am a little surprised, but I like it. It is easy to comb and just go. (In reality the thought of cutting my hair terrifies me.)

I found this dream to be powerful. My sister represented the angry addict in me, the one that's mad about the fact I can't "get high." That part is leaving me. Abandonment relates to leaving behind my old self, a release from control of the old self, which is very good news, even though it doesn't feel that way. The ditch and debris represent a clearing away, making my way through, including helping (loving) my inner child.

The kittens represent the independent me. I am able to care for myself. Three relates to my body, mind and soul, or the physical, emotional and spiritual sides of myself. I'm not able to pay as much attention to them as I would like because I'm too worried about being left out, which tells me I need to work on my issues so I can give full attention to the things that are important.

Again, the bicycle represents self-propulsion, an ability to make it on my own, which was preferable to taking the car (ego). The hair relates to external parts of my internal nature. What am I covering? The style, easy to fix and go, relates to keeping it simple.

November 5, 1996

Everything started happening in mid-October. I started an AWOL group in September, which stands for A Way Of Life, and is an extensive study of the twelve steps. We were on Step Four, I knew that a lot of stuff would be coming up for me, always does when we're working on fourth step stuff. But since this was not my first thorough one, the last one being the real cleanup of my past, I was not at all frightened or intimidated like I was with that last one. I got such tremendous relief after having completed it, I couldn't believe it.

I didn't really think I could ever get to a place where I didn't have shame about my past, but it happened. It was incredible, and I've been thankful ever since. Just like it says in the Big Book, I felt an incredible freedom from my past, and my pain, and I felt a new surge of life in me. Everything that happened after that point, has only been growth in this program I call life.

Because of that, I was actually looking forward to doing another 4th step, although I must say that at first I didn't think there would be that much to write, since my last one was 87 pages long. But, again I was amazed, and this one, although very different from the last, was very long too. Now I was ready to deal with character defects. I couldn't get to that point before because I had so much baggage from my past, too many regrets, too much shame.

I had to get some peace with where I'd come from before I could look at where I am. I was now ready to do that. We spent two weeks on Step 4 and one on Step 5, and during those three weeks I struggled like you wouldn't believe. Old thoughts, old defects, old everything began to reappear, and not only did it throw me totally off guard, I was sure it meant I was backsliding, failing in a sense at my own recovery.

It was as if the old, sick me, had come back and was invading my body and my life. I was again at odds with my daughter, and although I tried to hide it, I struggled, and I'm sure she sensed something wasn't right. I was filled with fear like I haven't felt since early recovery, and before. I felt the old, controlling side of me again, and I became way too aware and concerned with how others were living their lives.

I felt irritable, easily frustrated, and spent most of those couple of weeks angry, out of sorts, and exhausted! I was talking about it at meetings, but I kept finding myself saying, I don't know what's going on with me. As frightened, and frustrated as I was during that time, there was a tiny part of me, somewhere deep inside, that trusted what was happening. It was much smaller than the fear and anger, but it kept me working my program to the best of my ability, it kept me going to all my meetings, and praying.

It felt like such hard work. I wanted to run so bad. I fell into a lot of old behaviors. I found myself wanting to get high again. I began overeating again, feeling too full most of the time, and yet still thinking of what I could eat next. That horrible feeling of being so full and yet feeling so empty, that you continue to try to fill up, creating an even deeper feeling of void, and disappointment, and sickness.

It was happening all around me and I couldn't seem to stop it. I was taken right back to the 70's with my eating disorder, and again felt out of control. I didn't think I would ever have to deal with this again. While part of me was being pretty hard on myself, part of me wasn't. Part of me was accepting it, and trying to understand what was really going on. Part of me trusted it was growth, not deterioration, that was happening.

I haven't had to work so hard at serenity since early recovery. I haven't felt like I was white knuckling it, or "unraveling" since then either. It was so scary to me, and yet somehow I knew it was a good thing.

I've learned enough in this program to know that whatever needs to come up will be there, and the fact that "old" stuff was reappearing, told me that I hadn't *really* let go of a lot of it. If that were the case, I told myself, then let's deal with it now! It was another lesson in humility for me, because I thought I was doing so good. I guess too good, and I needed to be reminded that I will never be done growing. And that's okay.

Now it's okay. Now that I'm not struggling like I was, I can say it's okay, but boy, when I was in the midst of it, it was not okay. The whole thing caught me off guard, and didn't make a lot of sense, because this 4th step was a very positive experience. I enjoyed taking a thorough inventory, recognizing how far I've come, yet realizing where I need work. I was eager to do my 5th step, this time with my sponsor.

I met with her on the morning before class. That night we read Step 5 and discussed it, and were assigned Step 6 for the next week. But I didn't get the same "relief" I got the first time. Partly I know because I didn't have all the garbage to dump like I did before. I didn't need to be restored to dignity like I did the first time. I didn't get the same surge of spirituality either, and somehow felt I hadn't done it right, or that I'd missed something.

Nothing was missing. It was perfect. This time around things were exactly the way they were supposed to be, and now that I've processed the whole thing, I can see that. It was just a continuation of the feelings I'd been having for a couple of weeks. Nothing felt right, everything felt like a struggle. It wasn't until this past week, being on Step 6, and doing the readings, that I discovered what was really going on, and the awareness was amazing.

The little "preview" of Step 6, in the *Twelve Steps and Twelve Traditions*, said it all. I read, "Were entirely ready to have God remove all these defects of character. Step Six necessary to spiritual growth. The beginning of a lifetime job. Recognition of difference between striving for objective—-and perfection. Why we must keep trying. 'Being ready' is all-important. Necessity of taking action. Delay is dangerous. Rebellion may be fatal. Point at which we abandon limited objectives and move toward God's will for us."

Wow. I was amazed. I felt a surge of something rush through my body and a great sigh of relief. That's it! It's all been part of working these steps! It's all been growth! A good thing! Not backsliding at all, just God's way of revealing some things to me so that I might look at them one last time, making completely sure I'm entirely ready to have them removed. How incredible. What a gift. This is the part of the promises that makes sense to me now; we will be amazed before we are halfway through. The steps, it seemed, were working me.

I spent some quality time with God this morning, and I did a 4th & 5th Step about the past few weeks, and told Him I was entirely ready to have these defects of character removed. This past weekend I spent with the old me. I guess I had to. I indulged in all kinds of unhealthy behavior. The only thing I didn't do was drink or smoke, but I was definitely spending time with an old, familiar, and unhealthy, me.

That was okay too, because I know it was a farewell, a saying good-bye. There was grief and sadness associated with the process. My old self came back one last time, and I loved her, and let her go. Today I asked God to help me proceed with the new me, toward His will for me and my life, and I feel strengthened. Sad in a way, yet happy, relieved. Vulnerable, yet protected. I feel at peace, I feel serenity, I feel love for myself, and I feel hope for this new way of life.

Chapter 27

FEAR AND FRUSTRATION

November 5, 1996 - I dreamed I was in a house. There were other people around. I had a baby in my arms. The sweetest baby you've ever seen. She slept comfortably in my arms. I held her for the longest time, it was the most precious feeling I've ever felt. It was safety, security, and nurturing. I was trying to climb a stairwell or something and I had to lift her up to get through. She awoke, so I didn't try to go up.

This dream tells me that I'm getting very comfortable with my inner child, the infant self of me. I'm learning to nurture and love myself and that feels so good. When I try to "climb," and the baby begins to wake up, I stop, which tells me I'm not quite ready to disturb things, in other words, I don't want to go any further right now (kind of like "let sleeping dogs lie").

November 16, 1996 - Whew! What a frustrating dream! It started with some old friends. We were sitting at a picnic table, getting ready to leave after spending time together, a weekend or whatever. I had a bunch of awkward stuff to carry, like skis and volleyball poles. I had enough time to return the stuff and get home to get Megan to work.

I headed right to where I needed to go, but when I got to the front of the line for the volleyball poles, the guy abruptly said, "These aren't ours!" I was going to argue but then remembered that I had bought them, so of course they weren't rentals. I could keep them. It was kind of a hassle after waiting in line, but no problem. Then I was off to return the skis.

Everything was hard to carry. I just wanted to get rid of it and get home. I was running out of time. Here's where the frustration begins. The place where I had rented the skis in the first place (a long line of tables in an open area) was not where I had to return them. The rest of the dream consisted of the most frustrating and scary time I've had.

The area was a combination of a marketplace, carnival (no rides), and college campus. I would go in one building, maneuvering all this stuff, and come out another side, always expecting to recognize where I was, but always feeling more and more confused and lost. Then I realized that among all the stuff I was carrying, had to carry, I didn't have my purse. Panic! I had lost my purse and I really needed it. I had no idea where I could have lost it or who might have found it.

I was very much aware that it was past the time I was supposed to have been home to get Megan to work. Gregory would wonder what had happened to me. In the dream I felt frustrated and afraid. I didn't know what I was going to do. I couldn't seem to find my way back to where I had started, so I could tell where I was and where I needed to be. Somehow I kept going in circles, working really hard to hold onto all this "stuff," which kept slipping out of my arms. I would have to stop and rearrange it all to carry it.

I couldn't seem to get to where I needed to be. Finally I saw a familiar face. I desperately asked her for help with finding the ski place. She began leading me through buildings and stores. We went in one door, out the back, and into an alley. She seemed lost too. Then we'd turn around and go back the other way. Eventually, I lost her too. Now I was really scared and frustrated.

I remember worrying about my purse. It seemed to be a big loss. I tried to reassure myself that my drivers license was in there with my picture on it and my address. Maybe someone would call me with it or send it back to me. I decided not to worry about that right now. I just needed to find a phone and some money to call Gregory. Someone needed to come and get me. Clearly I couldn't find my way myself. This surprised me, since I'm usually pretty good at taking care of myself and finding where I need to go.

For some reason I had a dime in my pocket. I knew I needed to find another dime before I could make a phone call. I was walking across the lawn, a large patch of grass between buildings, like on a college campus. I saw a phone over on a building. It seemed so far away. I figured if I kept walking the direction I was, there would be a closer phone. A man rode by on a bike, kind of like a vagrant. I asked him if I could borrow a dime. He ignored me and continued on his way. Then a lady was walking toward me. By this time I was desperate, crying. I asked her if I could please borrow a dime. I'd lost my purse and my way and needed help. She was very sweet and gave me a dime.

I saw a phone up ahead. I got the other dime out of my pocket, after setting all the "stuff" on the ground, and started to use the phone. I looked down at everything, there was a lot—skis, a coat, some clothes, the poles. Underneath I could see my purse. I thought I'd lost it, but I hadn't. Relief. It gave me hope.

I put the two dimes in the phone, realizing that now it costs a quarter. I hoped a miracle would happen and the call would go through. I dialed the wrong number but hoped Gregory would somehow answer anyway. When no one answered, I hung up, realizing that if they did answer and it was the wrong number I would lose my money. I re-dialed and Gregory answered. He asked if I was lost. I said he had no idea how lost. I was crying and asked if he'd been able to get Megan to work. He said she decided not to go. This made me a little mad, but it was the least of my worries at this point.

I remember being able to see what used to be water in the background, the lake or something. Now it was a ski mountain. It looked gnarly, with huge moguls. It was snowing quite fiercely on the mountain. It seemed to be summer where I was. People were skiing the moguls like pros. It was out of place and character for where I was, but I thought, "Oh well, there's a big ski hill where there shouldn't be." That too, was the least of my worries at this point.

I cried and told Gregory I was staying right where I was. I had given up on thinking I could get myself out of this. Someone would have to come and get me. The next thing I remember, Gregory is waking me up with coffee, saving me from this terrible nightmare! I had a headache!

This dream was revealing in that it told me I was still trying to carry too much stuff, still trying to find my own way, and continue searching, even when all seems lost. Again I'm running late, which tells me I'm wasting valuable time. I lose my purse, which tells me I still worry about losing something of value. But after awhile I surrender, I know I need help and that I can't do this on my own. I ask for help. I find my purse, which reminds me that I haven't lost anything. The feeling I had about the ski hill being somewhere it shouldn't, was one of acceptance. The whole dream ended with me surrendering and accepting where I was, and that I needed help. (I can't do this on my own.)

November 22, 1996 - I don't remember too much about last night's dream except that I was on a motorcycle. I lost control or something, only I wasn't on it anymore. It went flying through the air and landed in someone's yard. I was in shock that the motorcycle could fly that far. I went over to get it out of the yard. The headlight was broken off and something else. I picked up the pieces and got on and rode away.

Well, I see I've moved from bicycles to motorcycles; where in my life do I want to be more masterful? But it's out of control which tells me I'm not quite ready for the power. The headlight represents vision, illumination. It's broken, but not lost. I still have work to do regarding mastering my own life, my vision. I'm not quite ready for the power.

November 23, 1996 - I dreamed I was outside of the recovery center. A woman came running out to greet me. It was Charlotte Carter, only really it wasn't, it just looked like her. She thought I was someone else as well. Just seeing someone who looked like Charlotte made me very sad. I took off on my bike, pedaling as fast as I could to a place where I knew I could grieve for her, because I never had.

I rode my bike up some stairs, then set it down and collapsed on the stairs. I began to cry and grieve, something I'd never allowed myself to do over the loss of Charlotte. Then she was there with me, comforting me, putting her arm around me, and allowing me to cry for her! It didn't seem at all strange to me that she was there. I knew she was really gone. It felt good to cry about her death, and it was wonderful to see her again!

This dream was quite clear to me. Charlotte was the minister at church, the one who I shared many dreams with. She was instrumental in leading me into dream work. She died earlier this year, and because she had moved away prior to her death, it was easy for me to pretend she wasn't really gone. I had never allowed myself to feel the loss, which she helped me do in the dream. It was a wonderful gift.

November 24, 1996 - I awoke very disturbed about a dream that frightened me. I felt so scared and unsafe. In the dream I was looking out my window. My husband was with me. There were people, one after the other, going down the sidewalk in front of our house. They were zombies, very methodically strolling by, very threatening. I was scared.

My cat wanted to go out. I didn't want to let her out, but I knew she had to go. She just sat outside the door. I called to her to come back inside, so I could lock the doors. I was afraid for her safety. By then the zombies had moved closer to the house and were coming up onto the porch from the side one-by-one. They were strolling in front of the window.

I was terrified and really wanted to get Gizzie back inside. Then I heard a dog and saw it jump from the side. All I heard was a slight sound coming from my cat. I didn't want to believe it, but I knew that the dog had gotten Gizzie. I woke up. It was terrible. I had such an uneasy feeling. I didn't want to go back to sleep.

I got up and went to the bathroom. It wasn't until I glanced out my window that a wave of relief came over me as I remembered where I was and what my life is like. Suddenly, I could remind myself that it was only a dream. I really am not, nor do I have to be, that frightened in my life. I was able to go back to sleep, having shaken off the dream.

This dream was about my fears. The zombies represent living death. What am I afraid to let go of? Gizzie represents the independent side of me, which is most likely what I'm afraid to let go of.

Later I dreamed that I was at a house with a bunch of people, like a meeting. A friend in the program was with me. We were outside on motorcycles. She was ahead of me and someone was between us. It was dark and none of us had our headlights on. I was nervous that I would get in an accident, yet I couldn't find out how to turn the lights on. I could see that Lynn couldn't turn her lights on either. I also couldn't remember how to drive the thing and I couldn't get it out of first gear. I was really frustrated.

It seems I'm still not ready for the motorcycle, at least not at full power (can't get out of first gear). I am having trouble with my vision. It's dark, but I keep moving. Fear kept me moving slowly as I tried to figure out how to turn the lights on. I know I'm still afraid of my own power, and the dream confirms it.

November 26, 1996 - I dreamed I was holding and loving a baby. It felt so good. He was so precious. Holding this child was the greatest feeling in the world. I don't know if he was mine or not, but I sure loved him.

I was with a bunch of people. We were in a big hall or something. There was going to be some kind of show. There were a bunch of women that were going to be modeling wedding dresses. I was going to model one as well. When I finally showed up at the last minute and put my dress on, I realized it was completely sheer on the sides and in spots. I was naked underneath.

I was trying to find something to cover myself with. I was hiding behind a wall from a couple of guys who were trying to look. I went into the bathroom to get a towel to cover my lower half when a hand reached out from the lower cupboard and grabbed my butt. I ran from the bathroom with the towel around me.

I'm nurturing and loving a baby, and it feels so good. I'm beginning to really love and nurture myself in my recovery, so that makes sense. Again, I'm dreaming about being partially naked in public, which relates to my fear of being exposed, now that I'm finishing the book. There's an underlying sense of fear in my dreams and in my life, and I'm aware of it, but it's not stopping me.

Chapter 28

GROWING UP

December 13, 1996. I feel overwhelming gratitude. An incredible feeling of humility and grace, and wonder. I found myself thinking about where I've come from, the mistakes I've made, the regrets I have, and I feel total acceptance about my past. Another one of the promises has come true for me, the one which says we will not regret the past nor wish to shut the door on it.

For a long time that was not true for me, and I didn't think it ever could be, but it is now. The feeling of gratitude for where I am now, and where my life is heading, gave me an incredible feeling of humility. I thought about a wonderful recovering person I've met in AA, who has been through a life that most of us could not even imagine, and yet she is healthy and strong today, and often cries tears of gratitude for the miracle that is her life.

I could relate to those tears of gratitude, and my own eyes filled with tears as I realized that *this kind of gratitude could not be felt if I did not remember the pain.* The meaning of that promise was fully realized at that moment, and it was a spiritual awakening. I have had so much healing. I have so much healing to do. But I'm okay where I am right now. I trust that I always will be.

That's not to say I won't be somewhere emotionally or spiritually, physically even, that I'd rather not be, but it does mean that with acceptance I can be okay with it. I guess if I could think of a word to describe this feeling it would be trust, and it feels good. All I have to do to keep it, is stay in the moment. That was something I could never do, I was either regretting the past or fearing the future. It's pretty easy for me most of the time. So much easier than trying to run the world!

An old behavior I've been acting out lately is codependence, worry. I was noticing some unhealthy behaviors in my daughter as well as in myself, and I was feeling helpless with both situations. She's been really codependent with her friends again, way too wrapped up in what they're doing, and she doesn't think they're doing it right.

She's been physically sick too. Not enough to get her down, but she can't seem to shake this cough and cold, even with medication, so I know she's lacking peace and serenity in her life. And of course, the codependent in me wants to take blame for that, since she learned it by watching me, and I want to fix it. Thus, the dream I had.

Megan and I were about to get on a ride. Actually it was an inner tube being pulled by a boat. It was a fast ride, dangerous even. I realized once we were on it and being pulled, that we didn't have our life jackets on. We were being pulled by a speedboat over rapids. It was the roughest river you could ever be on. I was freaked out that we didn't have life vests on. I thought if we fell off this thing we were going to drown.

I knew I could tread water and keep myself afloat, barely. But I knew there was no way I could keep both of us up if Megan grabbed a hold of me, which was very likely since she doesn't like water very much in the first place. Just then we were both thrown from the tube. We slammed into the water and went way under. I was surprised that we came to the top so fast. I was relieved to have my head above water.

Just as I was about to worry what we would do, I saw the inner tube right in front of me. I lifted Megan up and laid her across it so she could rest. She was tired. She was about ten or eleven in my dream (she's almost seventeen). I held onto the tube and rested in the water until help came, which I knew it would. The water was calm once we were in it.

This dream told me a lot of things, and helped me a lot. First of all, it obviously told me that I couldn't save my daughter, I can barely tread water myself. And that if I try to save her, we'll both drown. I also realized from the dream that I think of her as younger than she is, that she's not my little girl anymore, she's a big girl and has to save herself.

The other thing the dream told me was that we would be safe. Even though we got slammed into the water, we didn't get hurt. We went deep under the water, but we came up fast, before we could run out of air, and when we came up, the life preserver was right within our reach. The water was calm once we were in it. In other words, no matter how rough the water gets, it will always be calm at the end, and although we might get slammed a few times, we're not going to drown.

I talked to Megan about the dream, and about what I've noticed going on with her. She's so much like me, it helps her when I tell her about me. I'm just learning this stuff, and she can learn it too. She knows there's hope. She knows that as high-strung and uptight as she might feel, there's a way to relax, to be free from worry. I never knew that. She believes there's a different way, so that's all it takes. The dream reminded me that we're both going to be okay. I just have to take care of me. God is taking care of both of us.

December 15, 1996

I've figured something out. Before I quit drinking, my writing was always positive. I considered myself a writer of spiritual and inspirational material. When I was finally re-reading over the years, as the book was coming together, I discovered how BORING my writing during that time was. Well, that was my life during my drinking years. If you would have told me that, I would have denied it vehemently. But there it was in ink.

I thought I was doing so great, accomplishing my goals, living my dreams. No, I was just always on the edge of discovery. All the writing was, "I've figured it out," or "now I've got it!" Again and again and again. It was the weight issue for years. I always wanted to lose that last 10 pounds. It was the money issue for years. Time and again I had it figured out. But nothing ever changed.

The realization I had this morning was, I haven't been able to write about how really great recovery is. It was so rough in the beginning, that first year or so was hell, but now it's getting really good. I've worked a twelve step program diligently, sometimes stubbornly, sometimes regretfully, but it's paid off. I continue to incorporate it into my life. All the promises are true for me today, but I've been afraid to write about it.

In my writings before 1994, I wouldn't allow myself to write much about negative things, because I wanted everything to "look good." I discovered that my writings were not real. Everything was the way I hoped it would be, and much of it was, but the parts that weren't? Denial. So now I'm out of denial and willing to look at things. I realize I've been afraid to write about positive stuff, because at some level I'm afraid of appearing pollyannaish, like I see in my old writings.

But things are different for me today, and I need to write about that, I need to talk about it. That is, after all, the whole purpose of the book from the very beginning. *Recovering From Life* was always meant to be a triumphant story, a message of hope, but the real hope was never really there. It is now. I'm learning how to do life, with laughter and joy. I'm still in denial about some things, I still have work to do, and will always have work to do. But I don't have to worry about anything but today, today. I can enjoy each day, work through each challenge, and gain strength because I know I'm capable, and I am worthy.

I have to keep telling myself that, because a big part of me doesn't feel I am. But a small part does, so I'm going to fake it till I make it. It gets easier. It always gets easier. I've heard people in the program say it doesn't get any easier. It gets better they say, but it doesn't get easier. It gets easier for me every day. Some days are difficult. I have learning days, but that's what they are, days to learn more about myself. I'm glad when they're over. Some days are going to be hard, but as long as I stay sober, life gets easier. Staying sober is much easier than getting sober.

December 18, 1996

I'm in a phase where I'm not remembering my dreams real well, but just the small part I do remember has great meaning for me.

I was in a basement of some kind. The cement was very rough and uneven. I was looking around, checking it out. I saw a weird kind of spider that I'd never seen before. I hollered up at Gregory, "There's a spider down here."

As I turned to go upstairs I noticed, almost hidden and blended in with the rocks, was a little mouse. He was so tiny and cute. He was nibbling away at something he held in his hands, just chowing down. I turned and hollered up to Greg, "There's mice too."

Spiders represent patience, organization, the dark feminine force, the spinner of webs. They also represent fear to me (I don't like them). But the little mouse was most significant with what's been going on with me lately. When I looked it up it said, meek nature, quiet, minor problems, inner feelings, shyness. What small troubles are gnawing away at me?

That blew me away. I've been feeling like something was literally gnawing away at me, especially since I'm chewing my fingernails, so that was confirmed, I'm not crazy. But the best news this dream brought was the realization that this "something" I've been running from isn't a big thing after all, in fact it's a very little thing, represented by the smaller than average mouse.

It's about my unconscious fear, represented by the basement. I figured as much, but the dream confirmed it, and since it indicated what a small problem this is, it gives me the courage to move through it. It's just a little mouse, not worth all the attention I've given it. It's about the writing, the book. I know it's about the fear I have of revealing the real me. I've received so much healing, and I love who I am today, but I'm not at all proud of some of the things I've done, *a lot* of the things I've done.

I'm grateful for my life and my experiences because of what they've taught me, and I'm especially grateful that I'm not the same person I was before, but there's definitely a part of me that fears exposure (thus the dreams about being partially naked). There's the part that says, "Your daughter, nieces and nephews, and grandparents are going to read this."

I'm sure that's what most of this recent fear is all about. I was getting so close to actually putting this book together. I was feeling good every day with what I had accomplished. I was having a ball! Then I fall face first into the fear and I stop writing. I know that's what's going on.

As hard as I've worked at affirming what other people think of me is none of my business, still I want everyone to like me, I don't want anyone to judge me or my life. I would like it if I hadn't done some of the things I did. But I've learned honesty, and acceptance. I'm okay with who I am today, and what other people think of me *is* none of my business!

When I think of other recovering people reading my book, it feels good, and I remind myself of another one of the promises: no matter how far down the scale we've gone, we see how our experiences can benefit others. I know that it helped me deal with some of the darker stuff when I talked with people who had the same shame. I could love and forgive others for what they had done, but I didn't know how to love and forgive myself. Others did it for me, until I could do it for myself. They loved me until I could love myself. We do that for each other.

Chapter 29

SEARCH FOR SERENITY

December 18, 1996. So much has changed since I quit drinking, I can hardly believe it. I've said it before, no one but God & I truly know the extent of the transformation. I'm so grateful for the changes, even if I did kick and scream for awhile. I look around my house today, it's a mess. And that's a cool feeling (in a sick sort of way), because the gift is in the mess. No matter that I prefer my house to be in order, it's okay the way it is, for now.

It was never okay for now, it had to be clean, a place for everything and everything in its place. There were no exceptions, stress or no stress. Today I don't have that stress because I don't have the same expectations for myself. I want a clean house, and I will clean my house, but it's okay that I'm writing instead, it's okay that I'm finishing this book, and that's my job right now. My main job.

My other job *is* taking care of my family, cooking dinner, doing laundry and washing dishes, and I love that part of my life. I love being a homemaker, it's not always easy, and that's what I love about being a writer, I can do those other things that bring me joy, and still have a career I love.

Before I quit drinking I kept really good care of my house and family. Yeah, right, I ran them like a drill sergeant, forcing them into compulsive neatness and proper behavior! I was so busy keeping everyone and everything in perfect order that I didn't have time to be there for my family and children. I may have been there physically while my kids were growing up, but I was never there emotionally, and that's sad for me to admit.

I was so wrapped up in my own dysfunction that I couldn't see the gifts in front of me. I'm so glad that I've come to a place of acceptance with that, happy that I've made amends with the kids as best I could, and we've moved on. It's never too late to start having a wonderful relationship with our children, grown or not. That's what I choose to focus on today, being emotionally available to everyone close to me, and I feel that more and more in recovery.

Today the focus isn't on the house being clean (obviously), it never made me happy and they knew it. In the old days a house as messy as mine is right now would have put me in the worst mood imaginable, probably for a long time. But now, so what if the house is a mess, my daughter sees a contented mom, a happy person, ready to hear the events of the day and share a laugh (or tear).

That change alone is worth everything I've gone through in recovery. The calm person I am today as opposed to the hyper mess I was my whole life. That's a miracle. Anyone who knows me can see the change, and I never thought it was possible. I believed I was hyper and that was "just the way I am." Deep down I didn't believe you had control over things like that, I only dreamed of being as calm as other people seemed to be, to one day not feel so fearful, uptight, and insecure.

But I didn't think it was anything I could change. I'm sure that's what I liked so much about alcohol, it took away the insecurities. But since I've learned that change is possible, I've been on a quest for more peace! More serenity! That feeling of calm is something I treasure, and although I still get caught off guard every now and again, most things just aren't worth losing my peace over, it doesn't matter who's at fault. There are some things that just aren't worth fighting for.

All the things I used to think were worth the fight, are not. I'm so grateful for that. I guess what I'm feeling is tired, tired of the fight, it's not worth it. I guess that's what they mean by surrender. I feel like I've surrendered, I feel beaten, and what a relief the struggle is over! My whole value system has changed. Everything that was important to me is not.

I had an owl collection that I started when I was about 12 years old. By the time I sobered up I had 400 owls. Who the hell needs 400 owls?! I had a lot of "stuff." A year into recovery I had a yard sale and sold all but about 6 of them. I still love owls, I just don't need 400 of them. It was the "cleaning out" phase of my recovery and it was happening inside and out.

Everything I surrounded myself with represented my worth, my importance. Things I wanted, everything I had was the main goal in my life. Don't get me wrong, I like having nice things around me, I believe we're meant to live abundantly, but these things are not the goal any longer, they are just added gifts. It's about being who I am, doing what I love, and sharing myself and my life with people I love. It's about *people* for me today, and it was never about people before.

Another one of the promises of recovery is that we will lose interest in selfish things and gain interest in our fellows. I didn't understand that until it came true for me, continues to come true for me. There's a shift that takes place, and I believe it happens in meetings, where we learn how to accept others right where they are. No judgments, just a quiet ear and a look of understanding.

It's a safe place when we know someone else relates to our feelings. For me it started in meetings and began to flow out into the rest of my life. I see people in a different light now, all people. I used to think myself pretty open minded, non-judgmental and anything but prejudice. And today that is me, but it sure wasn't back then! I was accepting of "most" people, but not all.

Today I have knowledge of a deeper connection between all of us, and I recognize it in everyone I meet. There are still those people who seem to rub me the wrong way, but there's a big difference in how I see that now from before. Before it would have been totally about the other person. It's because you're this or you're that, or you do this or did that. Always about you. Today I know it's not about you at all. Sometimes that really pisses me off, but I'm grateful. I know that I wouldn't be feeling these feelings if there wasn't something I needed to take a look at.

I'm continually learning and growing, and if I can count on the fact that I will be healed, blessed even, once I deal with my issues, I want to have these awarenesses. I guess that's where the *courage* part of the Serenity Prayer comes in. I remember when the shift happened and I became willing to look at myself, when I allowed myself to do a "fear-less" inventory. I was scared to death, but I forged ahead, and did it anyway. I remember thinking, this is what courage feels like. As vul-nerable as I felt, it was a nice feeling. I felt like I was going to be all right because I trusted enough to go ahead and do what was suggested in the twelve steps.

I was willing to do the things that promised healing, no matter how painful it was. That's when I became open to change, and the learning continued. If I still need to work on my feelings of unworthiness, then I can be pretty sure I'm going to find myself challenged to look at that. If I'm still insecure about my children and my part in their lives (since I didn't give birth to them), you can bet my daughter is going to get glamour shots of her birth mother (my husband's ex-wife) for Christmas, and I'm going to have to deal with my feelings about that.

See how it works for me? I can be going on along just great, and maybe even start thinking I've got this thing figured out, and boom! Exactly what I've described happens. It makes me laugh now. It always makes me laugh. Sometimes I have to cry first, but I can laugh at myself at some point and that was something that never happened before. I couldn't laugh at all, my life just wasn't that funny. Today that makes me laugh. My life, when it wasn't very funny, is hilarious to me today.

I was also presented with something else I guess I hadn't complete-ly dealt with. I haven't had an urge to drink since I finally did a thorough fourth step, and I haven't missed a thing about my drinking days. Figured I never would. The other day a package comes from our friends back home. For my husband a wonderful gift set of my favorite wines.

The cutest, mid-size bottles I've ever seen. I was surprised at what it did to me. I couldn't believe I felt sorry for myself. I hopped right on the pity pot for sure, and threw in some self blame too. It wasn't that I wanted to actually drink the wine, it was because I couldn't shape up and learn how to drink right in the first place. Because I'm an alcoholic damn it, because I can't sit down to a nice dinner with my husband and enjoy a glass of wine that our friends sent from Idaho. Because I could-n't do it right, I don't get to do it at all.

I felt like a child in school, and I really had to take a look at why that was happening. It was later the same day the pictures of the ex-wife came, so I really had a learning day! I'm okay with all of it now, and I'm grateful. I just needed to take a look at some unresolved feelings and emotions that I only thought I'd dealt with.

I say the Grace Prayer every day, and I've prayed hard on the "reveal what needs to be revealed" part, because I want to know. I'm at a point in my recovery where I want to know if there's something I haven't dealt with. I've learned that I can come to terms with things in my life and I don't have to stuff my feelings. They never stay stuffed.

It's a process for sure, but I don't have to fix everything at once. I just have to work with this day, this moment, and I'll deal with the next moment when it comes. There are some confusing times in early sobriety, and sometimes the brain doesn't seem to be working at all. I remember being so confused sometimes, and many times I would just "draw a blank." I was told it was all a part of that first year physical healing, so I trusted it would get better. I was told the mind does return. It did. But boy, early on the kitchen thing, for one, was a nightmare.

For quite awhile I listened to my tape in the kitchen and it just worked for me. It kept me at a slower pace, where I used to just buzz around like a crazy woman. It kept me calm enough to think clearly, and that makes anything easier. Now I don't listen to music while cooking very often, but if I'm feeling stressed, or I don't feel like cooking, I can put the tape in and everything goes smoothly.

For me it was about replacing old habits with better ones! And the music thing was kind of strange in recovery. I was always a die hard rock and roll fan, and deep down I always will be, but for the first year and a half in recovery I couldn't listen to *any* music. There was so much going on in my head, and so many things I was learning, unlearning, I just couldn't add any more to it.

If I was in the car I couldn't stand to have the radio on (before I couldn't stand the silence). This caused me a little uneasiness at times when my husband was home and listening to his music, the way he likes it, loud, especially when the house was all tore up and there was no place to go to get away from it. When he was here and we were working on the house, I just accepted it and it was okay, but more and more I was craving the silence.

I hadn't thought too much about the fact that I'd lost my love for music, until it came back. I was washing windows one day, probably about a year or so sober, something I usually played music while doing, and the thought came to me that I wouldn't mind hearing some music. I got the radio and turned it on and it was so much fun. They played great songs, and I was happy, singing along. I was filled with joy and the music made the job much lighter.

It was then that I realized I had lost my love of music when I quit drinking. Now that my music is back, I find it's different. Again, I'm looking for the calm. I would just as soon put on my meditation tape while working around the house, or writing as I usually do, than have blaring music. I used to listen to the rock station, now it's easy listening. I still love live music, no matter what kind, so that didn't change. But nearly everything else did change.

I finally forgave myself for my past so I could begin to enjoy today, and tomorrow, thereby creating a new past. If I didn't learn how to forgive and love myself, I was never going to grow. If I didn't believe the promises that recovery offers I would never have made it. I said it early on, I didn't get into this program to be more miserable than I was when I was drinking. *Contented sobriety* was what I was looking for, and I was told it was possible.

I was willing to go to any lengths, sometimes kicking and screaming, but I went! My goal has been contented sobriety, and that's what I continue to find. My life doesn't have to be perfect today. I don't have to be in a perfect mood every minute. I can talk about things that bother me, and I can listen to others. I don't have to do this alone. I can make mistakes and it's okay.

It wasn't long after doing my fourth and fifth steps that I started writing again. It was then that I finally felt free enough to finish this book, healthy enough to somehow put an end to a story that will continue. Ready to focus on my recovery instead of the pain that got me here. I had to feel the pain, I had to do the work, but in the end what I found was hope, and freedom. What I found was exactly what I was looking for; Serenity.

Chapter 30

BLESSINGS

December 23, 1996. What a beautiful morning. It snowed in the night and the world is covered with the most beautiful white blanket. I was reminded of how many winters look like this, but this year we just haven't had as much. I was suddenly compelled to shovel the walks. It was still early so there wasn't much traffic. There was a blue tint to everything, and the street lamps glowed a soft golden color, which added to the peacefulness of the scene.

It stirred so much in me. Remembering the year I was a human snow shovel, spending many a morning out at this hour, with this peace. Then the year after that when I had no energy, and it was all I could do to keep our walks clear. And that was a struggle. And now. I feel good. I'm healthy. I don't mind shoveling the walks. It's not a burden, nor an obligation. I was filled with the spirit when I was out there. Everything was white. Everything looked peaceful and serene. It was right out of a storybook.

I was so grateful for the experience, because while I've recognized that all the shoveling I did that first year was running from myself, I'd forgotten that I was getting a lot out of it too. I know I kept shoveling anything and everything because I didn't want to go back inside and be alone with me. But it was just as much that I wanted to stay outside where it was peaceful and serene. It was very healing for me, and I'd forgotten that part.

It was good physical work as well, and I'm grateful that I can enjoy that experience today without being obsessive or avoiding it altogether. After the walks were done, I turned before going in, and just took in the scene. The lamp posts were still shining, and the blanket of white that covered everything, lay still in the quiet. I've learned to feel that stillness within me, something I'd never felt before, and today I can hold on to that feeling. If it goes from me, I can close my eyes and be right back outside at dawn, feeling the warmth amidst the cold, hearing the power in the silence.

January 9, 1997

Wow. I'm overflowing with gratitude for my life. At this moment it seems that everything is falling into place, gracefully. It's a miracle. I went to the women's meeting yesterday as always, but there was something different about this Wednesday, something special.

I really don't have any one way I get to a meeting on Wednesdays, I just always do. I spend every Wednesday morning with my mother, so if all else fails she can take me on her way home. Sometimes I get a ride with Lisa, in the summer I ride my bike. This Wednesday Katie said she would pick me up, and afterwards we'd get a bowl of soup. Tuesday Susie & I talked and she said she could pick me up for brunch and then a meeting on Wednesday, and I agreed before I remembered Katie & I had plans.

I called Susie back and we agreed to see each other at the meeting. The friendship between Susie & I has come full circle, and we're back to a place of love and acceptance. I'm grateful to have her in my life. When mom & I got back from our errands that morning there was a message on the machine from Lisa saying she could give me a ride if I needed one. I laughed, and told mom how crazy it was that I had three rides to the meeting, guess I *really* need to be there today.

The meeting was a good one, talked about relapsing after nine or ten years of "recovery," not just sobriety. Two women. It spoke to me big time, because I've had this feeling that it's not about the alcohol anymore, and for the most part I know it isn't, but I can never forget that I am an alcoholic, and therefore prone to drink, depending on my spiritual condition. That's what I try to work on.

The thing they both agreed they did was stopped going to meetings, stopped working their program, and I've heard this many times at meetings. I guess that's why I've always been so diligent about my program and my meetings. I don't want to go back to that old way of living, that scares me. It hasn't been easy trying to learn this new way, but it's paying off. I have mounds of serenity in any given day, and peace of mind which I never thought possible.

It's been a journey getting here, and I've been promised it will be worth all the work it takes, and for me today it is. This program feeds my soul in a way nothing ever has, and I don't want to lose that. Yesterday's meeting reminded me that I have to stay awake. I have to continue growing, I have much to learn. Most of the unlearning is over, that's where the pain was. Now I'm just learning, and growing, and changing. I must never stop wanting that for myself. I heard everything I needed to hear.

By the end of the meeting there were only four of us left, myself, and the other three who had offered me rides. The four of us prayed the Lord's Prayer, and then had a group hug that was wonderful! Then we all went to lunch. As I sat in the booth, three of my closest friends around me, it was a special moment.

Those three friends are all uniquely different. I connect with them each in a different way. It's not normal that we would all four be together at noon on Wednesday. I left the restaurant feeling overwhelming gratitude for sober friends, and special and dear ones at that, who all give me something unique. It's a miracle.

I've lived here for going on 10 years now, that seems so amazing. We moved here in 1987, and for most of those years I was aware that I didn't have a close friend to confide in, like I had back home. I had drinking friends, and friends who used me for whatever reasons, advice, direction, drugs, but a close connection of the heart that is found with girl friends, well, it's something to treasure, and rare to find.

All these years later I not only have a friend, I have many friends. This morning I met with another friend, as is our normal routine these days, for breakfast and wonderful conversation about spiritual things, life and learning. She is also a recovering alcoholic trying to live a spiritual life, and the things the two of us have in common are incredible. It's clear to both of us why we came together, and why this friendship is so mutually fulfilling.

I have yet another friend whom I meet for lunch, just around the corner from my home. We enjoy that hour twice a month, and she & I became fast friends. I also see her at the step meeting where we met. This morning in my quiet time I couldn't help but notice how blessed my life has become with friends. Never in my whole life have I had five friends as close as these are, all at the same time.

It's a testament to this program of recovery which allows us to find and nurture our true selves, thereby connecting with others with like minds and hearts. We all have the same goal. We're all doing the same thing, yet our lives are all quite different. Again I say it's a miracle, and I'm so grateful.

For me, that day was special. It was God's way of showing me something I hadn't taken notice of. I have a lot of friends. I have a lot of people who support me in my life, and just as importantly, I have lots of friends I can support. It's an absolute gift. Small miracles.

I also have to be honest about what else is going on. I am still running. Whether it's running into peace and serenity, or hiding in it, I'm avoiding some things that need to be done by me. I want to finish the book, I *need* to finish the book, and yet I've let every little interruption keep me from working. I'm here right now because I told myself enough was enough. I feel scared when I think about finishing it.

Part of me feels inadequate, afraid I don't know how to write a book, how to put it together, how to make chapters, what to call them, how to arrange the material. And then editing. Part of me wants to run the other way. Another part of me loves this part, thrives while in the midst of it. And it all comes together, like the first time.

Whether I ever do anything with that book or not, it was written. Made into book form. It's still special to me, I still had a wonderful experience in the creating of it. I know I can do that again, better this time. I look forward to that experience, yet somehow part of me is scared, wants to sabotage my efforts. So, I pray to do first things first, with faith and trust that I will be guided all along the way, just like always.

It was right after that I got busy and began putting this book together. It was being put together all along, I just didn't know it.

February 1, 1997 - Last night I remember dreaming a lot, although I don't remember much. What I do remember is that there were many runaway buses. They were going every which way. Somehow I gathered them together, like you would cattle. I remember feeling really happy about that, kind of amazed. They were big, vacant buses, on the loose.

I looked up bus in my dream book and it said; shared journey, mass transit. How does my personal power relate to mass consciousness? That's pretty powerful to me, and I knew the dream was significant when I woke up. I just didn't think I had remembered enough to tell me anything. The work I've been doing feels powerful to me, it is my personal power and I feel like I'm just now coming into it.

To ask myself how that relates to the mass consciousness is to get goose bumps, because that's exactly what it's all about. It's about everybody coming into their own, believing in love, choosing love, and recognizing the power we have to create whatever we choose. Mass consciousness definitely rules, so the more of us who believe in the goodness of life, the more power we have to create that in the world.

I just found myself thinking, "I hope I get that message across in my book." Then I realized that's probably why I had the dream. It's as if I needed to be reminded that the potential for influencing the masses is great. That's not to put on pressure, but rather to seize an opportunity. I've been moving through my fear, and it feels good. To quote a friend, I feel "peace in the fear." I'm scared to death, but one step at a time I know I can make it.

April 1997

I feel like this book could continue forever. So much has happened, and I've learned so much just since I "finished" it. From the events in my life this past week, to the dreams I've been having, it's clear that I need to get this book out. Here is the dream I had last night.

I was in a busy place, a huge auditorium with people coming and going everywhere. It seemed there were a lot of AA people here and there. There were tons of bathrooms everywhere, but not an available one in sight—and I really had to go. I was having to hold it and I was uncomfortable. It seemed that even when there were big rooms dividing different areas, the walls were made of glass so you could see into all of the other parts.

I walked into one part that seemed like a cafeteria. All the tables were full. I was wearing a short skirt and all the men started making a fuss and bringing attention to me. Everyone was looking at me. I sat down at a table (trying to hide), but I had to get up and go (literally). As I walked across the room I was self-conscious and uncomfortable, knowing that everyone was staring at me. To make it worse, I knew they could see right through my skirt, and my panty hose were falling down to expose my butt.

I hurried out. Again I was looking for bathrooms but all the stalls were full. It was as if people were getting ready for a wedding, or a bunch of weddings. A couple of AA friends were trying to help me (by being understanding). I was trying to minimize the situation (my needs). Then I found a toilet, but when I sat down and started to go, the door opened and men began walking past. There were walls around me, but they were made of glass. It was as if I was on display.

I was trying to figure out how I was going to clean up, stand up, pull up my panty hose, and pull my skirt down without anyone seeing my private parts. The toilet paper was like the rough brown paper used for drying your hands. I had a huge wad of it in my hand and was trying to figure out how this was going to work. Then the paper stuck to my hand. When I pulled it off it left a big wound, which began to bleed uncontrollably.

Now I was using the towels to try to stop the bleeding, and I was stuck on the toilet, not knowing how I was going to get up while keeping myself covered. Different people, mostly men, continued to stroll by and look at me. I was embarrassed that my hand was bleeding so badly. I tried to cover it up, but the blood kept soaking through the towels.

I stood up and tried to get my panty hose up, but now they were too short and wouldn't quite reach my waist. Instead they only covered half of me, and if I moved, they kept slipping down. I was so frustrated, from trying to pull them up and keep them up with my left hand, while trying to control the bleeding from my right.

That about says it all, don't you think? This is the vulnerable place I've found myself in right now. It's okay, it's just uncomfortable. I was able to finally go to the bathroom (cleansing and release), regardless of how exposed I felt. My right hand is significant because of the work I do, although I use both hands, which I was doing in the dream. I also relate the bleeding to cleansing, this time life-giving.

It's been just over three years since that March night when I prayed the right prayer and began to rebuild my life. I feel I've come full circle from where I was, and my life has never felt better. I believe in recovery. It's brought so much hope into my life, and I see healing everywhere I look. It's about everybody learning how to take care of themselves. It's about trusting others to do the same.

I believe we're entering into a generation of recovery. That's why coffee houses and bookstores are as popular as bars used to be. The sixties can't possibly work in the nineties, and more and more people are seeking healthier alternatives. We've decided we want to live. We saw what the "Me Generation" had to offer, and now I believe we're heading into the "We Generation." Together we can change the world.

I want to share two stories, and then I'm out of here. Miracles happen and dreams do come true, so I'm sure it was no coincidence that while doing the finishing touches on this book, I received some of my Grandma Sue's writings after twenty-two years of waiting. With all the work I did on anger in early recovery, it was the one issue that had not been resolved. It seemed fitting closure.

I was also reminded of the tree story, which was included in the first book, but has even more meaning today. A year before I stopped drinking, I had an interesting experience on a God walk at a spiritual retreat. It foretold of struggles to come, help that is available, as well as promising all would be well.

"I was enjoying a peaceful walk in the woods when I found a section of trees, all old and very tall. The area seemed clear because the trees were not real close together and their trunks went a long way up before there were any branches. Above though, all the trees touched and were a part of each other, creating a type of roof over the total clearing. It was a peaceful place to be, shaded and protected from the wind.

"I sat on a huge fallen tree that had a perfect flat spot for sitting, and newer trees grew up around it. In this area there were some downed trees, and I began to see that hard times had claimed these 'weaker' trees and that now they lay peaceful, although lifeless.

"As I began looking at the area even closer, I noticed there were trees that had nearly succumbed to the hard times, yet were thriving, because they were leaning on other stronger trees that 'caught' them and wouldn't let them fall. As I looked way up I could see that these weaker trees had curved their way upward to stand tall and healthy, full of life. And although at the base they leaned upon another, in the end they stood alone, strong and proud.

"I began to notice that the ones that had the roughest start, the ones that leaned the most, were the ones that grew the tallest, were the greenest, and looked the healthiest. I was amazed as I became aware of the similarities between the trees and us. I thought about how we're all God's creation, we all have life and we are forever growing and reaching upward.

"Then the most fascinating thing happened. I looked at the huge fallen tree I was sitting on, laying across the ground, and followed it to the left to see just how tall it had been in life, and to see if it had taken any others with it when it fell. I couldn't believe my eyes.

"I followed it about ten or fifteen feet when I noticed it began to curve slowly upward, straightening out ever so slightly until finally it was totally straight, huge and far reaching to the sky! As I compared its top to the others in the group I could see that this tree, this 'fallen,' supposedly dead tree, was the biggest and the healthiest of all those in the area!

"The one that apparently had been knocked down, stomped on and kept down for a very long time, emerged from the hardship to be the pillar of strength in that community of trees!"

I feel like one of those weaker trees. I've needed a lot of help, but I'm strong now and growing on my own.

*   *   *

Appendix One

THE TWELVE STEPS

1. We admitted we were powerless over alcohol—that our lives had become unmanageable.

2. Came to believe that a Power greater than ourselves could restore us to sanity.

3. Made a decision to turn our will and our lives over to the care of God as we understood Him.

4. Made a searching and fearless moral inventory of ourselves.

5. Admitted to God, to ourselves, and to another human being the exact nature of our wrongs.

6. Were entirely ready to have God remove all these defects of character.

7. Humbly asked Him to remove our shortcomings.

8. Made a list of all persons we had harmed, and became willing to make amends to them all.

9. Made direct amends to such people wherever possible, except when to do so would injure them or others.

10. Continued to take personal inventory, and when we were wrong promptly admitted it.

11. Sought through prayer and meditation to improve our conscious contact with God as we understood Him, praying only for knowledge of His will for us and the power to carry that out.

12. Having had a spiritual awakening as a result of these steps, we tried to carry this message to alcoholics, and to practice these principles in all our affairs.

THE PROMISES

If we are painstaking about this phase of our development, we will be amazed before we are halfway through.

1. We are going to know a new freedom and a new happiness.

2. We will not regret the past nor wish to shut the door on it.

3. We will comprehend the word serenity.

4. We will know peace.

5. No matter how far down the scale we have gone, we will see how our experience can benefit others.

6. That feeling of uselessness and self-pity will disappear.

7. We will lose interest in selfish things and gain interest in our fellows.

8. Self-seeking will slip away.

9. Our whole attitude and outlook upon life will change.

10. Fear of people and of economic insecurity will leave us.

11. We will intuitively know how to handle situations which used to baffle us.

12. We will suddenly realize that God is doing for us what we could not do for ourselves.

Are these extravagant promises? We think not. They are being fulfilled among us—sometimes quickly, sometimes slowly. They will always materialize if we work for them.

(From *Alcoholics Anonymous*, pages 83-4)

NOTES

From the book *Understand Your Dreams* © 1995 by Alice Anne Parker.
Reprinted by permission of H J Kramer, P.O. Box 1082, Tiburon, CA 94920.
All rights reserved. Pages 50, 52, 55, 56, 63, 122, 126, 127, 134, 136, 138, 140, 144, 157, 169, 180, 209, 216, 223, and 235.

From the book *Drinking, A Love Story* © 1996 by Caroline Knapp
Reprinted by permission of Dell a division of Bantam, Doubleday, Dell Publishing Group, Inc. Page 18.

From the book *Dreams: Your Magic Mirror* by Elsie Sechrist. Reprinted by permission of Subsidiary Rights Manager, Contemporary Books, Inc. Pages 116 and 117.

From the books *Alcoholics Anonymous* (The Big Book), Appendix One and Two, and *Twelve Steps and Twelve Traditions*, pages 43 and 212. Excerpts are reprinted with permission of Alcoholics Anonymous World Services, Inc. Permission to use this material does not mean that A.A. has reviewed or approved the contents of this publication, nor that A.A. agrees with the views expressed herein. A.A. is a program of recovery from alcoholism only - use of this material in connection with programs and activities which are patterned after A.A., but which address other problems, or in any other non-A.A. context, does not imply otherwise.

WHERE TO GET HELP

Alcoholics Anonymous
Grand Central Station
P.O. Box 459
New York, NY 10163
212-870-3199
FAX# 212-870-3003

Overeaters Anonymous
P.O. Box 44020
Rio Rancho, NM 87174-4020
505-891-2664

Co-Dependents Anonymous
P.O. Box 33577
Phoenix, AZ 80567-3577
602-277-7991

World Service Office of Narcotics Anonymous
P.O. Box 9999
Van Nuys, CA 91409-9999
818-773-9999

Al-Anon Family Group Headquarters, Inc.
World Service Office
1600 Corporate Landing Parkway
Virginia Beach, VA 23454
757-563-1600
FAX# 757-563-1655
800-356-9996

Adult Children of Alcoholics World Service Organization
P.O. Box 3216
Torrance, CA 90510
310-534-1815

The Self-Help Sourcebook
Finding and Forming Mutual Aid
Self-Help Groups
American Self-Help Clearinghouse
St. Clares Riverside Medical Center
Denville, NY 07834
201-625-7101

ORDER INFORMATION

Order *Recovering From Life* from your bookstore.

If unavailable at your bookstore, please send $14.95 plus $3.50 for shipping and handling for each book. If five or more copies are ordered send only $2.00 shipping and handling per book. Michigan residents add 6% sales tax.

Send _____ book(s).

PLEASE PRINT
Name: _____
Address: _____

_____
City: _____
State: _____ Zip: _____

Send check or money order(payable to Recovering From Life) plus above information to:

Recovering From Life
427 E. State Street
Traverse City, MI 49686